Learning through the Workplace

Learning through the Workplace

A guide to work-based learning

David Gray
Sue Cundell
David Hay
Jean O'Neill

T

Published in 2004 by:
Nelson Thornes Ltd
Delta Place
27 Bath Road
CHELTENHAM
GL53 7TH
United Kingdom

04 05 06 07 08 / 10 9 8 7 6 5 4 3 2 1

A catalogue record for this book is available from the British Library

ISBN 0-7487-6504-2

Page make-up by Northern Phototypesetting Co. Ltd, Bolton
Printed and bound in Spain by GraphyCems

CONTENTS

PREFACE

In the world of the 'knowledge economy', understanding what counts as knowledge, who possesses it, and how it is shared across an organisation is fast becoming one of the essential ingredients of business survival. Organisations operating in a fiercely competitive world have to stay 'ahead of the game', and most now understand that one of the most effective ways of achieving this is through the skills and knowledge of their workforce. This does not mean, of course, that these skilled workers can simply be recruited 'off the street' when required – like all precious commodities, they are in short supply. It means that organisations and businesses now have to apply much more thought, planning and resources to the training and ongoing professional development of their workforce, either through formal programmes of learning or training or through encouraging learning in less formal ways. It is perhaps then no coincidence that the concept of the 'learning organisation' has become so popular in the last 20 years – even if there is little general acceptance of what it actually means in practice.

For many individuals too, the old divisions between learning and work are beginning to erode. Work was what you did in order to earn a wage. Learning was what happened (in theory) at school, college or university, to prepare you for the world of work. Once in the workplace, you might receive some formal training on occasions, but most of the time you picked up what you needed to know on the job itself, often from people around you. This process, of course, still goes on. However, it is fast becoming the case that learning is seen as something you do continually whilst at work, both out of choice and by necessity. By choice because learning itself can be a life-enriching experience and one that can sometimes be transferred and applied beyond the workplace, such as back in the home or community. To use Leadbeater's (2001) terminology, it means 'authorship', where work (and learning) becomes a form of self-expression, embodying a sense of ownership, creativity and satisfaction.

However, learning also has to take place by necessity, because the nature of work in the modern organisation is changing. Organisational structures are being perpetually reorganised, job functions changed, merged with others or simply abolished. People are required to work more in teams, sometimes committing themselves to a range of diverse projects simultaneously. Communication, teamwork, and sharing knowledge and information are becoming increasingly essential traits of the modern 'knowledge worker'. This means that workers must not only be flexible and knowledgeable, but must learn in and through the work process – even learning how to learn because continual learning is now so essential.

Institutions of further and higher education are also waking up to the opportunities that workplace learning presents. Further education colleges have long been geared up for the delivery of vocational programmes focused on the needs of the workforce. Some universities also have years of experience in the delivery of one type of workplace learning programme – the sandwich degree – where, typically, one year of a four-year degree is spent in the workplace. Newer workplace learning programmes are also beginning to emerge, aimed at people in work who want to study part-time for an accredited award (such as a degree, certificate or diploma). These courses allow people to both study and work, but even more importantly, encourage participants to integrate and apply the academic and theoretical learning they acquire from the programme with their workplace practice. These workplace learning programmes often allow participants to claim for degree credits based upon their work experience, so recognising and rewarding their workplace learning.

THE SCOPE OF THIS BOOK

This book aims to explore and to explain how people learn, in and through the process of work, and how individual and group workplace learning can be promoted and supported. Chapter 1 maps out some of the developments in this process and traces the origins of workplace learning. We then look at the scale and types of training and professional development (including management development) being undertaken in the UK and examples of informal learning such as coaching and mentoring, and action learning.

In Chapter 2, we look at what may turn out to be one of the latest management panaceas – knowledge management (KM). In many ways, KM embodies many of the principles championed by this book. KM systems allow for, indeed can encourage, dialogue and communication between individuals and teams. In a sense, then, they can facilitate informal learning between people. They allow for the storage of documents and other knowledge artefacts, allowing people to access them and learn (a form of self-directed learning). They facilitate access to experts who can subsequently act as mentors or coaches, and they can also deliver e-learning programmes and log attendance at face-to-face courses (and hence facilitate the delivery of formal learning).

However, before we can really understand the process of workplace learning, we need to understand some of the fundamental principles and models of learning. Chapter 3 explores theories of learning, not necessarily to understand them in an abstract or academic way, but to inform later discussions on how people learn and how organisations can support individual learning.

As we have suggested, a major focus of organisational training has been on professional development, with quite a heavy emphasis on management development. However, there is a growing realisation that without underpinning knowledge and skills, none of this higher-level development will work. Chapter 4 therefore focuses on key skills. Developing appropriate key skills is important for an individual so they can improve their productivity and employability. They are also important if an organisation is going to survive and prosper in a competitive marketplace. The chapter looks at the reasons why key skills are crucial for an individual, an organisation and the national economy. A range of key skills is considered, and appropriate strategies for skill development are discussed. We also provide examples of how and where key skills can be assessed.

Chapter 5 deals with the issue of assessment in workplace learning. It includes an introduction to the key approaches in assessment methodology and explains, for example, the distinction between formative and summative assessment and criterion or norm referenced tests. The chapter also deals with issues such as reliability and validity in tests, and it outlines the ways in which assessment methods can be built into programmes of learning in the workplace so that testing and demonstrating achievement can become part of the learning process. The chapter is aimed at both learners and those who have responsibility for the learning of others.

Many people learn a great deal through the workplace – through the experience of doing their job, undertaking specific projects, and/or dealing with specific incidents. In Chapter 6, we provide strategies to enable staff to identify the knowledge, skills and understanding they have gained through work. The process of recognising, and assessing, prior experiential learning can help individuals make the most of appraisal schemes, support career opportunities, gain access to award-bearing courses, and gain credit towards awards. The process of structured and professional reflection enables individuals to identify exactly what they have gained through experience, the implications for themselves and their organisation, and how it will affect future actions and decisions.

The process by which this experience is presented is usually through the construction of a portfolio of evidence (Chapter 7). In this chapter, we consider the use of various types of portfolios for presenting achievement, reviewing progress and setting goals. We cover issues such as how portfolios can be used for different purposes, and who is available to support portfolio building. These are referenced to a web site so that you can access extracts from current portfolios (or other related material) to illustrate examples cited in the chapter.

Chapter 8 brings us to the point where we see what kind of learning organisation can be developed. It challenges us to be clear about our company culture, to measure our organisation against case studies of others, and to examine the way we operate, and who in our organisation are the enablers and facilitators of learning. Finally, you are asked to audit your own organisation and devise strategies to sustain and nurture a culture that encourages and enables learning.

WHO IS THIS BOOK FOR?

This book will, we hope, be of value to a wide range of audiences, including those who are planning workplace learning or professional development programmes (such as human resource managers or even line managers), individuals who want to understand how to nurture and support their own learning at work and organisations involved in the various elements of workplace learning. In summary it will be of use to:

- Managers of those in work who are studying for workplace qualifications at either undergraduate or postgraduate level, as part of their continuous professional development (CPD). This includes those registered as learners with LearnDirect.
- Those who support learners in work, including human resource managers, training consultants, line managers, careers guidance professionals, coaches, mentors and owner-managers in small and medium enterprises (SMEs).
- Teachers and facilitators working in further, higher and adult education, and especially those involved with professional development programmes.
- Students on professional initial teacher education programmes for the post-16 sector who need to understand the role of workplace learning and how it can be promoted, taught and assessed.

USING THIS BOOK

In using this book, you might like to read it sequentially from the first page until the end. However, you are also invited to make use of the Contents page and to dip into any of the areas that interest you. Essentially the first three chapters of the book set out the landscape by describing learning at work and how individuals learn. The chapters that follow are more specialised, getting down to the detail of how learning and skills can be supported, measured and assessed.

Running through the book you will see a series of case studies, framed around three contrasting organisations – a large, global corporate, an SME and a not-for-profit, voluntary organisation. We hope that by offering you these contrasting studies, we are able to show both the consistencies of how people learn within the workplace, and how the size and structure of organisations can affect the process and outcomes of learning in and through work. We also provide regular activities (which we hope you will actually attempt!) that are designed to provoke thought, reflection and learning. Some of these activities involve visiting web sites to provide you with material to supplement what you find in the book. You will also see boxes that contain additional, quite detailed material that you may wish to read but which are not necessarily central to the main text.

Within the book, you will find reference to both the terms 'training' and 'learning'. We generally use the term 'training' in the more traditional sense of technical or functional training, usually delivered by formal programmes (often to people lower down in the organisational hierarchy). One of the most important arguments of the book, however, is that modern organisations need to move away from such rather narrow concepts. We need to embrace the principle not only of learning through formal programmes, but also non-formal and incidental learning, i.e. learning in and through the process of work itself. And not just learning for the few (for example, in management grades) but across the entire organisation – generating both individual and organisational learning in a mutually reinforcing and enhancing dynamic. We recognise that training still takes place, which for the development of certain skills and capabilities is important for all of us. Learning, however, empowers individuals both personally and professionally and provides the bedrock for organisational success.

AND FINALLY SOME THANKS

We would like to thank our colleagues at Nelson Thornes for commissioning the book and especially to Claire Hart for her help and support during its production. We would also like to thank:

- Colleagues in the Business Operations Team, UniSdirect, University of Surrey, for their support and for acting as sounding boards for ideas.
- Martin Cundell, sculptor/designer, for encouragement and cooperation.
- James Clarke, Cougar-Automation, for information and feedback.
- Ray Edwards, Rachel Durrant, Bruce Jones, Peter Cooper, Nigel Jennings, Caroline Sackely, Danièle Brière, Judy Martin, Joseph McElligott and Alex Steward, for allowing us to use their work on the learnatwork web site!
- Jeff Ward of Surrey Satellite Limited.

- Jenny Cridland of BAESYSTEMS, for reading the relevant chapters and checking that our information is correct.
- The Royal Aeronautical Society and Lloyds TSB, for clarification of the issues that we raised with them.
- Owen Pugh and Andy Short (University of Surrey) for their patient IT support.

REFERENCES

Leadbeater, D. (2001) Learning and work – authorship. In: *The Future of Learning at Work: Executive Briefing*. Chartered Institute of Personnel and Development, London, pp. 33–39.

1 PROCESSES OF LEARNING FOR THE GLOBAL AGE

Objectives

After reading this chapter, you will be able to:

- Describe the broad spectrum of activities that comprise workplace learning, ranging from on-the-job training to management development.
- Outline the current provision of workplace learning in the UK, including its role in wider organisational strategy.
- Discuss the scale and quality of provision for CPD and management development in the UK.
- Outline the new kinds of skills and competencies required of professional development, such as problem-solving, negotiating, project management and conflict management.
- Discuss the methods commonly used to develop new skills and competencies, ranging from formal training programmes to on-the-job training, coaching, mentoring and action learning.

INTRODUCTION

The international economic system is becoming dominated by the new industrial and financial transnational corporations (TNCs), a process now usually referred to as 'globalisation'. However, globalisation involves more than just the growth of large companies. It is a term that has become synonymous with the championing of the free market, the removal of restrictions on the movement of capital and investment, and freedom of trade in all goods and services, including intellectual property. If the power of the TNCs is growing, this also implies that the power of individual nation states is receding. The extent and direction of these processes, however, are still matters of debate.

An important contributor to globalisation (and benefactor) is the growth of information technology (IT) (for example, the Internet, mobile phones, faxes, computers and digital television) and the changes this technology is bringing to business processes, attitudes and expectations. The Internet, for example, is not only giving businesses potential access to greater markets, it is changing business relationships to these markets. Businesses are using the Internet to connect both to their customers and to their supply chain. This means that companies have the potential at least to become **agile organisations**, understanding the needs of their customers in real time, and responding to these needs by rapidly sourcing production from their suppliers. Of course, the scale and pace of these changes is uneven across different countries, regions and business sectors.

It is clear, however, that the nature of work is changing. As Casey (1999) points out, globalisation means the restructuring of labour markets, high levels of geographical and occupational mobility for skilled workers (resulting in portfolio employment) and the marginalisation of the lower skilled. Hence, the wealth of an organisation is not based upon the shining chrome and reflective windows of its corporate headquarters, but on what its people (human capital) know and learn. In the new knowledge economy, the important issues become what counts as knowledge in an organisation, how this is transmitted and stored, who owns it, and how it is shared (or not shared). In other words, of rising significance is both individual workplace learning and organisational learning. Even if the scenarios just described appear somewhat idealised, elements of them, at least, are becoming a reality for a growing number of organisations.

In this book, we will often make reference to three case studies as a means of illustrating and elaborating our arguments. These are:

- Transglobal, a large-scale, transnational finance company, trading in four continents.
- Airsnack, an SME employing 200 staff, delivering food products for airlines.
- The Citizens Support Bureau (CSB), a not-for-profit, national organisation with a core staff of 400 but with over 3000 unpaid volunteers, supplying help and advice to those with financial, health or domestic problems.

We hope to show through these case studies how the size, structure and relationships between these organisations and the economic system impact both on the learning of individuals and, in turn, on the ability of their organisations to learn.

Let us first focus on Transglobal and how its growth has led to a multiplicity of learning needs, both for the organisation and for the people who work in it.

Case Study 1.1: *The growth of Transglobal*

Transglobal did not exist in the 1980s. It began life as the Assurance, a medium-sized, UK-based insurance company with modest aspirations. In 1989, however, a new chief executive took over and the Assurance acquired a similar-sized French company, making itself a pan-European operation. Two years later, this itself was acquired through an aggressive takeover by a Canadian company to form the fifth largest insurance company in the world. Transglobal was born.

The result, of course, was enormous internal change. The London and Paris headquarters were closed, and Toronto became the strategic global centre. The number of insurance 'brands' was rationalised and reduced. However, Transglobal harboured ambitions of being the world's leading insurance company and so was constantly on the lookout for new market opportunities and also to reduce costs. In 1994 all information systems operations were outsourced to an independent supplier, and in 1998, human resource functions went the same way. Other departments, however, were formed, including market research and communications. In 2002, a web site was launched, offering a new range of insurance 'products' to the growing Internet generation of customers.

In just 20 years, the organisation had completely reinvented itself. As a result, staff had to learn about new products, new markets, and new ways of working. The most significant knowledge areas of the company are now research, marketing and customer relations. This learning is supported by a corporate Transglobal University, launched in 2000. Nationally-based training departments have been closed, with the new corporate university supplying a broad range of web-based training programmes. These are designed to deliver underpinning knowledge that can then be extended and deepened, where necessary, by live training – an example of blended learning. Learning consultants (facilitators) are flown to wherever professional development is needed.

The entire organisation is performance-driven through the implementation of a competency framework. This identifies a set of core competencies that the organisation sees as central to its strategic mission. These core competencies are transmitted to all employees via the Transglobal University Intranet, and form the basis of the appraisal, promotion and reward system. Learning programmes are also provided, to help employees attain these competencies. Far from learning being based upon a 'wish list' of what employees want (or think they want), learning is driven through corporate business objectives that, in turn, drive and shape the core competency framework.

Beyond the core competency programme, a growing number of just-in-time training programmes are also delivered. These 'training objects' are small-scale, and focus on very specific skills needs or knowledge around a particular problem. Where these learning objects focus on quite generic subject areas (such as project management or IT applications), commercial, generic web-based programmes are bought for the web learning portal. However, the knowledge economy also means that there is widespread knowledge within the organisation itself that it needs to unlock. Hence, a group of knowledge experts who are willing to share their knowledge has been identified. Their work biographies, fields of expertise and contact details are made available through the web learning portal. This move is supplemented by the introduction of a mentoring system so workers can be supported and guided by more experienced and knowledgeable colleagues. A professional development programme for both mentors and mentees is being instigated.

In 2002, the web learning portal was reorganised so that an employee can gain access to:

- a list of the company's core competencies
- their personal appraisal records and competency profiles
- their personal development plans (PDPs)
- company HR regulations and access to the outsourced HR function
- online learning materials
- the knowledge experts' database
- a database of available mentors and guidelines on mentoring procedures.

The company realises that it still has some way to go in organising its competency framework. While, for example, it generates data on individual competencies, this is done on the basis of conversations between appraisers and appraisees and is paper-based. This is very time-consuming. There is also no way of easily seeing where competency gaps are arising, say, within departments. Transglobal intends to develop a competency assessment software application to speed up the process and to provide much-needed management data. However, despite these problems, Transglobal now sees itself as becoming a 'learning organisation', and one that is developing some expertise in the use of knowledge management systems.

How does the real world measure up to Transglobal? Well, most companies, even many large ones, have not completed this process, and some have hardly started. Many, however, are on the way. Performance management systems and competency frameworks are increasingly the norm in most large companies. Some organisations are developing their own corporate universities, sometimes within the framework of a KM system. What is common to most organisations is the realisation that employees are not simply a cost but a resource, and one in which the knowledge of the organisation resides. It follows, then, that learning, both individual and organisational, is not a burden but something that is central to competitive survival. In the next section, we trace how this situation has emerged.

THE PROCESS OF WORKPLACE LEARNING

Learning within the workplace is a diverse phenomenon, reflected by the fact that there are several terms used to describe it, e.g. 'work-based learning', 'work-related learning' and 'workplace learning'. For the sake of consistency in this book, we will use the latter term. Workplace learning is a complex concept because it encompasses such a broad range of learning activities, ranging from skills-based vocational training right through to strategic management development. It may be formal (for example an in-house company training programme), informal (a team meeting in which the exchange of ideas, and hence learning, takes place) or even incidental, i.e. occurring by chance. Marsick and Watkins (1989) suggest that incidental learning is a by-product of some other activity such as completing a task, an interpersonal interaction or just trial and error experimentation. Furthermore, Eraut *et al.* (1998) argue that formal learning in the workplace takes into account only a small part of what is actually learned at work. Most learning that takes place is informal, arising from the process of work itself, and from communication and interactions within the workplace.

Workplace learning is also complex because, as we have seen in Case Study 1.1, the nature of the workplace itself is being transformed, and therefore what needs to be learnt and how it is learnt is also changing. In a sense, learning *for* work is one of the functions of the compulsory education system, although views as to the effectiveness of the school system in this capacity remain mixed. As we mentioned in the Preface, learning for work could also include a work placement on a sandwich degree programme or professional development such as an accountancy or law course. The purpose of this book, however, is to explore learning *in* and *through* work. In this context, workplace learning can be distinguished from accepted, traditional approaches in a number of ways. For example, Raelin (2000) argues that workplace learning is different to classroom learning in that workplace learning:

- is centred around reflection on work practices; it is not merely a question of acquiring knowledge and a set of technical skills (although these can be important), but a case of reviewing and learning from experience
- arises from action and problem-solving within a working environment, which is centred around live projects and challenges to individuals and organisations; workplace learning also sees the creation of knowledge as a shared and collective activity, one in which people discuss ideas, and share problems and solutions
- requires not only the acquisition of new knowledge but the acquisition of meta-competence – learning to learn.

Workplace learning, then, is far from being merely the acquisition of formal knowledge or skills. It involves reflection on learning, learning through problem-solving and learning about learning itself.

Many companies have been eager to embrace workplace learning, because of its recognised importance to what Senge (1990) terms the 'learning organisation'. The learning organisation is one in which the learning and talent of individuals is encouraged and promoted so that the organisation itself begins to shape its future. This underlines the need for learners to develop the higher-level skills of analysis, evaluation and synthesis as well as the ability to be an independent learner and, in Schön's (1983) term, a reflective practitioner.

Hence, workplace learning is a process of **reasoned learning** through which both individuals and organisations move towards desirable and sustainable outcomes. However, this raises the question of whether individual learning and organisational learning are congruent and synonymous. In principle, the desirable outcomes and planned goals of individuals and organisations may diverge. Hence, workplace learning will only achieve the sustained development of the (learning) organisation if it can ensure that the personal development agendas of its employees are matched with its own organisational development.

Hence, the type of learning that takes place within an organisation is largely determined by the learning focus of the organisation, that is, how people learn within the organisation and what kind of learning is considered important. This, in turn, will be strongly influenced by the organisation's strategic goals, its flexibility and its willingness to take risks. Carr and Kemmis (cited in Matthews, 1999) suggest that there are three approaches to workplace learning: technical, interpretative and strategic. They argue that the **technical** approach, with its focus on the acquisition of specific skills or knowledge, is dominant within most organisations. Typically, skills acquisition becomes the focus of most training policy and the function of most training departments. The **interpretative** approach is more flexible, helping the learner to understand events and experience and to make personal judgements. Learning from past experience (reflection) is valued. Finally, the **strategic** approach involves the critical evaluation of underlying assumptions, values and beliefs, often through discussion in which ideas and opinions are exchanged.

Two observations can be offered about this classification. Firstly, the three approaches are probably hierarchical. In other words, learners may have to understand the technical elements of their work before they are in a position to make judgements and to reflect on their experiences. Critical evaluation of beliefs and values can only be enacted if one is first able to interpret events. Secondly, the approaches appear to reflect status and hierarchies within the workplace. Technical training tends to be provided for those at operational levels in the organisation, while strategic training and learning is generally the territory of management grades. Case Study 1.2 looks at whether a 'typical' new technology company can engage with these different approaches.

Case Study 1.2: *New learning at Airsnack*

Airsnack was established by two young catering graduates in 1997, to provide in-flight food for two medium-sized airlines. Within a year, it employed 10 people and now employs 200, producing food products for some of the world's major air carriers. In terms of location, it has moved from a home-based kitchen to a small factory unit on a high-tech estate. Knowledge and learning are what has made the company grow. It has not just been a question of packing food. The company has been careful to learn about the technical issues involved in serving food under pressurised flight conditions. It has also undertaken a process of continuous improvement in the nutritional qualities and presentation of its foods. The company has strived to become a 'learning organisation' in which learning must be rapid, shared and strongly linked to business needs.

To facilitate this, for example, Airsnack sponsors twelve employees on a Food Preparation and Cooking (NVQ Level 2) course at the local further education college, an example of technical training and knowledge acquisition. Also, within the company, partition walls have been knocked down to create open-plan spaces where people can see and interact with each other. Two designated coffee/meeting areas have been designed to facilitate communication and an Innovations Forum set up to generate new ideas. A monthly prize is awarded to the employee who comes up with the most interesting and innovative idea.

In practice, however, while these workers are highly innovative and creative, they are not very proficient at sharing their knowledge. There is competition to 'crack' problems before anyone else can, and an unhealthy 'them and us' culture has developed between those working on marketing and those involved with product development. Managers find it difficult to get their team members to actually talk to each other. So, in one sense, there is a lot of individual learning taking place in the organisation, but the learning of the organisation is being restricted. The Directors need to evaluate their personal leadership of the company, so they hire two executive coaches to help them with their strategic thinking.

We have seen in our case studies how two organisations of very different sizes have tried to make substantial changes to the ways in which they operate. Furthermore, external pressures from the outside world have meant that each organisation has had to pay very careful attention to its knowledge base and to its learning processes. However, this conscious, and often planned, attention to workplace learning is relatively new. In the next section, we trace the origins of workplace learning and show how it has evolved in a piecemeal fashion over time.

THE ORIGINS OF WORKPLACE LEARNING

In one sense, even at the very beginning of 'civilisation', people have learned at their work – from hunters learning to stalk their prey, to the first farmers, learning the importance of crop irrigation. As Jarvis *et al.* (1998) point out, one of the essential characteristics of human beings is that they have been innovators, but more importantly, they have then passed on their newly acquired knowledge to others. Both of these activities involve learning, but how this learning was transmitted depended on how the work to which it related was organised. In farming communities, for example, the household and family settings were the basis of production and therefore the transfer of knowledge. With the growth of towns and the early craft guilds, skills and knowledge were acquired through the apprenticeship system. The guilds both set the standard of knowledge required to enter the craft and ensured the continuation of this threshold standard by enforcing seven-year apprenticeships.

The development of capitalism, of course, smashed the guild system and heralded completely new ways of working and new sets of social relationships. In the craft systems, the craftsman (*sic*) possessed knowledge of the entire production process. Capitalism, however, broke the production process down through the division of labour. A worker now became only familiar with his or her own part of the production process. As Jarvis *et al.* (1998: 113) state:

> *This completely changed what learning was required. Workers should now know as little as necessary, rather than as much as possible. The source of knowledge was to be*

the employer and his organization, rather than other workers. Of course, workers continued to learn a lot informally, but only from other workers with very closely defined work roles.

In practice, of course, actual factory production was much more complex than this. Some workers did possess high levels of skill, but these people were often relatively well paid and in the minority. For most workers in the 19th and 20th centuries, training was limited to what they needed to know for a very specific work role. The development of skilled workers was still largely performed through the apprenticeship system. In terms of training, then, it was 'little for the many, rather more for the few' (Jarvis *et al.*, 1998: 114).

In the 20th century, the influence of people such as F. W. Taylor and Henry Ford meant that the process of increased division of labour continued, overseen by a rationalist analysis and planning of the production process. Managers, therefore, needed to acquire sophisticated new skills such as budgetary planning and strategic planning, as well as technical skills such as engineering. The training for much of the workforce, however, could be largely determined from their job descriptions. The training system that emerged from the Second World War was highly stratified, with quite distinct systems for senior managers, middle managers, skilled workers and unskilled workers. For senior managers, training was largely conducted outside the company, and was strongly influenced by government and professional associations. From the 1960s, universities began to involve themselves, influenced by the success of the university business schools in the USA. In contrast, training for the rest of the workforce was largely provided in-house, and was often seen as just one of the functions of the personnel department.

In the 1960s and 1970s, however, Fordist and bureaucratic approaches to management came under criticism, especially from writers such as Tom Burns and Tom Peters. New ideas began to emerge, based upon a critique of centralist notions of management and heralding the idea that managers and even workers themselves should have more discretion and influence over their own working processes. Successful firms had to adapt to the ever-changing external environment. According to Jarvis *et al.* (1998), four implications emerged from this:

- The demarcation between manager and worker began to break down.
- It became difficult to prescribe in advance all the knowledge and skills a manager and worker should possess.
- The organisation would have to respond to the changing external environment, rather than believing it could change it.
- Training had to move beyond the merely technical and win the employee's loyalty and commitment to the organisation – it had to change not only knowledge but attitudes.

The requirement that an organisation must be able to respond quickly to its external environment, and that its employees are key to this agility, meant that workers themselves were now seen as of central importance to the organisation. Hence, workers were no longer seen as 'employees' or 'personnel' but were (are) viewed as 'human resources'. Forward-looking firms restructured their personnel departments into human resource operations. Of course in some organisations, this was merely tokenistic, but over time, real changes in processes often emerged.

Firstly, there was the need to establish and retain employee commitment to the organisation and secondly, maintaining the idea of a planned training policy but one that recognises the importance of informal learning. Henceforth, the word 'learning' is often used in place of 'training'. Thirdly, there was the growth of new approaches to learning that did not depend on a transmission model, that is, a centralised training function telling people what they should know. What should replace the transmission model, however, has been problematic and has led to a variety of solutions, most of them framed around giving people greater responsibility for their own learning.

One such solution is to attempt to bring all learning, training and professional development work under one umbrella organisation, in the form of a corporate university. There are now over 1600 corporate universities worldwide, most of them in the USA, but a growing number in the UK and Europe (CVCP/HEFCE, 2000). The term 'corporate university', however, is used loosely to cover quite a disparate range of institutions, including:

- Partnership arrangements between a corporation and an actual university.
- Private universities and business schools with an orientation towards corporate needs.
- A university established by a corporation.

In the case of the latter, many of today's corporate universities have evolved from quite traditional company training departments. Indeed, some cynics would claim that many are still exactly this – only with rebranding. However, the rebranding process itself can provide opportunities for raising the profile of training and development activities. For example, in some cases it has been used to include training for strategic partners and supply chain organisations, and may involve partnerships with local college and university programmes. This raises the issue of qualifications and accreditation. In the USA, in particular, some corporate universities have taken the step of awarding their own qualifications, including degrees. In the UK, training programmes tend to be either non-accredited, or accredited by one of the main awarding bodies, through NVQs and usually involving further education rather than higher education level (Jarvis, 2001). Indeed, some private institutions have set themselves up as corporate universities to provide just-in-time, problem-based learning in 'bite-sized chunks' (see for example, NoonTime University, http://www.noontimeu.com). However, as Jarvis (2001) points out, these and the universities launched by corporations are not universities in the strictest sense of the word, being more concerned with operational than with academic competence. The following activity offers some examples of corporate universities.

ACTIVITY 1.1

For an example of a private organisation (Noontime University) that aims its products at the corporate sector, see http://www.noontimeu.com

For a well-known example of a corporate university, see the McDonalds Hamburger University at http://www.mcdonalds.com/corp/career/hamburger_university.html

The web site for the New Corporate University Review provides articles based upon the experience of both academics and practitioners in establishing and running corporate universities at http://www.traininguniversity.com/index.php

What has this rather breathless tour of workplace learning shown us? Firstly, it suggests that the changing global structure and goals of the economic system are affecting the structure and working practices of organisations. This affects both the products of learning (what should be learned) as well as the processes of learning (how it should be learned). Secondly, given the increased complexity of the global economy, and the necessity for organisations to be flexible and agile, command-and-obey forms of management are no longer tenable. In the knowledge economy, knowledge workers must have both the capability and the motivation to continually update their skills. This cannot be achieved through old-style training departments. Responsibility for learning is devolving its way down the organisation to line managers and employees themselves. This does not mean that the training function of organisations disappears completely – it means that it takes on a more facilitating role. Thirdly, it means that the focus of learning in the workplace is no longer based primarily upon the acquisition of formal knowledge. It must now also be collaborative and focused on solving real-life problems.

ACTIVITY 1.2

Evaluate the training provision in your own organisation. Does it exist? If so, what is the balance between it being centralised and devolved? Are individual employees expected to take responsibility for their own training or development and, if so, how explicit is this expectation? To what extent does your own organisation recognise or encourage learning beyond the remit of traditional training programmes?

WORKPLACE LEARNING IN THE UK

How does workplace learning in the UK compare with some of the workplace models we have just explored? Probably the honest answer is that the picture is not clear. This is because we rarely attempt to measure the impact of learning on organisations, particularly in terms of performance, output or efficiency. It is also because there is no national, comprehensive study of training, learning and professional development, although some Regional Development Agencies, Business Links and other 'gatekeeper' organisations are trying to map the mosaic of provision.

The Chartered Institute of Personnel and Development (CIPD) has, however, conducted a wide-ranging survey of over 500 UK organisations from a range of sectors and varying in size from 25 employees to large corporations (CIPD, 2001). From this we may at least be able to draw some tentative conclusions. The report endorses the idea, for example, that modern organisations are increasingly using the workplace itself as a source of learning and performance improvement. Yet there is still an underlying ambivalence about the strategic significance of learning and training. Results show, for instance, that while 40% of respondents believe that training does provide strategic support for business objectives, perhaps just as significantly, 45% of respondents did not reply to the question. While a healthy 86% of respondents said that senior managers and directors regarded training and development as an integral element of corporate strategy, almost half admitted that they found it difficult to get sufficient information or help from these bosses. On the other hand, a third of respondents stated that they never faced such difficulties, again reflecting an ambivalence in the findings.

For all the 'noise' about the new knowledge economy and the significance of training and professional development, the amount actually spent on training in the UK is dauntingly modest. As Table 1.1 illustrates, three-quarters of organisations spend less than £500 per head each year – although, as the report points out, these figures underestimate real totals. This is because training budgets do not always include many relevant costs (such as the salaries of those undertaking the training), and because organisations do not always measure every element of their training costs.

Table 1.1   *UK annual training budgets (CIPD, 2001)*

Annual training budget per head	% of total
Less than £100	41.4
£100–500	34.8
£500–1000	9.3
Over £1000	14.5
Total	100

What does this spending yield? According to Westwood (2001), not very much. For the UK, the average number of training hours undertaken per person per year is 99.5 (35 hours below the OECD average), compared, for example, with 218.7 for Ireland, 159 hours for the Netherlands and 143 hours for Poland.

Going beyond the issue of training under-funding, the provision of learning is far from evenly spread across organisations in terms of access. As Table 1.2 shows, whilst it is evident that most employees receive some on-the-job training (OJT), what is clear is that the main beneficiaries seem to be those in managerial and white-collar positions, rather than manual workers. The research found that the use of OJT was not linked to any difference in size of establishment, but was associated with possession of Investors in People (IiP) recognition and with the use of competence-based systems of training. According to the report, these factors may be mutually reinforcing. These findings tend to confirm those of Green (2000, quoted in Westwood, 2001) that while 71% of unskilled workers had received no training in the past 5 years, this figure was only 24% for those with degrees. If UK organisations, then, are becoming learning organisations, this seems to be learning organisations for managers. We will look at professional development and management training in more detail later in this chapter.

While coaching and mentoring are much less widespread than OJT, the imbalance of provision is just as pronounced. For management and professional grades in 63% of

Table 1.2   *The extent of structured OJT in the workplace (CIPD, 2001)*

Type of employee	Most do (%)	Sometimes (%)	None (%)
Management and professional	43.2	48.2	8.4
Other white-collar	53.6	40.4	6.0
Manual	29.3	23.7	47.0

establishments, some or most staff have a formally appointed coach or mentor. In contrast, 75% make no formal provision for their manual workers. This provision of coaching and mentoring is more likely in larger organisations, but there was no significant difference between sectors.

Another important finding is that 71% of respondents use a very structured approach to workplace learning, organising their workplace on the basis of formally defined competencies. Once again, you will not be surprised to learn that white collar and managerial grades are the prime beneficiaries. As Table 1.3 shows, OJT and face-to-face delivery are the favoured training methods. What seems to be significant here is the sheer formality of the training approach. While action learning, for example, is used, this is not on a regular basis by most organisations. In the UK, then, the practice of workplace learning contrasts sharply with some of the modern principles outlined in the previous section of this chapter.

Rather surprisingly, the use of IT-based training, such as computer-based methods and the Internet, appears quite modest. The rate of engagement with technical training methods, however, is increasing. The CIPD's survey for 2003 finds further growth, mainly amongst IT staff, middle and junior managers, and manual staff. The survey for 2001 also found a strong link between the use of computer-based training and competency-based approaches to training.

If workplace training is to engage with the notion of developing the whole person, it must encourage personal self-development. The CIPD (2001) survey found that 96% of training managers stated that they encouraged self-development in employees. However,

Table 1.3   *The extent to which establishments use different training methods and facilities*

	Regularly (%)	Sometimes (%)	None (%)
OJT	87.3	11.4	1.4
Face-to-face	84.3	14.4	1.0
Coaching/mentoring	59.4	32.1	8.6
Formal education	49.6	46.2	4.2
Conferences	43.4	50.2	6.4
Non-electronic open learning	34.7	51.8	13.5
CD-ROMs/DVD	28.9	47.6	23.5
Video	26.1	54.0	19.9
Intranets	23.7	34.5	41.8
Other computer-based learning	22.7	43.2	34.1
Internet	16.5	38.0	45.4
Action learning	14.7	36.5	48.8
Audio	8.4	38.8	52.8
Extranets	7.4	23.3	68.3

in terms of actual action, only 46% made any specific budget provision for it. Once again, where money is set aside, white-collar and management training is the most likely recipient. The conclusion of the CIPD (2001) report is that, while workplace learning is recognised as one of the most useful forms of training, relatively little attention is paid to it in practice. How can we explain this contradiction between verbal support for training and learning yet reluctance to finance it? The answers are probably numerous and quite complex, although an obvious explanation does present itself. The mindset of many UK organisations still sees training and professional development in terms of costs rather than opportunities for organisational sustainability and development.

This picture is further reinforced if we look at one sector in particular – SMEs. In 1999, small firms (1–49 employees) accounted for 38% of UK turnover, and employed nearly 45% of the private sector workforce (Smith *et al.*, 2002). In a study of 2000 SMEs, however, Hyland and Matley (1997) discovered a 'paradox of training', that is, a persistent inverse relationship between their positive attitudes towards training and their actual uptake of training that was largely insignificant. Indeed, of the 95% of owner-managers who displayed a positive attitude towards training, less than 14% of them had provided any training to their employees within the previous 12 months. One UK research project (Cambridge Small Business Research Centre, 1992) found that a number of characteristics influence the level of training in SMEs, namely:

- The size of the firm – larger firms provide more formal training than smaller ones.
- The ownership form of the employer – a subsidiary that forms part of a group is more likely to train.
- Age of the business – older firms tend to have better networks for accessing training.
- Industrial activity – those using advanced manufacturing technologies are most likely to train.
- Occupational status – those with professional and managerial status receive more training with unskilled workers the least.
- Technology – firms that place emphasis on research and development and who use new technologies are more likely to train.

Other factors encouraging training include the incidence of a buoyant local economy and the probability of a future expansion in recruitment. Smith *et al.* (2002) find that SME engagement with training has also been positively influenced if organisations apply for IiP status. The drivers for this tend to include the need to retain staff and to design a framework for people development. Yet despite these influences, Vickerstaff (1992) shows that many SMEs share common difficulties when it comes to accessing training:

- Resourcing training – many SMEs find the costs of training prohibitive.
- Time – often employees cannot be released for training because of work commitments.
- Locating training – SMEs are less likely than large firms to have access to qualified training staff; they also find it difficult to assess the quality of external training provision.

Evidence suggests that SMEs and their employees often require information and knowledge to solve immediate problems but lack the necessary channels of information (Marchmont, 1999). What is required is a new approach to KM that includes just-in-time learning. The Marchmont project also found that it is the role of senior managers within SMEs that is pivotal in driving the demand for learning.

Hence, while SMEs account for a significant proportion of the UK economy measured in terms of employment and turnover, they remain, with some exceptions, on the periphery of the training and professional development agenda. Probably not surprisingly, larger, more established firms tend to have a better track record, and IiP seems to have had a positive effect, at least amongst some firms. Certainly, the need to improve training and learning within the SME sector is still a high government priority.

CONTINUING PROFESSIONAL DEVELOPMENT IN THE UK

The term 'professional' is often used to describe a wide range of activities across many occupational groups, and usually encompasses those who, as a minimum, have a degree-level professional qualification. The number of people employed in professional roles has expanded considerably in the last 20 years, and is likely to continue to grow, as is the need for their continuing professional development (CPD). According to Madden and Mitchell (in Watkins, 1999), CPD comprises one or more of the following:

• Updating knowledge and skills.
• Preparing for a changing work role and new responsibilities.
• Increasing competence in a wider context.

However, it is predicted that the kinds of skills needed by professionals will change in response to globalisation and the dynamics of the world economic system. What we are likely to see is an increase in:

• The complexity of roles, as markets, products and organisational structures change.
• Skill requirements, with the new knowledge workers needing to develop higher-order problem-solving, negotiating, project management and conflict management skills – to name but a few.
• Teamworking, with work becoming increasingly organised through project or task groups, sometimes through virtual (online) collaboration.

Professional knowledge, then, is changing from basic procedural knowledge of 'what to do' to higher-order skills, as presented in Figure 1.1. Hence, knowledge workers need to move from Levels 1 and 2 – knowing what to do and how to do it (application) – to

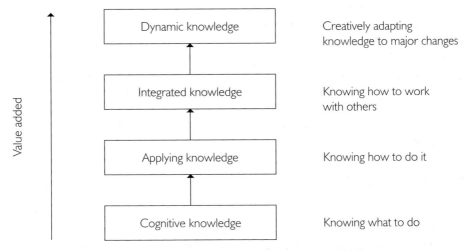

Figure 1.1 *Levels of professional knowledge (adapted from Watkins, 1999)*

collaborative skills for working with others. This can only be achieved by a deep understanding of an organisation's structures, systems and culture, with people working in teams and across disciplines and departments. According to Watkins (1999), those with dynamic knowledge (at Level 4) are able to apply and adapt the knowledge they have gained in the first three stages in order to come up with creative solutions in increasingly complex environmental conditions.

The term 'professional development' first came into use in the UK in the 1970s, but was only formally adopted by professional associations in the mid-1980s. Today, much of the professional development undertaken in the UK is through one of these professional associations, of which there are approximately 400 with more than 1000 members and 92 with a membership of between 200 and 1000 (Watkins, 1999). Some of these are statutory bodies, some trade unions, while others are chartered. Whatever their formal governance, in most cases these organisations have responsibility for professional standards, for initial and continuing education or training, for providing professional advice and for publishing journals and running conferences and events. Today, the education and training function is often passed on to institutions of higher education, with the professional associations retaining control over the curriculum content and course design. But the responsibility for undertaking CPD still rests with the individual member. However, a distinction needs to be drawn between whether a professional association holds a **sanctions** or **benefits** model of development. For the former, CPD is a formal requirement of membership, with strict guidelines laid down on the kinds of development activities to be undertaken – for example, formal accredited courses. Under the benefits model, usually found in the newer or developing professional associations, CPD is seen largely as an important but largely voluntary activity (Jones and Fear, 1994).

This situation, however, may be changing. According to Watkins (1999), a growing number of professional associations are establishing a minimum level of CPD as a requirement for membership. Especially for the (albeit small) number who require annually renewable practising certificates, for example, ongoing training and development have become essential. Watkins suggests that a minimum CPD requirement will soon be an established feature for all professional bodies. As we saw in Figure 1.1, managers need a broader portfolio of higher-order, cross-functional skills for them to survive at a competitive level, as well as good interpersonal skills. Some professional associations are now trying to break these down into specified competencies that can then provide the basis for programme development as well as a benchmark for personal development planning. Figure 1.2 outlines, at a general level, what these skills might be. It means going beyond specialised professional skills and developing coping skills, flexibility, working with others and the ability to cope with diversity and uncertainty.

ACTIVITY 1.3

Examine the skills outlined in Figure 1.2. Which of them might be a priority for your own organisation? How might people be trained to acquire them?

One of the implications of this diversity of skills is that individuals need to be able to manage their own development. A result of this has been the growth of what is termed the 'portfolio approach to CPD'. The practitioner builds up a portfolio of recorded activities

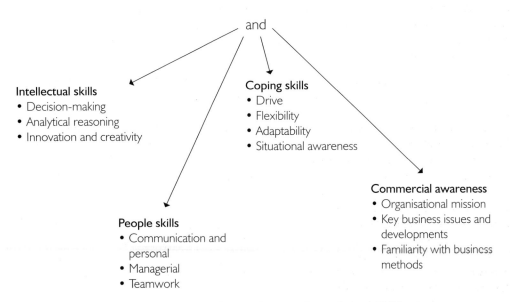

Technical and professional skills of the specialism

and

Intellectual skills
- Decision-making
- Analytical reasoning
- Innovation and creativity

Coping skills
- Drive
- Flexibility
- Adaptability
- Situational awareness

Commercial awareness
- Organisational mission
- Key business issues and developments
- Familiarity with business methods

People skills
- Communication and personal
- Managerial
- Teamwork

Figure 1.2 *Competencies required by professions (adapted from Watkins, 1999)*

(including formal and informal learning) and achievements, letters of commendation, records of mentoring sessions and PDPs. Chapter 6 discusses the Accreditation of Prior Learning (APL) and Accreditation of Prior Experiential Learning (APEL) – one approach to the recording and acknowledgement of development – while Chapter 7 discusses portfolios. This links well to a further recent development in CPD – the fact that there is less of an emphasis on 'inputs' (e.g. the number of courses attended) and more on 'outputs' in terms of what the individual is actually able to do. Hence, there is an increased focus on competence, types of competencies needed to perform a task and their measurement (see Chapter 5). According to Wilkins (1999), some professional bodies are now rewriting their CPD guidelines to allow for the recognition of prior and ongoing informal CPD.

Friedman *et al.* (2000), however, raise some concerns about this increasing emphasis on competence by highlighting a potential contradiction at the core of the professional development process. On the one hand, CPD is meant to enhance the personal skills and knowledge of the individual. It is an important component of personal development and lifelong learning. But on the other hand, professional associations need to reassure government and society in general that professional standards are laid down, monitored and adhered to. After all, professionals are handed a high degree of personal autonomy in their practice and a licence to grant who should be allowed to assume the mantle of professional 'authority':

> *As long as professional associations employ … the rhetoric of lifelong learning and personal development as well as assurances that CPD will provide some guarantee of competence, a fundamental confusion will continue to be fostered. CPD is burdened with twin aims which it cannot fulfil simultaneously.*

Friedman *et al.* (2000: 204)

MANAGEMENT DEVELOPMENT IN THE UK

In some senses, management development can be seen as one, but a very important, element of CPD as a whole. Indeed, a proportion of management development is undertaken through one of the various professional associations concerned with the development of managers, one of the largest of which is the Chartered Management Institute (CMI), which has over 90,000 members (see Box 1.1).

Box 1.1: The role of the Chartered Management Institute

One of the roles of the CMI is the delivery of management training programmes leading to NVQ/SVQ qualifications, including generic management awards such as a Certificate in Management (Level 3) and a Diploma in Management (Level 4), to qualifications focused on small businesses such as the Certificate and Diploma in Business Start-up. There are even specialist qualifications such as a Diploma in Energy Management. These qualifications are linked to the National Occupational Standards for Managers, the benchmarks for management performance, full members of the CMI gaining the award of Chartered Manager – 'the hallmark of the professional manager'. The aim of the award of Chartered Manager is to establish a hallmark of current competence and professionalism, to enable employers to identify managers who have demonstrated currency of management competence and positive impact in the workplace. In doing this, the programme will:

- provide managers with a structured CPD environment within which to develop themselves across the full range of generic management skills
- highlight a range of learning and development opportunities in support of this development
- provide access to a number of self-assessment diagnostic tools to monitor their progress.

The CMI system is discussed in more detail in Chapter 7 and web site details are provided in Activity 1.4.

Another important organisation is the Council for Excellence in Management and Leadership, established in 2000 by what was the Department for Education and Skills and the Department for Trade and Industry, to create a strategy for the development of managers and leaders of the future. The Council has completed over 30 publications, including reports and working papers dealing with issues such as corporate management and leadership, and studies on how UK business schools can make a better contribution to management education.

ACTIVITY 1.4

Look at the following web sites for UK professional associations concerned with aspects of management development:

Chartered Management Institute	http://www.managers.org.uk
Institute of Management Consultants	http://www.imc.co.uk
Management Standards Centre	http://www.management-standards.org
Council for Excellence in Management and Leadership	http://www.managementandleadershipcouncil.org

According to Mabey and Thomson (2000), in the late 1980s management development in the UK was reported to be poor in terms of both quality and quantity. Since then the picture has improved, in part at least because of IiP, which has encouraged organisations to design their management development programmes on competence-based principles. In their study, 61% of companies reported an increase in management training, only 9% a decrease, with 23% reporting no change (Mabey and Thomson, 2000).

One feature of this growth has been the rise in importance of external qualifications such as the MBA, now one of the best known qualifications in the world. First pioneered by the Harvard Business School, the traditional MBA makes use of real-world business case studies, rather than relying only on academic business theories. This model has remained largely unchanged since. European interest in MBAs began with the establishment of INSEAD in Fontainebleau, France, in 1958. In contrast to the US two-year programme, European MBAs tend to be for one year and are focused on an older clientele, in their late 20s or early 30s, i.e. people with more business experience. With the support of the UK government, the London Business School and the Manchester Business School were set up in 1964. Both adopted the US model with a two-year, full-time programme, while Warwick, Cranfield and Lancaster subsequently set up programmes using the one-year European model. Today, the USA still has the most MBA programmes, with over 600, but Europe is catching up. There are now more than 100 business schools in the UK, while it is estimated that there are about 100,000 managers studying for an MBA worldwide (Latreuille, 2001).

ACTIVITY *1.5*

The Association of MBAs (AMBA) is the independent accreditation body that assesses the quality of MBA programmes. Its membership includes qualified MBA students and Business Schools offering MBA programmes. Have a look at the AMBA web site at http://www.managementandleadershipcouncil.org

However, concerns are being expressed in some quarters that many MBAs, or similar accredited management programmes, are not meeting the needs of managers, because they teach management in a way that is divorced from its context (the workplace). Mintzberg (1999, referenced in Martin and Butler, 2000) accuses US business schools, for example, of directing MBAs at the 'wrong people' (full-time students with little real experience of management); using the 'wrong ways' (with too much emphasis on prescriptive case studies and disconnected theory instead of learning in context); and for the 'wrong reasons' (by creating a business class that believed they had the right to lead, just because of the qualifications they had earned in the classroom). In contrast, he advises that, in the future, MBA programmes should:

- be aimed at practising managers, i.e. students should be part-time and company-sponsored
- use action learning and reflective learning in which learning material is 'dropped in' at a time and within a context that fits real work situations
- dispense with 'silo' design in which participants come from functional backgrounds and focus on issues within these backgrounds, instead of trying to manage integrated business problems
- be international and collaborative to reflect the real world of business.

What is needed is a focus on **workplace** management development, with educational efforts linked into action learning projects, job rotation, and internal consultancy and mentoring schemes. It is worth noting that Hahs (1999) points to the fact that some of these improvements may already be taking place – some business schools are now looking to industry for advice in restructuring their MBA programmes. Others are including the study of a foreign language as part of the course or are using an overseas placement.

However, a large amount of learning is still informal, with on-the-job learning, coaching and action learning amongst the most popular methods for transmitting skills and knowledge. Whatever method is adopted, what is clear is that a key priority is senior management commitment to the issue of management development, made explicit through either policy statements, or a clear message that responsibility for this development emanates from management rather than being left to the individual. Hence:

> *Directing effort into the generation of a strategic management development policy, putting resources aside to support and sustain it and then taking an active role in co-ordinating its implementation constitute vital levers in the successful development of managers.*
>
> Mabey and Thomson (2000: 284)

That said, the role of management development as a strategic intervention in UK organisations remains far from consistent. As we have seen, however, there is an increasing emphasis on the development of management skills within a real, workplace situation and within a context. Coaching and mentoring are just two, but increasingly important, elements of this work-related focus.

COACHING AND MENTORING

According to the CIPD, 95% of the 500 organisations they surveyed in 2003 make use of coaching or mentoring (up from 85% in 2002) (CIPD, 2003). One of the problems faced in any discussion of coaching and mentoring, however, is that the two terms are so often used interchangeably. For the purposes of this discussion we will define mentoring as a relationship, often used internally within an organisation, whereby more experienced, often senior or executive managers, usually in the same speciality, provide support and a role model for less experienced colleagues. It is usually a fairly open-ended association, sometimes lasting months or even years, and is often associated with the mentee's career development. Many companies, particularly large ones, have specifically designed mentoring systems and written protocols. Mentors are selected (or even better, volunteer) and are given training in mentoring skills including listening empathetically and providing support, advice and feedback. Mentors are invariably not the mentee's line manager, as this would introduce an unhelpful power element into the relationship, and may even come from a different department or division in the organisation. One of the problems, however, that many organisations are facing is the shortage of experienced and suitable mentors. Some organisations are looking to ways of overcoming this problem through the use of e-mentoring (mentoring online) using IT solutions, but how effective this will be for what is largely a close, one-to-one relationship remains to be seen.

In contrast to mentoring, coaching is usually relatively short-term, and is performance, business and action-orientated. In the past, the term 'coaching' was often used quite restrictively to describe the passing on of training skills or even attitudes. Hence, it was often associated with OJT. Coaching within the context of management development was probably first used in 1958 by Myles Mace in a book on the development of executive skills (Eggers and Clark, 2000). His concept of OJT saw this as a process whereby managers used a job-development tool to generate greater productivity amongst their own employees. Hence, coaching was associated rather narrowly with job-skills development, rather than as it is today with the professional development of managers and executives.

Many modern organisations have coaching schemes, although they could often better be described as mentoring because they involve long-term support and advice from senior colleagues. One relatively new form that is coaching in its purest form is executive coaching. Two decades ago the concept hardly existed. Today, it would seem that most consultancy organisations are offering executive coaching services. There are currently about 10,000 executive coaches worldwide, but this figure is likely to increase five-fold in the next three or four years. Indeed, Eggers and Clark (2000) report that executive coaching is the fastest growing area amongst management consultancy companies and individual management consultants. A survey by the Hayes Group of 170 HR professionals found that more than half the respondents had established some form of coaching programme in the past 18 months. Intriguingly, 70% of respondents believed that coaching is more effective than traditional training development programmes in changing the behaviour and improving the performance of senior executives and 'high-flyers'.

Despite this, broad agreement on the nature, processes and functions of executive coaching has yet to be established. Downey (2003: 15) refers to it as 'the art of facilitating the performance, learning and development of another'. Carter (2001: 15) defines executive coaching more broadly as 'a form of tailored work-related development for senior and professional managers which spans business, functional and personal skills'.

The International Coaching Federation, however, also includes development beyond the workplace, seeing executive coaching as 'a process that is designed to help clients improve their learning and performance, and *enhance their quality of life*' (our emphasis) (ICF, 2003). The coached client is someone who wants to reach a higher level of performance, personal satisfaction or learning. In terms of relationship, the coach is not necessarily an 'expert' or 'authority' but someone who relates to the client in a spirit of partnership and collaboration. It is the client, however, who holds the ultimate responsibility for and ownership of the desired outcomes.

Case Study 1.3: *Workplace learning in the Citizens Support Bureau*

The Citizens Support Bureau (CSB) is a not-for-profit, national organisation whose aim is to ensure that individuals understand their rights and responsibilities and are able to gain access to the services they need. In practice, the CSB operates through a network of local, high street 'advice centres', which give mostly legal and financial advice to people who 'drop in'. There are over 100 full-time staff at the CSB's national headquarters and, generally, about two or three full-time and a small number of part-time paid staff at each of the local centres. There are also ten regional managers. The overwhelming human resources, however, are the 4000 unpaid volunteers who vary in background from local solicitors, teachers and accountants, to retired people.

The CSB in its present structure was formed 50 years ago, very much as a caring organisation that survived on the goodwill and commitment of its volunteers. After all, they do give their valuable time free of charge. However, particularly in the last 10 years, a growing weight of legislation and a burgeoning case load has forced the CSB to expand its full-time staffing at both national and local level. This in turn has forced the CSB to abandon its reliance on charitable funding and turn to the state for support. The CSB is now largely funded by national government, but this has meant that the organisation is increasingly subject to governmental pressures as to how it operates.

While recognising the valuable work the CSB performs, the government has been concerned that the service needs to become both more accountable and more 'professional'. Financial and auditing controls have recently been put in place, and national and local management committees set up. The CSB has also been 'encouraged' to place a higher emphasis on staff development and training, to be linked with a new professional qualification for both advisers and managers. The new qualification, a Diploma in Advisory Services, will be modular and work-related, that is, the assessment elements of the qualification will comprise analysis of live projects, and problems and case studies from the learner's own workplace. The Accreditation of Prior (Certificated) Learning (APL) and the Accreditation of Prior Experiential Learning (APEL) will also be recognised and counted towards the award. (We will look at APL and APEL in more detail in Chapter 6.) Hence, someone with legal qualifications will be given 'advance standing' and be able to count this towards the award, so gaining exemption from certain modules. Again, a manager or volunteer with, say, ten years' experience of financial counselling will be shown how to demonstrate evidence of this experience to gain advance standing and exemption.

In addition to this formal qualification, the CSB also initiates a coaching and mentoring system that is to be used particularly for guiding the much-needed influx of volunteers. A handbook, comprising a set of formal procedures for coaching and mentoring, is to be prepared and distributed to all staff. Furthermore, the skills of coaching and mentoring are designed as two modules of the Diploma in Advisory Services qualification. So, for example, those studying the mentoring module will carry out, analyse and reflect on these skills through mentoring a member of staff and by being mentored by their own CSB line manager.

ACTION LEARNING IN THE WORKPLACE

In contrast to coaching and mentoring, which usually focus on one-to-one relationships and interactions, action learning usually involves collaboration within a set or group. Unfortunately, as with coaching and mentoring, one of the problems of action learning is that it can mean different things to different people. As Marsick and O'Neil (1999) describe, many quite traditional programmes are given the 'badge' of action learning, but are far from being so in the accepted sense of the word. Weinstein (1995: 3) gives a quite specific definition of action learning as:

a process underpinning a belief in individual potential: a way of learning from our actions, and from what happens to us, and around us, by taking the time to question, understand and reflect, to gain insights, and consider how to act in future.

Participants on a workplace action learning programme will, typically, focus on live workplace problems and issues that could involve, say, their own managerial and personal development, the management of staff or teams, communication, or managing the implementation of a new IT system. In essence, learning is inductive. The learner starts with a problem, examines it from as many angles as possible, builds conceptual models and solutions, implements them and evaluates the impact. From its very inception by Revans (1982), action learning has also involved questioning. Hence, according to its classic formulation:

Learning = Programmed knowledge from the past + Questioning insight (L = P + Q).

Questioning insight occurs when people question and reflect on their direct experience. The key is finding the right question to ask. One very important potential outcome of the action learning experience is learning *how* to learn. This is because in most action learning programmes, time is set aside for the review of learning. Members also review the issues that emerge from group dynamics and processes and the work of others in their action learning sets. Some might also keep learning logs or negotiate learning agreements with a tutor.

Action learning as a concept relies on the understanding that the emphasis of any activity is about *the learning that arises from the process* rather than (though inextricably linked to) the solution to an actual problem. The development of a solution will draw on the skills of identifying and analysing experience, reflection and feedback. Its practices, therefore, draw heavily on models of experiential learning developed by people such as Kolb (1984) and Boud *et al.* (1985), and on principles of reflective practice espoused by Schön (1983) (see Chapter 3). Revans (1983) also emphasises the importance of systematic research in action learning and builds upon, rather than seeks to replace, the academic traditions.

Action learning is still a significant element of many formal programmes of learning, particularly those involved with personal and professional development. However, as Marsick and O'Neil (1999) suggest, who benefits from the action learning process depends, in part, on whether the focus of the project is the individual or the team. Projects pursued by individuals often have more of an emphasis on their own personal learning. In contrast, team projects often focus on organisational goals, even though individual growth may also emerge. However, the very power and dynamics of action learning mean that the outcomes of recommendations of projects can often challenge strongly held beliefs, processes or cultures in an organisation – and vested interests. Yet action learning is:

often the first step for participants in a journey toward greater awareness of the political and cultural dimensions of organizational change. For organizations, it is often a first step toward linking individual learning with systemic learning and change.

Marsick and O'Neil (1999: 174)

In some senses, then, action learning epitomises many of the positive features of modern workplace learning – the emphasis on individual responsibility for learning (but often linked to a group context), learning as part of CPD, and learning that is focused on the solving of real, live work-related problems.

Summary

- Workplace learning includes formal learning (through accredited or non-accredited programmes); informal learning (arising through interactions at work, from action, through problem-solving or through processes such as coaching and mentoring); or incidental learning (occurring by chance).
- Most learning at work is informal, but organisations pay insufficient attention to it and often fail to understand or encourage it.
- Workplace learning in the UK is becoming increasingly recognised as a source of performance improvement and includes on-the-job training, coaching, mentoring, and action learning through to formal education including professional qualifications and MBAs.
- An important element of workplace learning is CPD, much of which comes under the auspices of one of the professional associations. Some of these associations operate according to a sanctions model, where continuing membership is dependent on continuous updating of skills, qualifications or knowledge. Some of the newer professional associations are run more on a benefits model, where personal development is encouraged but largely optional.
- One feature of professional development, management development, has a patchy track record in the UK, although over the last ten years there have been signs of improvement both in quality and quantity. This is not just a matter of more MBA graduates. More management learning is delivered informally through coaching and mentoring and through problem-solving (sometimes through the use of action learning sets).

References

Boud, D., Keogh, R. and Walker, D. (1985) *Reflection: Turning Experience into Learning*, Kogan Page, London.

Cambridge Small Business Research Centre (1992) *The State of British Enterprise: Growth, Innovation and Competitive Advantage in Small and Medium Sized Firms*, University of Cambridge, Cambridge.

Carter, A. (2001) *Executive Coaching: Inspiring Performance at Work*, The Institute for Employment Studies, Brighton.

Casey, C. (1999) The changing contexts of work. In: *Understanding Learning at Work* (ed. Boud, D.). Routledge, London, pp. 15–28.

CIPD (2001) *Training and Development 2001: Survey Report*, Chartered Institute of Personnel and Development, London.

CIPD (2003) *Training and Development 2003: Survey Report*, Chartered Institute of Personnel and Development, London.

CVCP/HEFCE (2000) *The Business of Borderless Education: UK Perspectives*, Committee of Vice-Chancellors and Principals of the Universities of the UK, London.

Downey, M. (2003) *Effective Coaching*, Texere, London.

Eggers, J.H. and Clark, D. (2000) Executive coaching that wins. *Ivey Business Journal*, Sept/Oct.

Eraut, M., Alderton, J., Cole, G. and Senker, P. (1998) *Development of Knowledge and Skills in Employment*, Final Report of a Research Project funded by the 'Learning Society' Programme of the Economic and Social Research Council, University of Sussex Institute of Education.

Friedman, A., Davis, K., Durkin, C. and Phillips, M. (2000) *Continuing Professional Development in the UK: Policies and Programmes*, Professional Associations Research Network, Bristol.

Hahs, D.L. (1999) What have MBAs done for us lately? *Journal of Education for Business*, **74**(4), 197–203.

Hyland, T. and Matley, H. (1997) Small business, training needs and VET provision. *Journal of Education and Work*, **10**(2), 129–141.

ICF (2003) International Coaching Federation. http://www.coachfederation.org/aboutcoaching /nature.htm (accessed 14 April 2003).

Jarvis, P. (2001) *Universities and Corporate Universities*, Kogan Page, London.

Jarvis, P., Holford, J. and Griffin, C. (1998) *The Theory and Practice of Learning*, Kogan Page, London.

Jones, N. and Fear, N. (1994) Continuing professional development: perspectives for human resource professionals. *Personnel Review*, **23**(8), 49–60.

Kolb, D. (1984) *Experiential Learning*, Prentice Hall, Englewood Cliffs, NJ.

Latreuille, D. (2001) The Growth of the MBA. Guardian Unlimited. http://education.guardian. co.uk/mbas/story/0.10671.528563.00.html (accessed 1 February 2003)

Mabey, C. and Thomson, A. (2000) Management development in the UK: a provider and participant perspective. *International Journal of Training and Development*, **4**(4), 272–286.

Marchmont Project (1999) *Understanding SME Learning: The Challenges for the Ufi*, Report of Joint Marchmont/SME Cluster Group Workshop, University of Sheffield 10–11 November 1999.

Marsick, V. and O'Neil, J. (1999) The many faces of action learning. *Management Learning*, **30**(2), 159–176.

Marsick, V. and Watkins, K. (1989) *Informal and Incidental Learning in the Workplace*, Routledge, London.

Martin, G. and Butler, M. (2000) Comparing managerial careers, management development and management education in the UK and the USA: some theoretical and practical consideration. *International Journal of Training and Development*, **4**(3), 196–207.

Matthews, P. (1999) Workplace learning: developing an holistic model. *The Learning Organisation*, **6**(1), 18–29.

Raelin, J.A. (2000) *Work-Based Learning: The New Frontier of Management Development*, Prentice Hall, Englewood Cliffs, NJ.

Revans, R. (1982) *The Origin and Growth of Action Learning*, Chartwell Bratt, London.

Revans, R. (1983) Action learning: its origins and nature. In: *Action Learning in Practice* (ed. Pedlar, M.), Gower, Aldershot, pp. 3–13.

Schön, D.A. (1983) *The Reflective Practitioner: How Professionals Think in Action*, Temple Smith, London.

Senge, P.M. (1990) *The Fifth Discipline: The Art & Practice of the Learning Organisation*, Doubleday Currency, New York.

Smith, J.A., Boocock, G., Loan-Clark, J. and Whittaker, J. (2002) IiP and SMEs: awareness, benefits and barriers. *Personnel Review*, **31**(1), 62–85.

Vickerstaff, S. (1992) The management of training in the smaller firm. *Human Resource Management*, **5**(4), 32–37.

Watkins, J. (1999) UK professional associations and continuing professional development: a new direction? *International Journal of Lifelong Education*, **18**(1), 61–75.

Weinstein, K. (1995) *Action Learning*, 2nd edn, Gower, Aldershot.

Westwood, A. (2001) Drawing a line – who is going to train our workforce? In: *The Future of Learning at Work*, Chartered Institute of Personnel and Development, London.

2 Knowledge management in the workplace

Objectives

After reading this chapter, you will be able to:

- Define knowledge management (KM), and distinguish between data, information and knowledge.
- Describe and explain the growing strategic significance of KM.
- Explain why KM is as much about people and their learning as it is about systems.
- Explain the functions of a KM system in storing and disseminating learning as part of being a 'learning organisation'.
- Devise a strategy for introducing or modifying KM in your own organisation.

Introduction

In Chapter 1, we explored a wide range of issues connected with learning in the workplace, including workplace learning and some of its various facets, such as formal learning, coaching, mentoring and action learning. However, and particularly in the last ten years, interest has moved on to what has been termed **knowledge management (KM)**, of which formal, non-formal and informal learning are seen as a subset. In one sense, KM has been with us, in various guises, since the dawn of humanity. Even Stone Age societies evolved processes for survival that had to be understood and passed down (orally and through example) to each generation. Intellectually, one of the original sources of KM lies in Western philosophy in the work of, amongst others, Socrates, Plato and Aristotle, and in Eastern philosophy in the teachings of Confucius and Lao Tzu. Religion and philosophy have tried to understand the role and nature of knowledge and the role of individuals in thinking for themselves.

Societies have also had to develop processes for the capturing, transmission and development of knowledge. In medieval times, this was one of the functions of the craft guilds, while in more modern times it was the apprenticeship system that, for industrial workers, facilitated this process. Today, in a world of mobile workforces and dynamically changing skills, organisations are beginning to recognise the significance of the intellectual capital they possess and the need to manage it. KM as a coherent and debated concept, however, is not very old, as Table 2.1 demonstrates.

This chapter will look at some of the quite complex and diverse definitions of KM. It will also look at ways in which KM strategies and processes have been implemented, including the evolution of what are termed 'communities of practice' (CoPs). In reading this chapter, we would ask you to consider and reflect on how KM systems could be introduced or developed within your own organisation.

Table 2.1   *The development of KM, 1975 to 2004*

Year	Development
1975	Chaparral Steel, USA, bases its organisational structures and corporate strategy on an explicit management of knowledge
1980	Digital Equipment Corporation installs the first large-scale knowledge-based system
1986	The concept of the management of knowledge was introduced in a keynote address at a European management conference
1987	The first KM book is published in Europe (Sveiby and Lloyd)
1990	The Initiative for Managing Knowledge Assets (IMKA) commences
1991	Skandia Insurance creates the position of Director of Intellectual Capital. *Harvard Business Review* runs its first article on KM
1994	Consulting firms begin to offer knowledge services and seminars on KM for clients
1996	The European Knowledge Management Association is founded
2004	KM conferences held all over the world

WHY KNOWLEDGE MANAGEMENT?

Is KM important? Well, according to some commentators, the knowledge-based society has already arrived, and the only organisations that will survive in the new century will be those that can identify, value, create and evolve their knowledge assets (Rowley, 1999). Clearly, one problem is that the pace of change has become inexorably quicker. Given that the half-life of products (their market viability) is shortening and that it is becoming increasingly difficult for an organisation to sustain its competitive advantage, KM is one of the few tangibles that can be used to sustain advantage through efficiency and creativity (Davenport and Prusch, 2000). One problem is the fact that many organisations have downsized their staff levels and found that, as people walk out of the door, vital knowledge goes with them. The sheer scale of information, however, is also increasing. IBM, for example, estimates that the amount of corporate data doubles every 12–18 months, but that only 15% of this is structured: the rest is stored in a completely unstructured format – chaos management!

KM, then, is not just seen as a useful 'nice to have', but a tangible asset at the heart of business survival and success. However, what actually constitutes KM is open to debate. It also has to be conceded that the world of KM is overwhelmed by 'hype', particularly from those who have something to sell – such as vendors of KM software and systems. There is a danger that KM becomes a supply push (from developers) rather than a demand pull (from customers). Let us look, then, at the meaning of KM in more detail.

WHAT IS KM?

In a general sense, KM is concerned with the exploitation and development of the knowledge assets of an organisation so that its objectives can be further developed. It is defined by Neef (1999: 78) as:

. . . a critical set of policies and practices that will boost an organisation's competitive position in the new knowledge-based economy by optimizing collaboration and knowledge-sharing among employees and providing them with the information and knowledge that they need to improve operational efficiency, to innovate and to sense and respond to new opportunities in the marketplace.

This, of course, begs the question – what is knowledge? Davenport and Prusch (2000) describe it as a (difficult to define) mixture of values, contextual information and expert insights that provide a framework for evaluating and incorporating new experiences and information. We talk of 'pieces of information' but a 'body of knowledge'. Hence, knowledge is derived from making connections and comparisons between pieces of information and, in contrast to information or data, contains an element of human judgement. While information consists of facts and other data to describe a particular situation or condition, knowledge is used to receive information that is then analysed, interpreted and evaluated, in order to plan, adapt or implement – in other words, to learn then act.

Some kinds of knowledge are quite easy to identify and include the operation of basic processes, business plans, market research, patents, trademarks and customer lists. This is what Hildreth and Kimble (2000) term 'hard' knowledge. However, other forms of (soft) knowledge include internalised knowledge and experience, often known as tacit knowledge, which is much harder to define, recognise or measure. As Stewart (1998) comments, tacit knowledge also tends to be local and shared, if it is shared at all, and orally generated rather than in manuals, books or databases: 'it is created and shared around the watercooler' (Stewart, 1998: 73).

ACTIVITY 2.1

Think of when you started a new job. How easy was it to learn from 'old lags' in the organisation? Did you ever get the impression that they knew more than they were able or willing to pass on to you? How easy would it be for you to pass on to someone the skills of your current job?

Because knowledge is such a special commodity and in short supply, there is a market for it. Like any market, it operates through the forces of supply and demand. Knowledge buyers are those who have an issue or problem to solve. Knowledge sellers sell their knowledge usually for a salary (for example, as consultants). Hence, knowledge is more than just a set of ideas, concepts or procedures. If it contains an element of judgement, then it also incorporates expertise, something that can be difficult to identify, measure and share. As we shall see, this is one of the major challenges to a coherent KM strategy.

Sveiby (2001) suggests that KM has, over a period of only 10 years, been through at least three phases. The first phase was inward-looking and focused primarily on the implementation of IT systems such as project databases, best practice databases and Lotus Notes installations. The second phase began to look outwards, again with an emphasis on IT systems, but with more of a customer focus. The third (current) phase is the most interactive, combining IT with a customer focus through e-business, e-commerce and online transactions. Sveiby looks forward to the next phase of KM development that he predicts to be the 'people-track' or how people share knowledge:

> *The bandwidth of the human infrastructure is the trust between people and between management and employees. The human infrastructure requires investment just as the IT infrastructure does.*
>
> Sveiby (2001: 2)

Hence, this projected phase of KM is much more people and communication oriented. In summary, at a very basic level, KM could be said to consist of technology, people and the knowledge itself (but not necessarily in that order) (Figure 2.1).

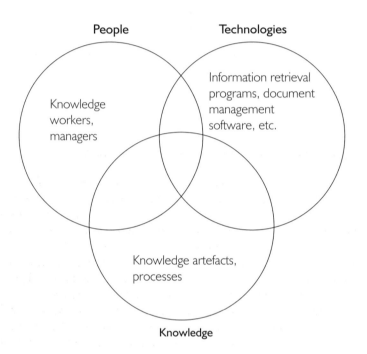

Figure 2.1 *KM as the interrelationship between knowledge, technology and people*

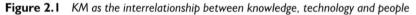

ACTIVITY 2.2

For an overview of what some 40 organisations are doing in the field of KM, go the web site http://www.sveiby.com/articles/KnowledgeManagement.html and take a look at the section 'Knowledge Management Initiatives Round the Globe'.

IMPLEMENTING KM

In the knowledge-based economy, it is essential that practitioners become both the creators and critical users of knowledge. But what can an organisation do to promote knowledge? Obviously, it has to have a coherent strategy, but it also has to understand how knowledge is created, transferred or blocked within its own structures. As Figure

2.2 shows, an organisation needs to pose itself questions such as what kinds of knowledge it creates, how it is captured and organised (when and by whom), how knowledge is accessed, when and why, and how it is used.

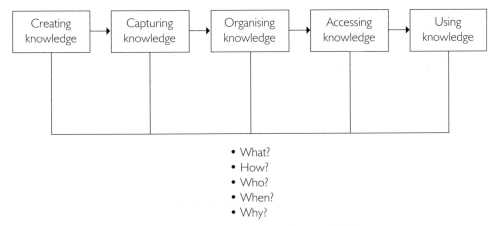

Figure 2.2 The stages of KM (adapted from Soliman and Spooner, 2000)

- **Creating knowledge.** Organisations have to encourage the creation of knowledge. This might occur through formal structures such as management meetings, research projects, feasibility studies or project planning, or informally through networks. However, if both a broader set of individuals and the organisation itself are to learn from this knowledge generation, the knowledge must somehow be captured.
- **Capturing knowledge.** As we discuss throughout most of this chapter, the prime function of knowledge systems is to capture (and disseminate) knowledge. Key issues here, of course, are what is worth capturing, and whose role this is.
- **Organising knowledge.** Organisations need to give careful thought to how the knowledge they capture is stored and structured if learning is to take place. This is because people who want to access knowledge artefacts (and learn from them) must be able to locate what they are looking for quickly and efficiently. Yet for a knowledge search to work, the depositor and searcher must each, independently, attribute the same name to that knowledge artefact. Devising a lexicon often helps both parties.
- **Accessing knowledge.** If KM systems are genuinely to facilitate the promotion of knowledge storage, sharing and therefore learning in organisations through accessing relevant knowledge must be a seamless process. The value of knowledge must exceed the time and effort needed to find it.
- **Using knowledge.** Having accessed a knowledge artefact, the searcher may note or even disregard its contents. But applying the new knowledge gained within the searcher's own workplace context may sometimes be problematic, particularly because the depositor's and searcher's work environments might be quite different. This begs the question of what learning needs to take place before people become competent in applying knowledge retrieved from a KM system to their own work situation.

Some of these issues can be resolved if an organisation finds ways of measuring or codifying knowledge and ways of getting people to know where the knowledge they need resides. Let us look at some of these issues in more detail.

Knowledge strategy

For KM to work effectively, it needs a clear and coherent strategy for its implementation, support from employees in the organisation at all levels, and a functional set of tools (so that everyone understands what knowledge is needed, what is being made available by whom and when). Rowley (1999) suggests a four-pronged approach to the creation of KM in an organisation:

- The creation of knowledge repositories and stores of knowledge and information. Repositories are much more than just documents – they add value and include stores of external knowledge (including competitive intelligence about other organisations), structured internal knowledge (such as research reports) and information that includes tacit knowledge (to the extent to which this can be captured). KM repositories could be something as basic as a filing cabinet; however, most organisations use dedicated software systems for storing information.
- The development of ways of improving access to knowledge, either through repositories or directly via key individuals or networks.
- The enhancement of the knowledge environment so that it is more geared up to knowledge creation, transfer and use. In terms of functionality, for example, audit programmes can be created to assess whether and how individuals apply knowledge in their decision-making (within the organisation, or learning about how people learn and apply their knowledge).
- The management of knowledge as an actual organisational asset to an organisation. Taking the notion of the 'balanced scorecard', for example, Rowley asserts that of the four dimensions – customer, internal processes, financial and innovation and *learning* (our emphasis) – the latter can be enhanced by KM activities.

Too often, organisations place an emphasis on creating a stock of knowledge (structure, storage and retrieval from a computer-based knowledge repository), when they should be more concerned with the *flow* of knowledge. Sometimes this will be about sharing best practices (learning from others). How often do people or teams develop a new idea, only to find that it already exists somewhere else in the organisation? This is much more to do with social relationships, how people work together and how they communicate and collaborate (Clare and Rollo, 2001). Many (some would say most) organisations suffer from the problem of 'islands of expertise' where knowledge is not shared, resulting in highly damaging consequences. These include the duplication of effort, repeated learning curves, a lower rate of innovation and lessons not learned.

Indeed, Nonaka (1996) argues that the knowledge-creating company is less about ideas and more about *ideals*. The key is personal commitment, with employees strongly identifying with the organisation and, above all, with its mission. This is where senior management can play an important role – by posing strategic questions. Who are we? Where should we be going? What do we need to know and how are we going to learn it? This means, in Nonaka's phrase, articulating the organisation's 'conceptual umbrella'.

Skyrme (2002) summarises an effective KM strategy into what he calls the seven 'knowledge levers' (Table 2.2). Essentially, this shows that a knowledge strategy needs to take into account external relationships (customer knowledge, stakeholder relationships and business insights) as well as internal processes (including organisational memory and the knowledge embedded in products and services).

Table 2.2   *The seven knowledge levers for KM strategy (adapted from Skyrme, 2002)*

Lever	Key activities
Customer knowledge	Developing deep knowledge-sharing relationships and understanding the needs of customers; identifying new opportunities
Stakeholder relationships	Improving knowledge flows between suppliers, employees, shareholders and the community
Business environment insights	Environmental scanning, including competitor analysis and market intelligence systems
Organisational memory	Knowledge sharing; best practice databases; directories of expertise; online documents, procedures and discussion forums; Intranets
Knowledge processes	Embedding knowledge into business processes and management decision-making
Knowledge in products and services	Knowledge embedded in products, e.g. in user guides, online search tools
Knowledge people	Knowledge-sharing fairs; innovation workshops; expert and learning networks; communities of practice

Knowledge generation

Knowledge is generated within an organisation, and is also acquired from outside it. One oil company, for example, gives a 'Thief of the Year' award to the person who has 'stolen' the best idea in applications development. The best way to generate internal knowledge is by setting up units or groups for that specific purpose – for example, through a research and development department. Knowledge is also generated by informal, self-generating networks (that may be formalised over time). This can be facilitated by the creation of physical space, or by granting time for informal meetings or electronic resources.

Knowledge codification

One of the problems with knowledge is that it is complex, diverse and diffused across an organisation, and – even worse – far from being documented and accessible, it is often only in people's heads (tacit knowledge). The aim of codification is to put organisational knowledge into a form that is accessible to those who need it, by making it organised, explicit and portable. When codifying, managers need to decide what business goals the codified knowledge must serve so that only *appropriate* knowledge is codified.

Mapping an organisation's knowledge is not achieved by gaining access to its organisational chart. This is not a knowledge map, it is only a diagram of reporting structures. One way to build up a knowledge map is to conduct a survey of employees to establish 'mini maps' of knowledge. Through snowball sampling, for example, those employees used for the knowledge mapping exercise could identify other suitable employees, etc. These knowledge maps could then be made available through electronic databases (an online Yellow Pages) such as through Lotus Notes or via the web.

Knowledge quality and maintenance

One of the dangers of KM is that knowledge itself can be created and stored in vast quantities – so vast that an organisation can become overwhelmed. And what about the quality of that knowledge? As Frank (2002) points out, sometimes the distinction between accurate and inaccurate knowledge is hard to draw. Hence, KM systems should be established that encourage the updating and revision of information. The outside world is in a continuing state of flux, so an organisation's KM systems have to continually reflect its changing circumstances. However, deciding when information has become obsolete is often difficult. One solution is to keep an 'outdated' (archived) version of the KM database that can be referenced – just in case.

Knowledge transfer

Not only must knowledge be mapped and codified, means must be found and enabled for its transfer. One of the simplest transfer mechanisms, of course, is through open discussions: 'In a knowledge-driven economy, talk is real work' (Davenport and Prusch, 2000). Conversations besides coffee machines or in the cafeteria are often occasions when people become aware of new networks, ideas or initiatives. This is one reason, of course, why organisations are increasingly aware of the importance of the internal design of their workspaces. A more open-plan environment, the deliberate provision of meeting spaces, and the co-location of teams are all ways that are used to encourage collaboration and the sharing of ideas through both formal and informal meetings. Sometimes, informal networks of individuals may develop, based around a common interest or work responsibility, which may, in time, develop into what have been termed CoPs (communities of practice) (see below).

Case Study 2.1: *Airsnack*

You will recall from Case Study 1.2 that Airsnack suffers from a lack of collaboration between those who work on marketing and product development. A 'them and us' culture has developed. To address this, the company has removed partition walls to create open-plan spaces. While people retain their individual desk spaces, these are 'fenced off' by low-profile partitions that attempt to create a physical compromise between some privacy and availability.

Rather than use separate product development and marketing teams, work is organised around specific projects, so small teams of staff work together. They are also encouraged to play together! For example, the two directors sponsor a company 'away day' in which several of these combined project teams compete at 'Paintball'. It is found that these team-building exercises do, indeed, encourage a more relaxed and friendly atmosphere within the workplace that facilitates dialogue, communication and the transfer of ideas – mutual learning.

ACTIVITY 2.3

Case Study 2.1 illustrates some approaches that might facilitate the transfer of ideas within a workplace. Can you give any examples from your own place of work that promote knowledge transfer? Do you have any new ideas that have not been tried yet, but should be?

Knowledge workers

For KM to work effectively, institutions need to create a set of roles or functions that are linked to the work of capturing, distributing and using knowledge. The most successful organisations are those where KM and sharing are part of everyone's responsibility. In addition, some organisations are beginning to create new kinds of posts that are specifically linked to the management of knowledge, such as:

- **KM workers**, whose role is to extract knowledge from people and to put it in a structured format, and to maintain and refine the knowledge over time. These people tend to have a vital mix of skills themselves – hard skills (such as technical abilities and professional experience) with soft skills (an awareness, for example, of an organisation's culture and policies).
- **Managers of knowledge projects**, whose skills must include project management, change management and technical expertise.
- **Chief Knowledge Officers (CKOs)**, whose role is to 'evangelise' KM, to develop a KM strategy, and to design and implement KM systems including libraries, databases, research centres and computer networks.

If 'knowledge is power', then those who possess it may be less than enthusiastic in sharing it with others. A suitable reward system comprising incentives (as part of performance-related pay), accolades and prizes might be initiated to motivate collaboration. For example, BAESystems has an award entitled 'The Chairman's Award for Innovation'. Ideally, though, participation in KM should be seen as a reward in itself, if only because, in principle, being involved in KM should make everyone's jobs easier. However, even if the motivation to participate in a KM process exists, some people are just not very good at expressing their ideas or transmitting knowledge to others. Sometimes, as well, the hierarchical structure of organisations inhibits or prohibits the sharing of knowledge. So, what can be done?

Unlocking knowledge

Of course, even with a deliberate KM strategy or the design of collegiate workspaces, problems may still remain. For example, information, as we have suggested, is often highly context-sensitive. If a worker from one part of an organisation reads a document submitted by someone to the KM repository, working in a different environment, can the lessons be transferred, even if, at a superficial level, the issues are the same? Knowledge transfer may also be inhibited by personal or organisational friction. There are ways, however, in which the transfer of knowledge can be enabled, some of which are noted in Table 2.3, and most of which are linked to the facilitation of collaboration, or the generation of incentives for collaboration.

ACTIVITY 2.4

Evaluate your own organisation for the ways in which knowledge is blocked. Think of systems, organisational structures and people. Following the example of Table 2.3, think of ways in which this knowledge flow can be unblocked.

Table 2.3 *Knowledge friction and possible solutions (adapted from Davenport and Prusch, 2000)*

Friction	Possible solution
Lack of trust	Build relationships through face-to-face meetings
Different cultures, vocabularies, frames of reference	Create common ground through education, discussion, learning, job rotation, building a common language
Status and rewards go to knowledge owners	Evaluate performance and provide incentives based on sharing
Intolerance of mistakes or need for help	Accept and reward creative errors and collaboration – create a 'no-blame' culture

COMMUNITIES OF PRACTICE

We have seen that much of the debate around KM focuses less on software and KM systems than on the need for human collaboration and communication. Where this crystallises into some kind of informal network, this is sometimes categorised as a CoP. The concept of CoPs was developed by Lave and Wenger (1991), who described how newcomers learn from 'old-timers', by participating in certain tasks relating to the practice of the work community. In time, newcomers come to participate fully in the activities of the community and, through an informal process, earn their status as legitimate members of it. CoPs are *not* the same as teams. In teams, status is often derived from your position in the hierarchy. In CoPs, it is *earned* through participation.

A CoP is characterised by Ward (2000) as a group of people related in some degree by a number of common features:

- A common purpose – there is a fundamental reason for the group of people joining a community.
- A common cultural context, culture being a collective identity. Inwardly this includes values, beliefs, attitudes and behavioural norms; outwardly, culture is a way of expressing inward identity through language, rituals, traditions, artefacts and events. Language is especially important for enabling clear communication and for creating meaning amongst members.
- Co-location – all community members share a common physical and/or virtual space. Strong community relations usually require some degree of physical co-location – even if this is just occasional.
- A common timeframe, with the community interacting with each other over a similar period of time. The closer this gets to synchronous, real-time interaction, the stronger the sense of community.
- Voluntary participation – community members choose who constitutes fellow members, and members choose whether to participate. Most communities within the workplace are also informal and often invisible to the formal organisational mechanism. Because they are informal and voluntary, participation is more dynamic and enthusiastic. However, without formal guidance, the potential benefits may not accrue to the organisation.

It is clear, then, that CoPs are informal networks. While members will often meet, these contacts should not be scheduled on a regular, timetabled basis, but when the need arises. When they happen, the meetings will operate on open agendas, so any issue can be raised and discussed. Some CoPs also make use of facilitators, whose role is to facilitate the process of learning. This role might involve helping the group to set the agenda, keeping the group focused and handling any conflict that arises. However, the main function will be to assist the process of communication and the learning that arises from this process. Such learning might be generated by After Action Reviews, whereby the CoP asks itself: What worked? What did not work? How can we do it better next time? This learning needs to be made available to the CoP and possibly other CoPs across or beyond the organisation. The famous and illusive 'no-blame culture' is essential for CoPs to feel comfortable about disseminating this kind of honest self-reflection.

An organisation might set up a CoP with a budget that might, in part, be used to hire a facilitator, but such financial donations must not come with any conditions attached. CoPs must be totally independent to act.

Liedtka (1999) emphasises the human and 'caring for others' element that binds together a CoP. Caring means respecting the autonomy of other members and helping them. This does not necessarily mean agreeing with all they say or do, but offering a combination of challenge and support. But essentially, learning to *care* is central to one's ability to take part in the community. According to Liedtka, a CoP based on an ethics of care will be able to sustain competitive advantage in a changing marketplace. This is because its members will have developed meta-capabilities that allow them to think strategically, to learn, and to collaborate and redesign processes on an ongoing basis.

Of course, one of the essential features of CoPs is that, by their very informal nature, they change their membership and even their purpose. Often networks may also have multiple, shifting and overlapping membership and participation. Different, but related, CoPs may sometimes be brought into collaboration or alignment through what Ward (2000) terms 'boundary spanners'. Sometimes people acting as relationship brokers, facilitators or change agents may undertake a boundary spanner role. At other times, members of different CoPs may come together in multi-community events such as joint meetings of web masters or content managers or joint meetings of professional organisations across an enterprise. Even documents (such as plans, projects or reports) can perform a boundary spanner role if they are worked on by a 'constellation of communities'. It has to be conceded, however, that many of these concepts and activities are operating in the world of web and IT development, but are far less common in other spheres of organisational activity. Box 2.1, a case study of CoPs within IBM taken from Gongla and Rizzuto (2001), is perhaps typical.

In modern organisations, many people communicate with internal colleagues and teams and also with external contacts by email. So if a CoP is formed, is email, or a computer conferencing tool, the best medium for of communication – in other words, can a CoP be virtual? An online community will have more chance of success if it transparently serves the needs of its members and if it clearly helps them all to work better. Hildreth and Kimble (2000) also claim that there is some potential for virtual working. For example, email can be used to transfer and share a document that the CoP wishes to discuss. But if, for example, learning is required through seeing a task performed, then face-to-face contact is usually essential. We also saw earlier that legitimacy is key to

Box 2.1: CoPs at IBM

A KM programme, which was heavily dependent on the forming of CoPs, was founded in 1995. By 2001 there were over 60 knowledge networks and about 20,000 participants. How did these CoPs emerge and develop? Gongla and Rizzuto (2001) identify a five-stage model, given below. Note, however, that not all CoPs go through all five stages. Some may stay at certain stages whilst some may even revert to a previous stage.

	Potential Stage	Building Stage	Engaged Stage	Active Stage	Adaptive
Definition	Community is forming	Community defines itself and formalises operating principles	Community implements and improves its processes	Community demonstrates benefits from KM and its own work	Community uses knowledge for competitive advantage
Functions	Connection	Memory	Access and learning	Collaboration	Innovation and generation

At the Potential Stage, people must identify and link to each other. They need to exchange information on what they do and what they are interested in. The kinds of technology used to facilitate this process include the telephone, email, bulletin boards and forums.

At the Building Stage, people need to learn more about each other, to share experiences and build a common vocabulary. Roles and norms are created through asking questions such as: Who are we? How do we react to each other? What is our purpose? Technology used to support groups at this stage includes a common repository that is accessible across the globe.

The Engaged Stage involves participants making a commitment to their community and performing their agreed roles. The community also expands beyond the core team, with group memory and tacit knowledge being shared with new members. The organisation with which the CoP resides may also now be accessing community members and trying to benefit from their activities. The organisation may also begin to intervene in the community – either to support it, or to redefine its scope and mission. At this stage, technologies used might include tools that help the CoP learn about itself – electronic surveys, analysis tools and portals and 'Yellow Pages' of members.

The Active Stage is based upon collaboration, with group members focusing on business problems and opportunities, often circumventing organisational barriers. The community reaches outwards to other communities across the organisation to share knowledge, with the organisation wanting and expecting value from the community's activities. Technological help comes in the form of collaboration and decision-making tools.

In the final Adaptive Stage, the core focus is on innovation and the generation of business solutions. However, the community is often too valuable by this stage to be left to its own devices and the organisation may actually convert the community into a business unit. Yet the community itself may not disappear entirely – it may become more covert, go 'underground' and drop back to a previous stage of the community process. At this stage, the community employs whatever technology it deems necessary and may pilot and experiment with new technologies.

becoming a member of a CoP – how easily can this be gained if communication is virtual? There are, at present, no definitive answers to these questions. The following case study illustrates some of the issues that arise when a CoP operates largely through virtual media.

Case Study 2.2: *CoPs at Transglobal*

Being a multinational organisation, Transglobal has IT support teams all over the world. Five years ago, an internal survey found that there were many different (and often mutually incompatible) IT platforms in existence. A decision was taken that only two core IT support teams should operate, one based in the USA and one in the UK. Over a period of about two years, an informal CoP developed both within each team and also between the teams. People often communicated with each other either by email (individual to individual, or individual to group), via telephone, voicemail, video link, or Microsoft NetMeeting.

Despite this, it was found that over a period of time the momentum of communication between the teams slackened. A decision was therefore taken to have biannual 'get-togethers', with one meeting in the UK and one in the USA. These meetings allowed for problem areas to be debated in more depth. Above all, though, they helped to develop relationships and to develop identity and confidence amongst and between group members. It was found that, after each meeting, the momentum of virtual communication peaked, at least for a while.

ACTIVITY 2.5

Taking the information provided in Case Study 2.2, and using your own experience, how comfortable would you be working in an entirely virtual CoP? Do you currently have any completely virtual relationships? Do you have any where you mix virtual with face-to-face contact with a colleague? Does the face-to-face element help the coherence and function-ality of the relationship?

KM SYSTEMS

Few other business trends are so wrapped up with IT systems as KM. According to Hildebrand (1999), 'knowledge management is in danger of being perceived as so seamlessly entwined with technology that its true critical success factors will be lost in the pleasing hum of servers, software and pipes'. But what do KM systems look like, and what differences do such systems make? Alavi and Leidner (2002) distinguish between three phases in which IT has been used to assist managerial and professional decision-making:

- Management information systems (MIS), processing vast amounts of information that are distributed across the organisation.
- Decision-support systems (DSS), providing tools for ad hoc decision analysis for specific decision-makers.

- Executive information systems (EIS), which provide updated and often real-time information to senior and middle managers.

The new and emerging KM systems, however, are moving beyond the gathering and distribution of 'data' or 'information' towards the creating, storing, organising and dissemination of 'knowledge'. These KM systems differ from traditional information management tools in that they are capable of handling the richness and content of the information, and not just the information itself. But what does a more sophisticated KM system consist of?

Gallupe (2001) distinguishes between three levels of KM technologies. Level 1 consists of KM tools such as expert systems, database and document languages (e.g. C++) that provide the basic building blocks for a KM system. At Level 2 there are KM system generators such as Lotus Notes, which can be used to build a variety of specific KM systems. KM generators are usually self-contained technologies that consist of a number of tools such as document management software, intelligent agents (programs that can filter out the knowledge that users really want) and groupware that helps groups or teams to communicate and collaborate. Level 3 comprises the specialised KM systems themselves. For example, in Figure 2.3, these specialised KM systems have been built for auditing, clinical and human resource purposes.

Figure 2.3 provides a conceptual picture of the relationship between KM tools, generators and actual systems. But in a practical way, what could a KM system look like? How would it function and what would it do? Figure 2.4 provides an idealised picture of such a system.

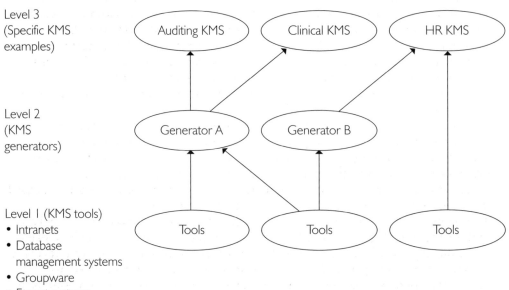

Figure 2.3 *Levels model of KM system (adapted from Gallupe, 2001)*

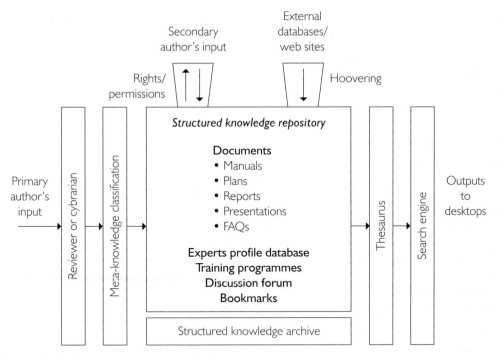

Figure 2.4 *Idealised representation of a KM system*

Keeping Figure 2.3 in mind, let us examine some of the features and processes of this KM system in turn:

- Review and evaluation – in principle, anyone in an organisation (see primary author's input) can contribute to the structured knowledge repository, that is, a place where knowledge can be stored – in this case, a dedicated set of servers. However, because the knowledge drawn from the KM system is going to be utilised within the organisation, it has to be valid, useful and robust. Hence, specially appointed reviewers evaluate the quality of all incoming documents. Sometimes this role may be undertaken by a librarian or resource centre organiser acting in the role of cybrarian. To prevent chaos, meta-knowledge classification is used, so documents are stored in accordance with a structured classification scheme.
- Structured knowledge repository – the repository itself consists of a wide array of knowledge artefacts. The most common will usually be documents of various kinds such as plans, reports and presentations, plus competitive intelligence about other organisations. They may sometimes also include news and data feeds from organisations such as Bloomberg and Reuters. The repository may have been designed and built using KM tools and generators, as described in Figure 2.3.
- The repository will usually contain a discussion forum that allows for both debate and for the threads (subjects) to be searched for information. Users can bookmark and store any knowledge artefact on their own computer hard drive. Note that what are termed 'secondary authors' can also gain access to documents (subject to appropriate permissions) and add to or change them. The system rationalises itself by noting how many 'hits' each document is receiving and removes those documents that are infrequently retrieved into the structured archive. Through computer

conferencing, for example, participants can launch a subject (thread) for group discussion, read other threads, or read and then post a reply within a thread. As Gundry and Metes (1996) show, computer conferencing is an ideal medium for structuring knowledge, because it works through threads that actually create a structure.

- Another important element of a knowledge repository is the facilitation of access to knowledge experts. Sometimes such experts may be self-appointed – volunteers who want to share their expertise and understanding with others. Often, they will be 'encouraged' by the organisation to offer these services, perhaps by a financial inducement, but more likely just on the basis of earning the plaudits of the workplace community. Such experts may provide information on an ad hoc basis or even perform the role of coach or mentor. Software systems may allow for the searching of an expert's database by subject area.

- What about formal 'learning'? Many organisations, and especially those that have declared themselves to possess virtual or corporate universities, also offer suites of learning programmes. These range from interactive software application training programmes to courses in higher-level management skills (although, currently, the former tend to predominate). These learning programmes are usually made available in the form of either a timetable of courses that can be booked online or e-learning programs that can be directly accessed through the KM system. A management information system is available to keep a record of courses completed and attendees. If linked to CPD, a personal (and sometimes confidential) e-portfolio could be kept of courses attended and qualifications gained, as well as personal notes and reflections (as illustrated in Chapter 6).

- Hoovering external web sites – this rather bizarre-sounding term summarises how KM systems are used to gain access to the servers of external organisations, to search the public areas of their web sites, and to import information based upon the specification of key words. In some cases, a company might target a rival organisation and use the search software to import competitive intelligence that is distributed to individual desktops on a 'need to know' basis. So, for example, an organisation that is planning the launch of a new product or service might hoover information from competitors on a similar range of products or services.

- Outputs – a KM system is useless if it cannot be searched effectively. However, with large stores of knowledge, it becomes difficult to locate precise information. This is aided by the use of search engines and a thesaurus, which guides the user as to the appropriate terms that can be used when making a search.

CRITICAL SUCCESS FACTORS FOR KM

We have looked at some of the models of KM and some of the processes involved in the communication of knowledge within an organisation. But if you are faced with the prospect (or opportunity!) to introduce KM into an organisation for the first time, what kind of *practical* steps is it sensible to take? Table 2.4 provides a summary of the kinds of processes that it is important to consider, including how to get started, organising roles and responsibilities, providing incentives for KM workers, and ways of facilitating the flow of knowledge and learning.

Table 2.4 *Knowledge elements and the possible actions to be taken to implement them*

KM element	Possible actions
Getting started with KM	
Get senior management support, and get them to send a message that KM is important accross the organisation	Devise a plan Offer a presentation Find successful case studies
If beginning to establish a KM system for the first time, start on a small scale	Decide on what is feasible in relation to budgets, timescales, current organisational culture
Roles and structure	
Set up organisational structures with clear sets of roles and skills – for example, new roles like chief knowledge officer, knowledge reporters, editors and network facilitators	Locate and provide positions for KM enthusiasts and evangelists
Get senior management to articulate the organisation's conceptual umbrella – what does the organisation need to know, how is it going to learn?	Link KM plans clearly to organisational plans, aspirations, mission
Incentives	
Make the development and use of KM linked to financial rewards	Find ways of measuring who shares knowledge within the organisation
Supply motivators tied to the organisation's compensation structures	Link evidence of sharing with rewards/appraisal scheme
KM flows and uses	
Ensure that those who access and learn from knowledge also have the power to act	Store and provide access to knowledge that has practical or operational value
Take steps to measure the flow of knowledge and assess its contribution to the bottom line	Evaluate which documents or artefacts are accessed, by whom and with what organisational impact
Encourage CoPs	Award them a budget, but do not seek to influence their aims, processes or agendas
Create multiple channels of KM transfer	Create working spaces and time for face-to-face meetings and dialogue through which learning can take place

Case Study 2.3: *Getting started with KM at the Citizens Support Bureau*

You may recall that the Citizens Support Bureau (CSB) employs full-time staff, but is also supported by a large number of unpaid volunteers. Given the move towards the 'professionalisation' of the service, it is now important that these volunteers are fully conversant with the management and operational procedures of the CSB. The CSB does not have the funding or resources to establish an expensive fully functional KM system, so how can knowledge be shared between the existing full-time employees and the large 'army' of volunteers?

The national management committee devises a simple but, in this case, probably the most effective idea. For the transmission of knowledge from the centre to the volunteers, a series of short, subject-focused staff handbooks are designed and issued. These cover issues such as: the history and mission of the CSB; its current roles and responsibilities; the management, reporting and committee structure; the functions and responsibilities of staff; health and safety, including personal safety when talking to clients. To capture their extensive knowledge, volunteers are asked to submit (either handwritten or word processed), short 'knowledge-bite' articles that, if selected, are published in the organisation's new internal monthly newsletter.

These steps at least begin the process towards a two-way flow of information, and help to capture some of the knowledge of volunteers who might easily walk away from the organisation. Above all, the approach relies on existing technology and so can be implemented quickly and without the need for large-scale cultural change.

ACTIVITY 2.6

If your organisation does not currently have a KM system, reflect on what scale you would recommend the organisation starts at. How easy would it be to elicit senior management approval and commitment? How could you go about planning the implementation of a KM system, and who should be involved?

SUMMARY

- KM comprises a critical set of policies and practices that optimise collaboration and knowledge sharing among employees and provide them with the information, knowledge and learning that they need to improve operational efficiency, to innovate and to sense and respond to new opportunities in the marketplace.
- A flexible and highly functional KM system can provide a haven for the storing and retrieval of knowledge, in a form that is structured and therefore, in principle, retrievable. It can facilitate communication between individuals and groups (including CoPs) and, vitally, provide direct access to key experts in the organisation, from whom people can glean expert knowledge (and learning).
- KM is much more than just information systems – at the heart of KM is the motivation and willingness of people to share knowledge and learn from each other.

- For KM to be successful, organisations need a clear strategy for generating knowledge, codifying it, maintaining its quality, and facilitating its transfer to where it is needed (*when* it is needed).
- Getting started with KM involves getting the commitment of the organisation at senior management level, being realistic about the initial scale of developments and providing incentives that encourage people to use the system.

REFERENCES

Alavi, M. and Leidner, D.E. (2002) Knowledge management systems: issues, challenges and benefits. In: *Knowledge Management Systems* (ed. Barnes, S.), Thomson Learning, London, pp. 15–55.

Clare, T. and Rollo, C. (2001) Capitalising knowledge: corporate knowledge management investments. *Capitalising Knowledge* **10**(3), 177–188.

Davenport, T.H. and Prusch, L. (2000) *Working Knowledge: How Organisations Manage What They Know*, Harvard Business School, Boston, MA.

Frank, U. (2002) A multi-layer architecture for knowledge management systems. In: *Knowledge Management Systems* (ed. Barnes, S.) Thomson Learning, London, pp. 97–111.

Gallupe, B. (2001) Knowledge management systems: surveying the landscape. *International Journal of Management Reviews*, **3**(1), 61–77.

Gongla, P. and Rizzuto, C.R. (2001) Evolving communities of practice: IBM Global Services experience. *IBM Systems Journal*, **40**(4), 842–862.

Gundry, J. and Metes, G. (1996) *Team Knowledge Management: A Computer-Mediated Approach. A Working by Wire White Paper* (http://www.knowab.co.uk/wbwteam)

Hildebrand, C. (1999) Does KM = IT? *Intellectual Capitalism* 15 September 15 (http://www.cio.com/archive/enterprise/091599_ic_content.html)

Hildreth, P. and Kimble, C. (2000) Communities of practice in the distributed international environment. *Journal of Knowledge Management*, **4**(1), 27–38.

Lave, J. and Wenger, E. (1991) *Situated Learning: Legitimate Peripheral Participation*, Cambridge University Press, Cambridge.

Liedtka, J. (1999) Linking competitive advantage with communities of practice. *Journal of Management Inquiry*, **8**(1), 5–17.

Neef, D. (1999) Making the case for knowledge management: the bigger picture. *Management Decision*, **31**(1), 72–78.

Nonaka, I. (1996) The knowledge-creating company. In: *How Organizations Learn* (ed. Starkey, K.), International Thomson Business Press, London.

Rowley, J. (1999) What is knowledge management? *Library Management*, **20**(8), 416–419.

Skyrme, D. (2002) Developing a knowledge strategy. http://www.skyrme.com/pubs/knwstrat.htm (accessed 26 November 2002).

Soliman, F. and Spooner, K. (2000) Strategies for implementing knowledge management: role of human resources management. *Journal of Knowledge Management*, **4**(4), 337–345.

Stewart, T.A. (1998) *Intellectual Capital: The New Wealth of Organizations.* Nicholas Brealey Publishing, London.

Sveiby, K. (2001) http://www.svelby.com.au/KnowledgeManagement.html (accessed 26 November 2002).

Ward, A. (2000) Getting strategic value from constellations of communities. *Strategy & Leadership*, **28**(2), 4–9.

3 HOW DO WE LEARN?

Objectives

After reading this chapter, you will be able to:

- Describe some of the important models of learning processes that are used to explain learning among adults.
- Use and apply a variety of diagnostic tools for the assessment and development of your own learning skills.
- Assess your own tendencies towards deep and meaningful learning in some areas and superficial or surface learning in others.
- Develop your own learning skills and behaviours in a professional context.

INTRODUCTION

The title of this chapter is a bold question. Most of us can say a few things about what we have learnt in the past but to be precise about how we learn is not easy. This chapter may help – at least it may help you to think more precisely about your own learning and the learning of others. This chapter is by no means, however, a systematic review of the various theories and practices of learning. There are many books that have already done this well and some excellent titles are recommended in the final activity for the chapter.

The first part of the chapter is an introduction to some of the important theories of adult and professional learning. In particular, the chapter includes a detailed discussion of experiential learning, an analysis of the different ways in which different people learn and an explanation of why many of us simply fail to learn from situations and experiences in which we could. The middle section of this chapter is largely concerned with deep (as opposed to surface) learning. This is an important theme in education. Deep learning is meaningful; it is about change in what we as individuals know and understand. Surface learning is superficial, and it is about learning to repeat information we have not digested for ourselves. The last part of the chapter is about different types of learning and it includes descriptions of some of the different tools that you may wish to test and use to develop your learning skills. Concept mapping, for example, is introduced as a tool that aids deep and meaningful learning. Finally, the conclusion focuses on the 'learning professional' and what we can do to learn more in the process of work.

LEARNING FROM EXPERIENCE

This is a book about workplace learning and at work most of our learning begins with an experience. That is to say it is experience of a new situation or a new realisation that what one has been doing could be done better that is often the incentive for learning. In 1975, Kolb and Fry published a simple model of the Experiential Learning Process (now widely used in education and workplace learning and commonly referred to as Kolb's Learning Cycle) (Figure 3.1). Kolb and Fry's model states that all learning begins with a concrete (i.e. a real world) experience. Then through reflection, the learner begins to make abstract generalisations about the experience, and finally plans a new course of action as a result. Thus Kolb and Fry describe four phases to the process of learning from experience:

- The concrete experience.
- Reflection on the experience.
- Generalisation and abstraction of the experience.
- Testing these generalisations by new actions.

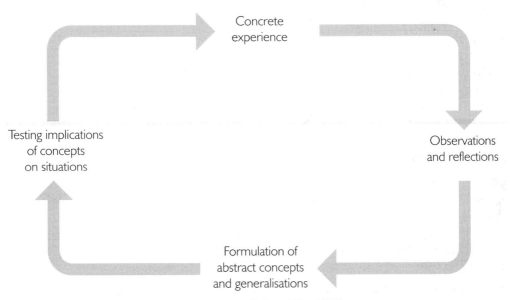

Figure 3.1 *Kolb's Learning Cycle (adapted from Kolb and Fry, 1975)*

Kolb and Fry's ideas have probably had more impact on how people now think about learning from experience than any other single theory. However, many others have since built on their approach and developed it. Wolf and Kolb (1984) used Kolb's Learning Cycle to illustrate the fact that different people learn differently. Briefly, they reasoned that some people would be better attuned to different stages of the learning cycle and that individuals would have specific preferences for different learning styles as a result. Each style they described is actually determined by an individual's ability to move from one stage of the cycle to the next:

- People who are good at reflecting on their concrete experiences they termed **divergers**.
- People whose particular strengths are in the making of abstract conceptualisations from reflective observation they called **assimilators**.
- Those who turn abstract thoughts into active experiments they named **convergers**.
- People whose strengths lie in carrying out plans that involve them in new experiences they called **accommodators**.

Of course the power of this approach lies not only in being able to recognise your own style, but, because learning requires one to pass through all stages of the cycle, it illustrates the need to develop skills in unfamiliar styles.

ACTIVITY 3.1

Take a few moments to reflect on something you recently learnt at work. Almost any example will do from the use of a new piece of software to dealing with a colleague. Where did the learning experience begin? Is it true to say that it began with an experience and ended with a new way of doing things? Did the learning process pass through phases of reflection and abstraction in between? Does this systematic way of thinking about learning from experience help you to describe your learning meaningfully? Could it help you to identify steps or phases in the learning process that you 'skate over' or simply ignore?

A similar (but perhaps more comprehensive) approach was developed by Peter Honey and Alan Mumford a few years later (Box 3.1). This, too, describes four principal learning styles (or approaches to learning). However, Honey and Mumford went on to develop a Learning Styles Questionnaire that can quickly be used to help identify individual strengths and weaknesses as a learner. Furthermore, by testing their questionnaire among many thousands of people from different walks of life, Honey and Mumford have provided a robust framework for comparing different styles reliably among different professions and between the sexes. Case Study 3.1 describes some of the ways that Honey and Mumford's learning style questionnaire can be used in businesses.

Like Wolf and Kolb (1984), Honey and Mumford actually argue that everyone has some ability in each of these styles and that all four phases of the learning cycle must be passed through for learning to occur.

Box 3.1: Honey and Mumford's approach to learning styles

The Manual of Learning Styles (published by Peter Honey and Alan Mumford in 1992) is effectively a manual and work book for trainers. It introduces the major themes of learning and it provides a questionnaire for diagnosis of individual learning styles. Activities and learning to develop learning skills are also supported and the book provides statistical data on many different professional populations for comparison. According to Honey and Mumford, learning is a continuous and lifelong process and it is best thought of as a spiral in which each turn includes experience, review, conclusion and planning (all broadly similar to the four phases of learning described by Kolb and Fry, 1975).

There are four styles described by Honey and Mumford:

- Activists – those who involve themselves fully in new experiences.
- Reflectors – those who stand back to ponder experiences and observe from different perspectives.
- Theorists – those who adapt and integrate observations into complex but logically sound theories.
- Pragmatists – those who like to try out new ideas, theories and techniques to see if they work in practice.

Key reference: Honey and Mumford (1992). (Note that this book is sold with permission for photocopying the Learning Styles Questionnaire and accompanying handouts so that it may be used in group work.)

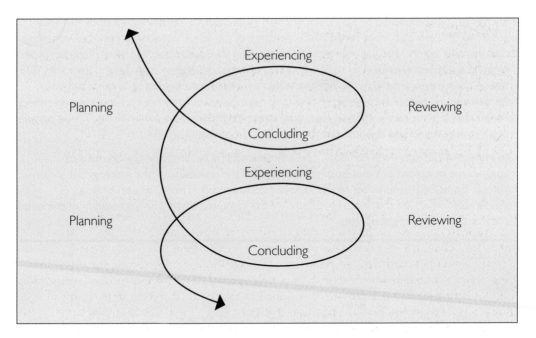

The following quotes from Honey and Mumford's book serve to illustrate the usefulness of their approach:

> *It is patently clear that people vary not just in their learning skills but also in their learning styles. Why otherwise might two people, matched for age, intelligence and need, exposed to the same learning opportunity react so differently? One person emerges enthusiastic, able to articulate and implement what has been learned. The other claims it was a waste of time and nothing has been learned. The question we all face is why, with other factors apparently constant, one person learns and the other does not.*
>
> *... The case for helping people to be more efficient learners ought to be self evident, yet many trainers still give insufficient recognition to it. It is perhaps the most important of all the life skills since the way in which people learn affects everything else.*
>
> Honey and Mumford (1992)

Case Study 3.1: *Training programme selection at Transglobal*

As Transglobal grew and assimilated the training and staff development programmes of the various organisations it comprised, so the need to systematise the availability and provision of staff development increased. At the suggestion of one senior board member with considerable experience in human potential development, a programme of 'learning workshops' was instigated across the company in order to help staff understand their learning styles and needs. This was facilitated by the use of Honey and Mumford's questionnaire, even though many different workshop facilitators were involved in the delivery of the programme in the different branches of the company. The approach enabled individuals to identify whether or not they were likely to learn best from face-to-face teaching in the 'classroom' or in seminar/workshop situations, and others who are more suited to learning through supported workplace practice. The same approach was used to help managers reflect on how they manage and how they can improve their management styles. For example, 'activists' were helped to understand how their behavioural tendencies generally provided opportunities for others to observe and reflect on what they do but rarely provide their staff with planned learning experiences. These people were also supported and encouraged to develop their abilities.

The impact of this approach has been considerable and by far the majority of staff and managers are in agreement that both the quality and the suitability of the training that is now taken by Transglobal employees have improved considerably. There has also been a considerable impact on the 'learning culture' of the organisation and an acceptance of the need for learning is now commonplace.

ACTIVITY 3.2

Purchase or borrow a copy of Honey and Mumford's book, *The Manual of Learning Styles*. Use it to assess your own strengths and weaknesses as a learner. Does this help you to better understand learning situations that particularly suit you and others you find difficult? Does it suggest styles that you need to develop to become a better learner? You might also assess the learning styles of a number of colleagues and discuss the result with them.

See http://www.peterhoney.co.uk/main and http://adulted.about.com for a variety of different learning style assessments and other tests.

LEARNING AND NON-LEARNING

Now that we have examined David Kolb's model of learning and looked in some detail at Honey and Mumford's approach to learning styles, we will begin to explore one of the most interesting models of adult learning from the educational literature. This is Jarvis's Model of Adult Learning.

Jarvis began to develop his model simply by asking adults to describe their own experience from potential learning situations. Importantly, he found that almost invariably the individual described him or herself first when they began to talk about their learning experiences. For example, people often began with: "Well I found myself in this new situation at work and . . .", or "I was given this new job to do and I began to see that . . .". Perhaps this is not surprising; when most people are asked to describe something they have learnt they begin by describing themselves and the situation they found themselves in at the time. But importantly, it led Jarvis to construct his model, not as an abstraction of the learning process, but as a description of change in the individual. Then, when Jarvis looked in detail at what individuals experienced, he found three distinct types of description of learning (or the absence of learning). In the first case, some people seemed to learn nothing from situations in which there was actually a potential for change. People simply went on repeating their mistakes or thinking about things in outmoded ways, even when confronted with evidence of their mistakes. This Jarvis called **'non-learning'**. Second, some people appeared to change their behaviour and acquired new skills but often without really understanding what they had done and why. This Jarvis called **'non-reflective learning'**. Finally, a third group reported deep changes in their thinking, understanding and behaviour as the result of reflection. Jarvis logically called this **'reflective learning'**. Thus Jarvis concluded that there were three broad outcomes of potential learning situations: non-learning, non-reflective learning and reflective learning (Figure 3.2).

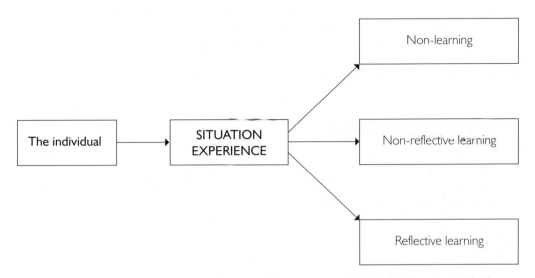

Figure 3.2   *The three broad outcomes of potential learning situations (adapted from Jarvis, 1992)*

There is a variety of ways in which individuals can pass through situations and experience without learning. If the individual thinks there is nothing to learn (presumption), or if they think that the potential learning in the situation is not worthy of attention (non-consideration), then the person will remain reinforced but unchanged by the experience. Neither of these two routes require active reflections on the experience. If, however, the individual does reflect on their experience, they may still remain unchanged if they reject it. As an example, Jarvis *et al.* (1998) cite an older person (or a younger one) experiencing the complexity of a modern city and exclaiming: 'I don't know what the world is coming to!', instead of probing into it and learning about it.

ACTIVITY 3.3

Take time to reflect on a recent experience from which you consider you have learnt nothing. Are the routes to non-learning that Jarvis suggests appropriate descriptions of this outcome? Is it true that there was nothing to learn from this situation and could it be that there was an alternative to presumption, non-consideration or rejection?

Memorisation and skills learning play an important part in Jarvis's model but, in his model, memorisation can also lead to non-learning. This is because memorisation can be trivial. Skills are usually acquired through imitation and role modelling. However, there is a big gap between learners who have watched practical demonstrations of a skill and claim to be able to repeat the task, and those who can actually perform the task for themselves. Memorisation can lead to learning on its own (this is what Jarvis means by non-reflective learning). Only when memorisation is integrated with practice, evaluation and/or reasoning and reflection does it lead to reflective learning that includes the ability to apply skills and knowledge to unique or novel situations.

Case Study 3.2: *Role model learning at Airsnack*

The ability to produce food to a high quality but at speed has always been important at Airsnack. In the early days, new recruits to the business were shown the facilities and talked through all that was required of them. Then they were 'let loose' in the kitchen and monitored. This proved time-consuming and often wasteful. Subsequently a period of role model induction was introduced. People starting out in food production at Airsnack were appointed a mentor or senior colleague, whom they were expected to shadow for the first two weeks and who would be responsible for showing them the ropes. Although this was a definite improvement it was common to find that, at the end of the induction period, new staff knew all that was expected of them and how it should be done, but in practice they would invariably get stuck. Mentors were too often called away from their own tasks and spent considerable time 'putting their junior colleagues right'. New staff were often able to describe what it was they did wrong and they were even aware of how they should have done their job correctly, but simple errors in practice were common. Theoretical understanding of the task was being grasped, but putting what had been learnt into practice proved a drawn-out business. At Airsnack, this problem was resolved by reversing the roles of the mentor and the learner. For a two-week period of induction the new recruit was only given the broadest description of what was required of them in each task they were employed to do. Then they were allowed simply to get on with it, finding their own way round and discovering for themselves all the steps involved. The mentor simply watched and gave direction and advice as required. In this way skills were rapidly acquired and by the end of the two-week period most new staff were operating with confidence largely independently of their mentors. The approach had other benefits too – mentors had time to reflect on the ways things were done by convention and often new and more efficient ways of doing things were discovered. Furthermore, the process proved excellent at helping new staff to form relationships, both with their senior colleagues and with their new fellow staff.

Contemplative Learning, **Reflective Skills Learning** and **Experimental Learning** are all examples of reflective learning (in Jarvis's model) and lead to change and increased experience. Contemplative learning involves reasoning and reflection, evaluation and memory, but may not always include reference to the wider society or the broader context of the individual's situation. Contemplative learning usually takes place after a situation has passed. After a crisis, for example, you may take time to sit back and calmly reflect on the reasons for the situation and what might be done to prevent it happening again. Reflective skills learning is in evidence when people 'think on their feet' and innovate to solve problems (sometimes apparently without thinking). Excellent reflective skills are usually important traits of good managers and of people working in customer service. Here the ability to deal with potential conflict situations and to resolve them quickly and efficiently largely depends on an ability to reflect spontaneously and not to react hurriedly. Similarly, reflective learning skills are paramount in any form of problem-solving – whether the problems to be dealt with are cognitive or technical. Finally, experimental learning is learning that is achieved through practice. It is of course reflective because it requires the ability to think squarely about an issue, to take meaningful action and then to reflect on how well the action worked to solve the problem. This sort of learning ability is common among those who have strong activist tendencies (see the earlier discussion of Honey and Mumford's approach), and also frequent among particular groups of workers. Computer programmers, for example, often have well-developed experimental learning skills and will frequently solve problems by experimenting with new and ever-evolving pieces of code until the problem is solved.

ACTIVITY 3.4

At this stage you should ask yourself which of these learning (or non-learning) experiences are most common to you and how non-learning experiences could become more profitable. Think carefully about Jarvis's model of learning and about reflective learning processes in particular. Could you use Jarvis's approach to design a programme of learning for yourself or for others? List the activities that you could include to promote reflective learning and what things you could do to avoid non-learning.

MAKING LEARNING MEANINGFUL

We have already seen that where learning occurs it can be reflective or non-reflective. Another way of describing this difference would be to use the terms meaningful and surface learning. Meaningful learning would be equated with a deep understanding of a subject, whereas surface learning would refer to the mere acquisition and memorisation of information. This sort of distinction between deep and surface learning or meaningful and rote learning has been the focus of considerable recent research.

Two important studies of adult students at the UK's Open University have shown that how people conceptualise learning (simply what they think learning to be) can be very different (Marton *et al.*, 1993; Säljö, 1975). On the one hand, some learners describe learning as an increase in knowledge, memorisation and increasing ability to apply knowledge. On the other hand, some learners think that learning is an increase in understanding, the seeing of things in different ways or change as a person. This gives a total of six different conceptions of learning that can be further arranged into two groups of three (Table 3.1).

The key differences between surface learning (or learning by rote as it is sometimes called) and deep (or meaningful) learning are illustrated in Box 3.2.

Table 3.1   *Six conceptions of learning (after Marton et al., 1993)*

Surface learning conceptions	Deep learning conceptions
1. Increasing one's knowledge	4. Understanding
2. Memorising and reproducing	5. Seeing something differently (i.e. the referential aspects of understanding)
3. Applying (i.e. understanding how knowledge can be used in the referential aspect of knowledge)	6. Changing as a person

Box 3.2: Differences between deep and surface learning

	Learning as the acquisition of information	Learning as the grasp of meaning
KNOWLEDGE	An increase of knowledge or information about a subject usually acquired by the gathering of unrelated facts and seldom related to what is already known **SURFACE**	A deep increase in the understanding of a subject involving the grasp of underlying principles so that new facts and information are given meaning and are related to what is already known and understood **DEEP**
APPLICATION	An ability to apply new knowledge to particular tasks and problems but usually this is not transferable **LOCAL**	An ability to apply newly understood meaning that is generally transferable to a variety of different tasks and problems by analogy and deep understanding of underlying principles **GENERAL** (i.e. transferable)
ENDURANCE	An ability to recall newly acquired information that is usually only short-term because facts are not related to others by understanding and what is known is not tested and applied in other contexts or situations **SHORT TERM**	A long-lasting change as a person that is reinforced by the repeated testing of new attitudes and ways of doing things in different situations **LONG TERM**

Key references: Biggs (1987) (a book that includes the study process questionnaire (SPQ) that can be used for self-assessment of learning strategies); Marton *et al.* (1993).

Where learning is primarily an increase in knowledge, emphasis is placed on an ability to recall and apply this knowledge. Where understanding is the primary purpose of learning, learning can result in long-lasting change to the individual and an ability to apply what has been learnt in novel or unique situations. This is illustrated in Figure 3.3 and appears to be highly consistent with the distinction between non-reflective and reflective learning as we have already seen described in Jarvis's model.

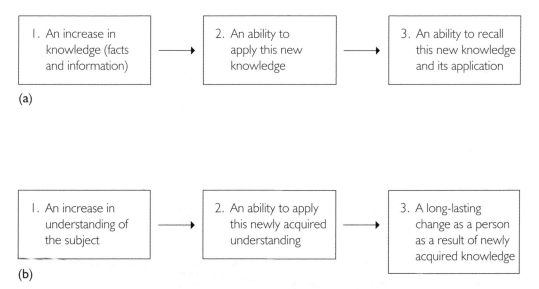

Figure 3.3 *Learning as an increase in knowledge or an increase in understanding (adapted from Entwistle and Marton, 1994): (a) learning as an increase in knowledge; (b) learning as an increase in understanding*

ACTIVITY 3.5

Briefly interview a number of your colleagues and fellow learners to determine the different ways that they describe their own learning. See if you can classify their conceptions of learning in the same way that Marton *et al.* (1993) and Säljö (1975) did. Do you think that some of your colleagues are likely to learn more deeply or meaningfully than others? Discuss your thoughts with those you have interviewed.

CONCEPT MAPPING

Concept mapping is a simple technique developed by Joseph Novak at Cornell University to promote meaningful learning (Novak, 1998). Briefly, concept maps are diagrammatic descriptions of knowledge (like spider diagrams or mind maps). Concepts are displayed on a page in boxes and arrows are drawn between related concepts. These arrows must then be labelled with a 'linking statement' that explains the relationship between the two concepts. Together each pair of concepts and their linking statement form a series of propositions that describe exactly what the author of the map understands about a particular subject. Concept maps should be organised hierarchically, with the 'big ideas' at the top and the details placed peripherally in order to exemplify the picture of the topic that exists in the author's mind. The process is difficult, often requiring repeated rearrangement, and must not be confused by the addition of too many concepts (usually 20 concepts per map is an upper limit). Box 3.3 explains the principles and methods of concept mapping.

In the course of learning anything new, concept mapping does much to show how the breadth and depth of understanding changes over time. Successive maps exist as a record of increasing knowledge and understanding and, in particular, help to reveal specific misconceptions where they occur. Kinchin *et al.* (2000) report the use of concept mapping in this way and show how learners with different 'cognitive maps' of the source topic can be helped or hindered by the approach.

Box 3.3: Concept mapping

Concept maps are powerful educational tools and excellent aids to learning. Making a concept map is simple. For any topic, all the concepts that you think to be important should be written down in boxes (see below). Then each concept should be linked with an arrow and each arrow labelled to explain the nature of the link. Concepts should be arranged hierarchically (inclusive concepts at the top and more specific concepts or even examples toward the bottom). No concept should be written more than once although there is no limit to the number of links that can be used, and links can bridge two or more hierarchical levels. This is the concept map – a simple diagram that shows everything you think to be important about a topic in a structured and logical way.

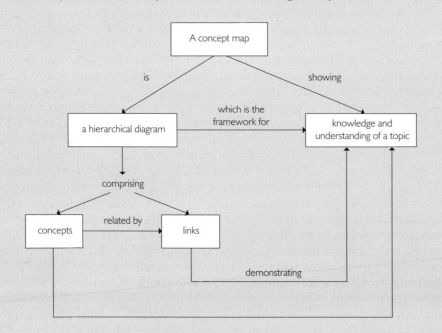

The most powerful use of concept mapping is as a method of tracking conceptual change. Draw a concept map of a topic you are about to study and then draw a new one when your studies are done. If meaningful learning has taken place your second map should show you how you have incorporated new ideas with your earlier views and you should be able to see just what has changed. Concept maps are also revision and study aids and they can facilitate group work where different people must share and include many different views and positions (for example, see Hughes and Hay, 2001).

Key references: Novak (1998); Hughes and Hay (2001).

ACTIVITY 3.6

Make a concept map to describe 'learning'. Do not be tempted to use more than 20 concepts and ensure that all the links you draw are appropriately labelled. Try to reflect on how this process has tested your understanding of learning. How many concepts in your map were new to you before you began reading this chapter? Have you been able to link new concepts to the older ones in your mind meaningfully? When you finish this chapter try to make another map without reference to the one you have just done; then compare them. Look to see if you can find evidence of meaningful learning that has taken place and reflect on how the process of concept mapping itself has (or has not) helped you to learn.

Case Study 3.3: *Concept mapping and organisational purpose in the Citizens Support Bureau*

All ten regional managers of the Citizens Support Bureau (CSB) try to meet at least once a year for an 'away weekend' at which they discuss and resolve issues that affect them all. Before the last meeting it was decided that a fundamental review of their mission and goals should be undertaken. To help them in their task the group hired the services of a professional workshop facilitator and used concept mapping to set about a detailed exploration of how they each saw the purpose of the organisation. On the first day of the meeting the facilitator introduced the principle of the method and then the ten managers, working both in groups and individually, produced a series of concept maps to describe (a) the internal structure and functioning of the organisation, (b) the external operations of the organisation and (c) the organisation's future. Needless to say the process generated considerable discussion but slowly patterns and clear specific differences began to emerge from the individuals' maps. Some had much clearer ideas about how the organisation needed to change in the future, for example. Overnight, the facilitator was able to analyse the maps that had been produced that day and the following morning the managers were presented with a summary of their work. This included tables showing the concepts that were common to all participants, and tables showing the unique contributions that were made by only one person. The group then set about concept mapping again, this time struggling to produce a unified map that included the important themes common to all the unique individual contributions that were finally deemed to be valuable by the group as a whole. By the end of the second day, the team had a completed map for the organisation and its future development that was owned and valued by all the participants.

THE EMOTIONAL COMPONENT OF LEARNING

A variety of emotional distractions can be a barrier to learning. These include the general feeling of distress, worry about friends, family or work, feeling bad about oneself, a lack of sense of curiosity, tiredness and being 'turned off' by the thought of learning.

To maintain a clear and inquiring mind is not always as easy as one might suppose, but certainly it is a prerequisite for new thinking or the making of new links between new ideas. One must be both motivated to learn and free of stress. Lucas (2001) gives the following advice to learners:

- The brain needs physical relaxation to function well so exercise is good.
- Mental effort uses energy and frequent short breaks are therefore useful.
- The brain needs to see the big picture as well as the details, so break up the big picture into small chunks, but step back mentally from time to time and revisit the whole.
- Use different learning approaches as often as you can; if you have been listening for a while, try writing, for example, as this brings different parts to bear on the subject.

For many of us, the first thing we do when we set out to learn something new is to 'shout for help'. At least, most of us ask 'an expert' or reach for an authoritative textbook. However, this may not be the best place to begin at all. As we have already seen, starting with what we already know about a subject is actually more appropriate than starting by trying to find out what others think. Concept mapping (Box 3.3) a new topic, for example, even before doing anything else at all, is often the best way to start. Concept mapping means trying to put down and link up all the concepts you have in your mind about a topic – and this is tough, especially if the topic is new and you are rather too willing to say 'I don't know anything yet'.

There are several reasons why this engaging with what you don't know is a good place to begin. First, with some effort, you may be surprised to find that in fact you know a lot already, and when this happens it is a boost. Second, the mental effort and the fact that you are starting by being active can bring you to a very energetic start to your learning. Third, by engaging your mind (to think) and your hand (to write and set out your thoughts on the page) you are already bringing in more than one part to your learning; visual material is good too, because the retentive properties of the visual memory are excellent (see Shepard, 1967). Finally (and perhaps most importantly), you are voluntarily exposing yourself to the experience of what you don't know. This effort to explain something (even when you don't think you know a topic at all) is excellent exercise for the mind. As Reif (1987) says: 'There is good evidence that students who self-explain when learning or problem solving perform better in subsequent tests.' It is also the 'not knowing' and the depth to which one is prepared to experience the 'not knowing' that is, according to Jarvis (1992), the fundamental spur to learning.

We have already described how what something means to a person can fundamentally determine how it is experienced. According to Marton and Booth (1997), understanding this fact is key to understanding what it means to learn:

> *The way in which we experience a certain phenomenon, the specific meaning it has for us, is the most fundamental aspect of learning. Learning is learning to experience. Being good at something is to be capable of experiencing or understanding it a certain way.*

THE LEARNING PROFESSIONAL

There is little doubt that change in the working lives of professionals over the last 30 years or so has done much to promote the need for flexibility and an ability 'to learn' from work. Middlehurst and Kennie (1997), for example, have documented the many changes that affect the working lives of professionals (Table 3.2) and report the general tendency towards knowledge use, teamworking and decision-making at local or partner levels in most organisations.

Table 3.2   *Changes affecting professionals (after Middlehurst and Kennie, 1997)*

From	To
Expectation of a 'job for life'	Reality – 'no job is safe'
Generally single employer (increasing specialisation)	Multiple employers (and potentially multiple careers
Develop a single specialist skill	Adaptable and flexible – multiple skills required
Careers planned – vertical hierarchical promotion	Plan your own career – horizontal/lateral development

In particular, regular updating and reskilling is thought to be important by many and essential by some. Furthermore, the importance of generic and transferable skills has increased. Skills such as negotiating, gathering and managing information, and using and controlling technology have become essential. As McNair (2001) points out, the idea of a career has undergone considerable change – referring less and less to a planned progression through a recognisable career structure and more and more to the (post hoc) construction of someone's work history as a coherent story. But many believe that it is not only individuals who must respond to these changes by learning and developing, it is their organisation too. Pedler *et al.* (1997: 10), for example, state that:

> *Today's organisational leaders are experiencing a conscious shift. Where they sought excellence, they now seek learning – not only to achieve excellence, but to stay that way through being flexible, intelligent and responsive.*

These issues and goals of the learning organisation have already been explored in Chapter 1 and are discussed further in Chapter 7. However, a discussion of the role of the learning professional in this broader context is given here. This is important because never before have individuals been so encouraged to take responsibility for their own learning.

One of the most frequently cited descriptions of the development of expertise is the five-stage model of Dreyfus and Dreyfus (1986) (Box 3.4). Briefly, this approach suggests that people can be transformed by learning and progress through developmental stages from novice to expert. This is achieved through deliberate practice and the making explicit of what was earlier tacit and implicit, thus opening professional practice to critical reflection and review (Charness, 1994).

ACTIVITY 3.7

Choose one or two of the common duties for which you are responsible in the workplace. Use the Dreyfus and Dreyfus model (Box 3.4) to locate your performance. Next write a detailed description of what each job entails and do as much to explain the *meaning* (its importance, its relation to other functions of your organisation, its significance for others, etc.). Reflect on how this may help you to see yourself as an 'expert' and how others may experience and benefit from your expertise.

> ## Box 3.4: The Dreyfus and Dreyfus five-stage model of professional competence
>
> Dreyfus and Dreyfus (1986) describe five stages of skill acquisition from the novice to the expert:
>
> 1. The <u>Novice</u> follows limited rules to acquire a new skill.
> 2. The <u>Advanced Beginner</u> still applies rules but with greater flexibility.
> 3. The <u>Competent</u> performer carries out goal-directed plans.
> 4. The <u>Proficient</u> performer has accumulated enough experience to see what is most important in a situation and to make decisions accordingly.
> 5. The <u>Expert</u> no longer relies on rules but is able to act intuitively without consciously thinking about his or her ongoing activity.
>
> This model has been criticised because little explanation of the development process is given, but according to Dreyfus and Dreyfus (1986) someone at a particular stage of skill acquisition can always initiate the thought processes characteristic of a higher stage, but will perform badly when lacking practice and concrete experience. The model represents a progression and reflects a change from the analytical behaviour of a 'detached' novice to the involved and intuitive skilled behaviour of the expert.

This approach to 'expert knowledge' has actually been developed further by Tynjälä (1999), who suggests that experiential learning and reflective thinking are the processes by which individuals develop and become transformed. According to Tynjälä, there are seven characteristics of the expert:

- An advanced ability for problem-solving.
- A considerable amount of specific knowledge.
- An advanced ability to organise this knowledge.
- An ability to use the relevant knowledge effectively.
- A creative ability that includes the ability to create new knowledge.
- A tendency towards apparently intuitive actions without obvious thinking or decision-making.
- A practical ability and the tendency to use and synthesise knowledge and skills to the desired ends.

It is these seven attributes that are developed by meaningful learning and according to Tynjälä (1999), there are actually seven steps or conceptual changes that take place as these are acquired:

- New concepts (or ideas) are added to existing prior knowledge.
- Old or existing concepts are redefined, specified or rejected.
- Specific aspects of both old and new concepts are linked in new ways.
- The learner begins to move from one category of explanation to another, broadening and specifying what is known and understood, both at the same time.

- A theoretical viewpoint is added so that what is known and understood is generalised and embedded in applicable theory.
- One theoretical view is replaced with another (or sometimes alternative views are held simultaneously).
- A single explanatory framework is formed that is robust and applicable to a variety of different and sometimes novel situations.

This sequential framework for the development of 'expert knowledge' has allowed Tynjälä (1999) to state seven principles for the development of expertise. These are shown in Box 3.5 and provide a powerful tool for the planning and management of both one's own learning and the learning of others.

Box 3.5: Seven principles for expert development

In his important monograph on 'expert knowledge', Tynjälä (1999) develops seven principles for developing expertise. These are as follows:

Principle one: Emphasis should be placed not on memorising and reproducing knowledge, but on using and transforming it

Principle two: Acquiring and using knowledge are not separate phases of expert development; rather knowledge is learned by using it

Principle three: Knowledge is used especially to solve problems

Principle four: Stimulating learners thinking activities and enhancing their thinking about the learning process and self-regulative skills are embedded in the study of content knowledge

Principle five: Social interaction has a central role in the learning process.

Principle six: Assessment of learning is embedded in the learning process.

Principle seven: Learners must be involved in the assessment of their own learning.

Finally, despite the considerable emphasis on the theoretical frameworks of professional development explained in this chapter, it is also important to reflect on the importance of the individual's approach to their own learning and their own professional development. Sandberg's work on competence in the workplace (Sandberg, 1994) shows that commonly it is the way of experiencing work that is the most important determinant of ability. More often than not it is the meaning that a job has for an individual that is actually the most important determinant of how well the job is done. Engineers, for example, who voice the best (the most reasoned and articulated) opinion of what a job entails are usually those who were most favourably reported as 'experts' by their colleagues and peers. In Sandberg's research, it was found that ability was not associated with the number of years a person had held a particular job, nor with the number of hours of training they had achieved, but only with how they had come to understand the job itself. Learning and experience are important, but only to the extent that they develop meaning.

ACTIVITY 3.8

There are a number of excellent texts that can be recommended in order to help you to explore further the theory and practice of learning. *The Theory and Practice of Learning*, by Jarvis *et al*. (1998), and *Learning, Creating and Using Knowledge* by Novak (1998) are particularly recommended. The chapter 'Learning to Work and Learning to Learn' by Barnett (2002) in Reeve *et al*. (eds), *Supporting Lifelong Learning*, Volume 2, is also particularly useful because it deals efficiently with work-related learning.

SUMMARY

This chapter has dealt with a variety of 'learning theories' and explored the benefits they can bring to those wishing to learn. A knowledge of the learning processes is indispensable for effective learning and for the development of individual learning strategies that will save time and effort and give results. One of the key features of adult learning is the willingness to accept responsibility for one's own learning and development, and finding out as much as one can about how we learn as individuals is a fundamental part of this responsibility. It is clear that we experience many situations in the workplace from which we learn little or nothing; improving and developing our reflective learning skills will undoubtedly help us to develop and grow professionally. However this chapter has placed considerable emphasis on the distinction between 'deep' or 'meaningful' learning on the one hand and 'surface' or 'rote' learning on the other. The ability to learn meaningfully and to make meaning out of one's everyday workplace experiences is likely to be the hallmark of those of us who seek to be expert and professional.

This chapter has introduced:

- Kolb's learning cycle.
- Honey and Mumford's learning styles questionnaire.
- Jarvis's model of adult learning.
- Descriptions of deep or surface learning by Marton and Booth (1997) and Säljö (1975).
- Novak's concepts of meaningful and rote learning.
- Concept mapping.
- The Dreyfus and Dreyfus model of professional competence.
- Tynjälä's seven principles of expert development.

REFERENCES

Barnett, R. (2002) Learning to work and working to learn. In: Reeve, F., Cartwright, M. and Edwards, R. (eds) *Supporting Lifelong Learning, Vol. 2: Organizing Learning*. Routledge, Falmer, London.

Biggs, J.B. (1987) *Student Approaches to Learning and Studying*, Hawthorn, Victoria, Australia.

Charness, N. (1994) Expert performance: its structure and acquisition. *American Psychologist*, **49**, 725–747.

Dreyfus, H. and Dreyfus, S.E. (with Athanasiou, T.) (1986). *Mind over Machine. The Power of Human Intuition and Expertise in the Era of the Computer*, Blackwell, Oxford.

Entwistle, N.J. and Marton, F. (1994) Knowledge objects: understanding constituted through intensive academic study. *British Journal of Educational Psychology*, **64**, 161–178.

Honey, P. and Mumford, A. (1992) *The Manual of Learning Styles*, Peter Honey, Maidenhead, Berkshire.

Hughes, G. and Hay, D.B. (2001) Use of concept mapping to integrate the different perspectives of designers and other stakeholders in the development of e-learning materials. *British Journal of Educational Technology*, **32**(5), 557–571.

Jarvis, P. (1992) *Paradoxes of Learning*, Jossey Bass, San Francisco.

Jarvis, P., Holford, J. and Griffin, C., (1998) *The Theory and Practice of Learning*, Kogan Page, London and Sterling, Kansas.

Kinchin, I.N., Hay, D.B. and Adams, A. (2000) How a qualitative approach to concept map analysis can be used to aid learning by illustrating patterns of conceptual development. *Educational Research*, **42**(1), 43–57.

Kolb, D. and Fry, R. (1975) Towards an applied theory of experiential learning. In: *Theories of Group Processes* (ed. Cooper, C.L.), Wiley, London, p. 217.

Lucas, B. (2001) *Power up your Mind*, Nicholas Brealey, London.

Marton, F. and Booth, S. (1997) *Learning and Awareness*, Lawrence Erlbaum, Mahaw, NJ.

Marton, F., Dall'Alba, G. and Beaty, E. (1993) Conceptions of learning. *International Journal of Educational Research*, **19**, 277–300.

McNair, S. (2001) Social, economic and political contexts. In: *The Age of Learning: Education and the Knowledge Society* (ed. Jarvis, P.) Kogan Page, London and Sterling, USA, pp.16–26.

Middlehurst, R. M. and Kennie, T. (1997) Leading professionals: towards new concepts of professionalism. In: *The End of the Professions? The Restructuring of Professional Work* (ed. Broadbent, J. *et al.*), Routledge, London.

Novak, J.D. (1998) *Learning, Creating and Using Knowledge: Concept Maps as Facilitative Tools in Schools and Corporations*, Lawrence Erlbaum Associates, Mahaw, NJ.

Pedler, M., Burgoyne, J. and Boydell, T. (1997) *The Learning Company: A Strategy for Sustainable Development*, 2nd edn, McGraw-Hill, London.

Reif, F. (1987) Interpretation of scientific and mathematical concepts. *Cognitive Issues and Instructional Science* **11**, 395–416.

Sandberg, J. (1994) Human competence at work: an interpretive approach. Dissertation thesis, University of Göteborg, Sweden.

Säljö, R. (1975) *Qualitative Differences in Learning as a Function of the Learner's Conception of the Task*, Acta Universitatis Gothoburgensis, Gothenburg.

Shepard, R.N. (1967) Recognition memory for words, sentences and pictures. *Journal of Verbal Learning and Verbal Behaviour*, **6**, 156–167.

Tynjälä, P. (1999) Towards expert knowledge? A comparison between a constructivist and a traditional learning environment in the university. *International Journal of Educational Research*, **31**(5), 357–442.

Wolf, D.M. and Kolb, D.A. (1984) Career development, personal growth and experiential learning. In: *Organisational Psychology: Readings on Human Behaviour*, 4th edn (ed. Kolb, D. *et al.*). Prentice Hall, Englewood Cliffs, NJ.

4 KEY SKILLS FOR THE INDIVIDUAL AND THE ORGANISATION

Objectives

After reading this chapter, you will be able to:

- Describe appropriate key skills for staff in your organisation.
- Recognise why key skills are important for an individual, an organisation and the national economy.
- Identify appropriate strategies for the development of key skills.
- Identify how and where key skills can be assessed.

INTRODUCTION

Many business, professional and educational organisations have adopted a key skills approach towards the development of:

- benchmarks of standards and quality
- audit tools to identify strengths, gaps and needs, both in terms of individuals and an organisation
- portability and recognition of achievement.

Key skills have a relevance to an individual's personal as well as professional life. An organisation needs to ensure that they have identified the right key skills needed by staff to enable the company to survive in a competitive marketplace, and be there in the future. National, and local, agencies – including government agencies – consider key skills are needed for a healthy national economy, and there is targeted funding for the development of specific key skills, particularly if a skills deficit has been identified.

TOWARDS A DEFINITION

Although there is no definitive definition of the term 'skills', the definition from the Skillsbase Labour Market Information Database (http://www.skillsbase.dfes.gov.uk), is comprehensive:

> *Skill is the ability to perform a task to a pre-determined standard of competence. It is acquired through formal and/or informal learning and through practice.*

Box 4.1 lists definitions of different skill types drawn from Fallows and Steven (2000), from government papers (Performance and Innovation Unit, 2001) and from the Skillsbase Labour Market Information Database.

Box 4.1: Skill types

Key skills. The word 'key' in this context is generally taken to mean important and the term is becoming synonymous with the six National Key Skills developed through the Qualifications and Curriculum Authority (QCA) (see Box 4.2). Some organisations will have additional key skills in their list. However, the word 'key' has a useful second meaning – an instrument used to release a lock. This can be considered as a useful metaphor for unlocking the door to effective working, career development, etc.

Transferable skills. The implication in this term is that skills developed within one situation are also useful when transferred into another situation – either from education to employment, or from one job role to another.

Generic skills. Transferable skills that can be used across occupational groups. These could include the key skills mentioned above, particularly the six National Key Skills, as well as reasoning skills, work process management skills, and personal values and attitudes such as motivation, discipline, judgement, leadership and initiative.

Common skills. 'Common' in this context refers to the universal nature of the skills. They are seen as relevant to each and every person, regardless of the discipline or career, and are required in all occupations.

Core skills. Here the implication is that the skills have to be central to a person's experiences, whether within education or employment.

Basic skills. These are seen as the minimum requirement for operating in most occupations and usually relate to literacy, numeracy and basic IT skills.

Vocational/occupational specific skills. The specific 'technical' skills needed to work within an occupation or occupational group. They will often be those capabilities described within Occupational Standards developed and published by Sector Skills Councils (who are replacing the National Training Organisations, which previously had responsibility for developing National Occupational Standards). Some vocational skills may also be transferable across occupations. These may include local functional skills (e.g. operating specific pieces of equipment) or employee-wide skills (e.g. specific working methodologies).

Cognitive skills. These primarily involve thinking, reasoning and the use of knowledge.

Manual skills. These mainly rely on hand/eye coordination.

As can be seen from Box 4.1, some skills are 'occupation-specific', such as welding, book-keeping, silk screen printing, i.e. they are narrow specialist/technical skills required for a specific job and are not generally transferable to other occupations. What we are considering in this chapter are generic skills that can be applied to all occupations – skills such as communication, the ability to work with others, and the ability to solve problems. We'll call them key skills, but be aware that there are differences in perceptions as to what the components should be – and we'll look at a number of sets of key skills in this chapter. If you wish to go into more depth on issues such as history, epistemological arguments and theoretical rationale then Bennett *et al.* (2000) give an excellent overview.

If you are involved in areas such as recruitment of staff, appraisal, or staff development programmes, you need to be clear about the key skills appropriate to your particular organisation – whether they are occupationally specific or generic. These key skills may be unique to your organisation, defined by a professional body, and/or be synonymous with the National Key Skills detailed in Box 4.2.

Some lists, or 'sets', of key skills are based on the needs of industry to be competitive, whilst others take a wider view and focus on skills for personal and professional life. The National Key Skills developed by the QCA (see Appendix 4.1) are the skills you are most likely to meet in the UK if your organisation is providing placements for further education students, or if you are involved in vocational awards such as Modern Apprenticeships.

Box 4.2: National Key Skills

Key skill	Components (based on Level 3)
Communication	Discussions; oral presentations; reading and obtaining/synthesising information; writing documents
Application of number	Planning an activity and interpreting information; carrying out calculations; interpreting results and presenting findings
Information technology	Searching for and selecting information; developing information; presenting information
Working with others	Planning activities; working towards objectives; identifying and reviewing progress
Improving own learning and performance	Setting targets; using a plan; reviewing achievements and progress
Problem-solving	Recognising, exploring and describing problems; generating ways to solve problems and comparing them; planning and implementing options; checking, describing results and reviewing approaches

There can be the danger of getting trapped into thinking of key skills in a narrow way rather than remembering the wider context. Val Zolingen (1997), cited in Brown (1999), stresses the importance of knowledge, insight, skills and attitudes – and the interaction between these. They are:

> *that part of a durable core of an occupation or group of related jobs, with the possibility of transfer to other, new jobs within that occupation and of innovations within that occupation, which contribute to the development of a person's occupational competence and facilitate transitions within the career.*
>
> Brown (1999: 78)

She also identified the following personal attributes as being important:

- self-reliance
- perseverance and creativity

- the ability to adapt oneself to the corporate culture
- showing a critical attitude to work and one's own interests.

The Skillsbase Labour Market Information Database (http://www.skillsbase.dfes.gov.uk) identifies additional personal attributes, such as:

- motivation
- judgement
- leadership
- initiative.

Not all of these personal attributes can be described as key skills, nor can they be developed and assessed within formal and/or informal training programmes. However, they can be promoted by your organisation in a way that encourages its staff to operate, and to interact.

Key skills in further and higher education

The majority of programmes in further education now include the six National Key Skills, and many colleges have developed specific procedures to ensure that key skills are central to a student's personal and professional development. New members of staff may have certificates demonstrating achievement of these key skills at specific levels.

You will also meet recruits from universities who have achieved specific key skills. A number of universities are using the National Key Skills, but many are developing their own list of key skills that incorporate the six National Key Skills. In his report on higher education, Dearing (1997) recommended that key skills should have a place in all degree-level programmes as they were 'the key to the future success of graduates whatever they intended to do in later life' (1997: 133). The report emphasised the skill of learning because of:

> *the importance we place on creating a learning society at a time when much specific knowledge will quickly become obsolete. Those leaving higher education will need to understand how to learn and how to manage their own learning and recognise that the process continues throughout life*

> Dearing (1997: 133–134)

The Association of Graduate Recruiters has commented that it is impossible to imagine that the skills needed in the workplace will remain the same in the 21st century, and it suggests that:

> *In the 21st century the most significant challenge for graduates will be to manage their relationship with work and with learning. This requires skills such as negoti-ating, action planning and networking, added to qualities like self-awareness and confidence. These are the skills required to be 'self-reliant' in career and personal development: skills to manage processes rather than functional skills. They are as valuable in education as in the workplace and as valuable to organisations as to individuals.*

> Association of Graduate Recruiters (1998: 5)

The new recruit may wish to continue the development of their key skills within the context of work. Is there the opportunity in your organisation?

Key skills from employers

So which – if any – key skills do employers and employees identify as being important? Research by Harvey *et al.* (1997) suggests most employers want individuals who:

- are intelligent
- are adaptable
- are flexible
- can deal with change
- are quick to learn
- can work in teams
- are able to communicate well
- have good interpersonal skills
- can use high-level skills such as analysis, synthesis, and multi-level communication.

This list reflects earlier comments from the Head of Education Policy at the Confederation of British Industry, who felt that the common denominator of the highly qualified would be the ability to think, learn and adapt. He went on to underline the importance of personal transferable skills such as problem-solving, communication and teamwork.

The Council for Industry and Higher Education has examined the mismatches between the expectations of academics and employers about the skills undergraduates should learn. It focused on English, engineering, hospitality, tourism and sport – 80% of employers surveyed identified the ability to be flexible and respond to change as a key success factor at work. Other skills employers saw as important were time management and integrity for engineering, and learning and numeracy skills for hospitality, tourism and sport graduates. Employers also sought more creativity and management skills in graduate engineers, and relationship-building skills and productivity in English graduates.

In 1997, Green decided to update previous surveys he had undertaken and ask respondents – mainly employees – about the use of current skills compared with those needed five years earlier. He found that there was a higher level of competence now required in skills such as problem-solving, communication, social skills and computing. The information was used to generate new estimates of changing skill needs across the country and details are held on the Skillsbase Labour Market Information Database (http://www.skillsbase.dfes.gov.uk). It has been projected, for example, that the demand for problem-solving, communication, teamworking and computing skills is likely to rise up to at least 2010 (Green *et al.*, 1998). Felstead *et al.* (2002), in their research, identified that in 55% of jobs, computing skills were either essential or very important, but the nature of the job would determine the level of IT skills that were required.

Skills Insight undertook research into what was needed by employers and concluded that: 'the most rapidly growing need is for more effective communication skills, including client and professional communication, horizontal communication, and verbal skills. This is especially the case for corporate managers' (Skills Insight, 2002: 16). As expected, the skills required by employers tended to vary with the type of vacancy, but it was found that there was a priority placed on communication skills and customer-handling skills. However, in management occupations the most required skills were teamworking, management skills and problem-solving.

The key skills for an occupation may be defined within specific National Occupational Standards drawn up by Sector Skills Councils (which are now replacing National Training Organisations). These usually form the basis for vocational qualifications such as National Vocational Qualifications (NVQs). The competencies detailed in these National Occupational Standards have been identified by employer representatives as being vital for an occupation. The key skills may feature as explicit units within the standards, but in many case they are integrated into all units. QCA (1999d) has produced a useful booklet, written primarily to offer practical advice to standards setting bodies and research organisations about how signposting of the six National Key Skills in National Occupational Standards could be undertaken. The results can be used to quality assure the standards and improve the efficiency of training and assessment. A signposting analysis of the standards can also show a profile of the key skill content of roles as 'it is not at all unusual for that profile to show wide variations between one key skill and another since different roles require different levels and combinations of key skills' (QCA, 1999d: 8).

Towards consensus

How far, then, is there agreement about key skills? Can there be agreement if we are looking for key skills that cross occupational sectors and levels of responsibility? Marshall and Tucker reviewed the different models in 1992 (cited in Bennett *et al.*, 2000), and considered that there was an emerging consensus on the skills needed for a successful economy, and that these were:

- capacity for abstract thought
- ability to solve real-world questions
- ability to communicate well in oral and written forms
- ability to work well with others.

Ten years later, this still provides a concise overview of the necessary key skills. These then need to be articulated in a way that is meaningful for our own organisations.

Bennett *et al.* (2000) proposed a framework that is comprehensive for the development of key skills, based on the four skills of:

- management of self
- management of information
- management of others
- management of task.

The skills are generic and so can be applied to any discipline or job. The subsets within each of the four areas are intended as examples rather than as a rigid set of skills and so can be adapted to any context (Table 4.1)

There are further examples of sets of key skills in the case studies you will meet in this chapter. In Case Study 4.1, Transglobal has identified relevant key skills for the organisation, and the details have been put onto the Intranet. This provides the

Table 4.1   *Model put forward by Bennett et al. (2000: 31–32)*

Management of self	Management of information
• Manage time effectively • Set obectives, priorities and standards • Take responsibility for own learning • Listen actively and with purpose • Use a range of academic skills (analysis synthesis, argument, etc.) • Develop and adapt learning strategies • Show intellectual flexibility • Use learning in new or different situations • Plan/work towards long-term aims and goals • Purposefully reflect on own learning • Clarify with criticism constructively • Cope with stress	• Use appropriate sources of information (library, retrieval systems, people, etc.) • Use appropriate technology, including IT • Use appropriate media • Handle large amounts of information/data • effectively • Use appropriate language and form in a range of activities • Interpret a variety of information forms • Present information/ideas competently (orally, in written form, visually) • Respond to different purposes/contexts/audiences • Use information critically • Use information in innovative and creative ways
Management of others	**Management of task**
• Carry out agreed tasks • Respect the views and values of others • Work productively in a co-operative context • Adapt to the needs of the group • Defend/justify views or actions • Take initiative and lead others • Delegate and stand back • Negotiate • Offer constructive criticism • Take the role of chairperson • Learn in a collaborative context • Assist/support others in learning	• Identify key features • Conceptualise issues • Set and maintain priorities • Identify strategic options • Plan/implement a course of action • Organise subtasks • Use and develop appropriate strategies • Assess outcomes

benchmarks for staff for job roles, performance reviews, personal and professional targets. In Case Study 4.3 the key skills relevant to an advisory service are integrated into a diploma.

ACTIVITY 4.1

Consider the skills needed by staff within your own organisation. Can you identify four key skills that all staff in your organisation should have? Are there key skills that staff in specific departments should have? If you work for a large organisation, with diverse operations, identify two key skills required by one particular section that are not key for another.

Key skills and their component parts

The identification of the key skills required, whether generic key skills that go across the whole organisation or those required within specific occupational areas, is only the first step. When considering key skills such as communication or teamworking, there is a need to consider the component parts so that staff know exactly how to perform these skills, or what to do to develop them.

Communication

The component parts of communication may be writing skills, oral presentation skills, and/or negotiation skills. There will be different definitions in different organisations, and different priorities across occupational groups. For example, in one company:

- A secretary will need to be able to demonstrate their ability to use different writing skills, and communicate over the telephone.
- A buyer in the same company will require good negotiation skills.
- A project manager will need good presentation skills.

A joint report from the DTI (Department of Trade and Industry) and CBI (1997) commented that all levels of a company needed good communication. For example, a leader should be able to communicate their vision of where a company is going, welcome and encourage feedback, and provide regular team briefings.

Teamworking

The components that make up the overarching skill of effective teamworking include the ability to:

- initiate
- consult
- request advice
- provide alternative ideas
- weigh up different viewpoints.

These, in turn, require the interpersonal skills of listening, reflection and tolerance (Bennett *et al.*, 2000: 125).

In addition to identifying the components of a key skill, there is also a need to consider the level of skill required. For example, a member of staff who has a responsibility for marketing to prospective clients is likely to need a higher level of presentation skills than a financial administrator. Box 4.3 gives examples of level differentiation relating to the National Key Skills, published by QCA (1999a, b). There is far more detail in the key skill specifications, and insufficient space here to detail the full range. Further information can be found on the QCA web site (http://www.qca.org.uk).

Appendix 4.2 contains extracts from Management NVQs at Levels 3 and 4. As a number of key skills may be in the area of management (e.g. managing self, managing resources, managing teams), the Management NVQ units can provide you with useful information to draw upon relating to component parts, and identification of different levels, of competence.

Box 4.3: National Key Skills differentiation

Focus: Communication – presentation skills

Level 2:	Level 3:
Speak clearly in a way that suits your subject, purpose and situation Keep to the subject and structure your talk to help listeners follow what you are saying Use an image to clearly illustrate your main points	Speak clearly and adapt your style of presentation to suit your purpose, subject, audience and situation Structure what you say so that the sequence of information and ideas may be easily followed Use a range of techniques to engage the audience, including effective use of images

Focus: Problem-solving

Level 2:	Level 3:
Identify the problem, accurately describing its main features, and how to show success in solving it Come up with different ways of tackling the problem Decide which options have a realistic chance of success, using help from others when appropriate	Explore the problem, accurately analysing its features, and agree with others on how to show success in solving it Select and use a variety of methods to come up with different ways of tackling the problem Compare the main features of each possible option, including risk factors, and justify the option you select to take forward

WHY SHOULD ORGANISATIONS FOCUS ON KEY SKILLS?

The National Skills Task Force (Department for Education and Employment, 2000) argued that skills levels are one important factor in determining UK competitiveness, and factors such as the level of capital investment, the supply of skills and the utilisation of skills by employers are key in determining economic growth and productivity. It went on to highlight the link between low UK labour productivity and the comparative poor levels of skills, with the comment that a relatively high proportion of the UK population of working age lacked basic and intermediate skills – both technical and key skills – and that we were not keeping pace with other industrialised countries. Economic and industrial change increasingly demands a workforce that is flexible and adaptable. For

ACTIVITY 4.2

Consider one of the key skills you identified in Activity 4.1. Identify the component parts of the skill. Now consider two members of staff with different levels of responsibility. What difference would you expect from them in the way they demonstrated this key skill? What levels of competence should they have?

companies, retraining and deploying employees to support more efficient and effective operations, and integrating new technologies, will be crucial to remaining competitive (Department for Education and Employment, 2000: 56).

When we are considering key skills, we are considering these in relation to all levels of responsibility. A global productivity study by Proudfoot Consulting (2001) showed that poor management in terms of inadequate planning and control and insufficient day-to-day supervision was the biggest single reason for productivity loss, equating to 65% of lost time. The study found that managers tended to wait for problems to arrive instead of planning effectively, and that they wasted a disproportionate amount of time on administration and manual tasks. They failed to delegate effectively and therefore failed to concentrate on the problem-solving aspects of their role.

Proudfoot Consulting also found that productivity levels across the countries studied (which included the UK, Austria, Germany, France, Hungary, South Africa, Australia, Japan and the USA) were just 57%, with the UK having one of the lowest productivity levels of 48%. Although they acknowledged that productivity loss was due in part to poor working morale, IT-related problems and an inappropriately qualified workforce, a number of these issues could also be linked with the skills (or lack of skills!) of management. There was enough scope for an increase in productivity without capital expenditure, and companies were urged to examine their business practices – particularly areas such as planning, management systems, existing IT and staff morale. If companies were serious about competing in global markets they had to address the productivity issues, which meant addressing skills issues – technical and key skills.

It is important to prepare organisations for the future – the world of work is changing, and different skills are needed. The country, and companies, needs an adaptable workforce who can cope with:

- globalisation
- intensification of competition
- technological innovation
- customisation of goods and services
- improved access to information, primarily through new technologies
- demographic change
- changing patterns of work – there is an increase in areas such as flexible working practices, part-time working, shift work, teleworking, homeworking, and zero-house contracts.

Permanent contracts are no longer a significant feature in employment; established career paths have disappeared and new industries have emerged. Many of the current jobs didn't exist 30, or even five, years ago. The second report of the National Skills Task Force (Department for Education and Skills, 1999) summarised the demand for key skills in the labour market, commenting that a number of interrelated trends in technology, working practices and in the industrial structure of employment have increased the need for key skills, and the demand for these seems set to increase further.

Consider the following points (Proudfoot Consulting, 2001):

- Of UK firms seeking to improve product or service quality, 70% will require additional high-performance skills such as teamworking and customer handling.

- The net growth in employment over the last 25 years has been in 'new jobs' such as design, finance and leisure services, which demand a different kind of intermediate or higher-level skill, for example creativity and problem-solving skills.
- There is a need for analysis, synthesis and problem-solving in 76% of jobs, and employers expect workers to take responsibility for finding better ways of doing the job.
- There are 55% of jobs in which computers are essential or very important – and the figure is rising. Only one-third of workers in these jobs think they have the computing skills to maximise job performance. The proportion of jobs in which Internet use is essential or very important is 24% and rising.
- Counselling, advising or caring for customers or clients is becoming more important and is seen as essential or very important in 51% of jobs.
- Of the 20% of firms reporting an internal skills gap, deficiencies in communication (54%) and customer care skills (51%) were most commonly reported.

ACTIVITY 4.3

Imagine you have been asked to speak, very briefly, to an executive meeting of your organ-isation on why key skills may be important. Identify three main reasons why the organisation should focus on key skills – these should form the basis of your presentation.

DEVELOPING KEY SKILLS

As key skills are important from three perspectives – national, organisational and individual – then it follows that key skills are important at the recruitment stage, the utilisation stage, and in the development of employees. They are important both from the organisational standpoint of enhancing capability and filling skills shortages and from the individual's need for continuing personal and professional development.

Key skills at the recruitment stage

When recruiting, it is important to know the key and technical skills required for the position and so make informed judgements about the profile of skills required from a candidate for recruitment purposes. Many employers say that, in a new recruit, they are looking for the ability to work with others/be team players, the ability to use initiative and problem-solve, and leadership potential (Lester, 1998). However, when interviewing, how do they judge these – what criteria do they use? For example, if you identify that effective team management is important, have you:

- defined this key skill, and its component parts?
- defined the level required?
- identified strategies to find out if the interviewee has the skills at the right level – what evidence are you looking for?

If this skill is important to your organisation, is there opportunity for a new member of staff to develop further in this area?

In some geographical areas of the country it can be difficult for an organisation to recruit people with the required skills, and therefore there is an added impetus to look at its own staff to train to meet any skills shortage.

Development of employees

An Employers Skill Survey commissioned by the National Skills Task Force (Department for Education and Skills, 2001) looked at skill shortage vacancies and found organisations had:

- hard-to-fill vacancies caused by a lack of job applicants with the required skills, qualifications or work experience
- internal skills gaps where a significant proportion of existing staff in a particular occupation were not fully proficient at their current jobs.

The survey found that the types of skills sought by employers for internal skills gaps tended to lean more towards generic key skills than is the case for technical skill shortage vacancies. Communication skills were required for 41% of all internal skills gaps, with teamworking, customer handling and technical/practical skills cited for around a third each of these.

A report by the Performance and Innovation Unit (2001) envisaged the UK as a society where government, employees and individuals actively engage in skills development to deliver sustainable economic success shared by all by 2010. The writers of the report defined workforce development as activities that increase the capacity of individuals to participate effectively in the workplace, thereby improving their productivity and employability. They perceived the responsibility of investing in training as lying with the individual, with business and with government. They see the benefits of education/training affecting individuals through increased earnings, and on a company through increased productivity. For individuals, lifelong learning and retraining will be essential for both employability and career progression.

Dearden *et al.* (2000) found that training significantly boosts productivity, and this was further confirmed in a joint DTI and CBI report published in 1997. The report commented that winning companies unlock the potential of their people, which includes the creation of a culture in which employees are genuinely empowered and focused on the customer. Further details relating to support for learning can be found in Chapters 1 and 8 of this book.

Organisational culture and context in the development of key skills

Many organisations have had to change to be effective in today's operating climate, and the changes can challenge new recruits as well as those who have been in the company for some time. The only certainty now appears to be change.

There are different organisational structures, ranging from hierarchical, with rigid vertical structures, to more horizontal structures, or a possible matrix. There are different cultures, which may tend towards authoritarian or democratic. These and other factors will affect the strategies and approach to the development of key skills. An overview of the factors that can affect the development of key skills is given in Box 4.4.

There will always be the need to balance the needs of the individual member of staff, the needs of the team, and the needs of the organisation. What is crucial is that there is overt

> ## Box 4.4: Factors affecting strategies used to develop key skills in an organisation
>
> - Culture of the organisation.
> - Size of the organisation.
> - Working environment.
> - Whether there is the opportunity to develop within the job, e.g. through team meetings, managing projects.
> - Whether there is the opportunity to try things out – and to take responsibility for actions.
> - Whether there is perceived support from senior management for the development of key skills.
> - The attitude of line managers/training officers (as attitudes to key skills held by managers determine staff's attitudes).
> - Personality of individuals – how they view key skills; whether they consider skills are innate or can be developed.
> - Whether there is a human resource department that organises training centrally, or whether training is devolved.
> - If full responsibility for the development of key skills is devolved, is it devolved to the individual, or to teams, or to line managers?
> - Role of appraisal.
> - Whether the organisation has IiP status.

support from senior management for the development of key skills, and individual members of staff are made aware of their significance as part of recruitment, appraisal, internal promotion and CPD.

For those involved in IiP standards, the development of key skills can contribute to the four principles, particularly when identification, and then development, of targeted key skills is a partnership between the individual and the organisation. For example, there may be feedback from self-assessment and/or appraisal, and then the inclusion of outcomes in professional development plans. There is, therefore, possible contribution to all of the IiP indicators.

Involving staff

If an aim of the company is to promote a more skilled workforce, then there is a need to engage people in learning. Individuals need to see the relationship between key skills, personal progression and professional effectiveness. QCA discovered that the attitudes to key skills held by other staff, particularly senior management, determined the attitudes of those focusing on developing key skills (LSDA and Learning for Work, 1999).

Problems can occur when there is a mismatch between what is said and what is implied through the ethos of the organisation. For example, the culture of the organisation may not support strong teamworking, but in appraisal there is considerable emphasis on this. Your company may say they encourage initiative, and that staff can learn from their (minor?) mistakes, but they may not allow for any risk-taking by staff, and may penalise staff for any mistakes they make.

Some companies have the same benchmark targets that go across an organisation, with no scope for targets relating to an individual's CPD. Not all members of staff need to aim for the same level of competence in a key skill – it depends upon the requirements of the job.

ACTIVITY *4.4*

Consider the culture of your organisation, and the context in which you operate, and then:

1. Identify three factors that will support the involvement of staff in the further development of key skills.
2. Identify three factors that may not help or encourage staff to become involved in key skill development.

Identifying the key skills to be developed

A key skills audit can help an organisation identify keys skills – which are its assets – and skills shortages – which are its weaknesses. For some skills gaps, the recruitment of new staff may be the appropriate way forward. However, it may be that recruitment is not an option because it is difficult to find people with the required skills, or because the organisation cannot afford to employ additional staff. In these circumstances it is more appropriate to identify relevant in-house staff who could be encouraged and supported to develop the required skills.

An analysis of an individual's key skills against a profile for their occupational roles can enable training activities to be more precisely targeted – both from the organisational standpoint of enhancing capability and filling skills shortages, and from the individual's need for continuing personal and professional development.

The process of self-assessment, as well as appraisal, can be used by an individual to identify both their strengths and areas that need improvement – both for their current job and for the future. Feedback – formal and informal – can contribute to this process. However, criteria are needed against which an individual can benchmark their own key skills. This can be seen in Case Study 4.1, where staff at Transglobal have clear details of the core competences at different levels.

Case Study 4.1: *Transglobal*

Staff review their key skills, or core competencies, through the Intranet, and there is a Training Needs Analysis tool already available detailing these core competencies. These are at four levels, approximately equating to NVQ standards at Levels 2, 3, 4 and 5.

These core competencies were identified in collaboration with a higher education establishment, and an analysis tool developed for use by staff. Where appropriate, the details from the self-assessment will be taken forward to appraisal, when there will be further discussion of the evidence demonstrating achievement of these core competencies.

There is, therefore, the ability to self-assess against core competencies that include:

- The communication of ideas and information effectively in oral and written form.
- Effective time management.
- The setting, planning and meeting of personal developmental targets.
- The setting and meeting of professional targets, priorities and standards.
- Supporting others in learning.
- The use of mathematical techniques.
- Working well with others, including in a team context.
- Using IT appropriately.
- Solving problems, identifying options where appropriate and implementing a course of action.
- Using initiative within a professional context.
- The effective handling of information/data.
- Being customer orientated within one's own operating context.

There are four levels for each core competence. In addition, there are specific professional skills needed for the person's work context. Strategies for development can include the following:

- through the web
- through the in-house mentoring system
- through attendance on in-house as well as external courses.

Staff are expected to identify the key skills, or competencies, to be targeted in personal action plans, and to reflect on personal development, including learning gained through undertaking their job.

If an individual is undertaking a programme such as a modern apprenticeship, whether at foundation or advanced level, then the minimum requirement for key skills will be identified in the standards. For example, there will be the key skills inherent within the NVQ standards, and in addition they will probably have to demonstrate achievement of some of the National Key Skills at specified levels. If a member of staff is registered for a programme such as a part-time Higher National, or a degree, then the specifications for the award will contain details of relevant key skills, and the standards required. In Case Study 4.2, John targets presentation skills as a key skill he wishes to develop within a certificate course at the local college – the minimum benchmark being criteria in the National Key Skill of Communication, Level 3.

Case Study 4.2: *Airsnack*

John identified, with his line manager, a certificate course at the local college that would help him in his job. He would also gain an NVQ at the end of the course. As part of the qualification, John is expected to gain the National Key Skills, through both work-based projects and external exams. It is compulsory to take communication, application of number and IT.

If he wishes, John may also gain accreditation in the remaining three National Key Skill areas of problem-solving, working with others and developing own learning. Achievement of these key skills will be through negotiated projects with his tutors, and evidence from the workplace. He will be supported in putting together a portfolio of evidence to demonstrate achievement of the assessment criteria.

Although there are key skills at Levels 4 and 5, it is expected that Level 3 be achieved as a minimum. The generic criteria are set down in the national standards, and the context is determined by the work of the employee/student.

John wishes to improve his presentation skills, which is a component part of the key skill of communication. At work he has to present the findings of a recent investigation into client complaints at a team meeting. He speaks with the team leader and they agree that he will give a presentation to his team colleagues using PowerPoint. His colleagues and his team leader will provide feedback on the way he communicated his findings through the presentation. This will identify what was successful as well as where there could be improvements. John needs to provide evidence for his portfolio, and so will have:

- his own personal reflection on how well he gave the presentation
- written feedback from the team leader, who will incorporate the comments of the team
- a copy of the PowerPoint presentation.

Another opportunity for developing a key skill – that of problem-solving – presented itself when a colleague identified a problem with the structure of the database the company was using to record the nature of client, and passenger, complaints. It was proving difficult to analyse the information and forecast any trends. John was given the task of working with other staff, and with their main clients, to identify requirements for a database, and to create a database that would meet these needs. John kept a record of actions undertaken, including reasons for these, and the outcomes. He also included implications for staff and the company.

Training strategies

There are many different ways of gaining key skills and these will usually reflect the nature of the organisation. Strategies may include in-house programmes, external support, formal input sessions, informal learning through self-directed learning, and interaction with colleagues. Training needs and availability of resources for the development of key skills will vary, and not all training has to be through formal courses/formal interventions. A number of different strategies can be seen in the case studies.

There has been a growing debate about the 'transferability' of key skills, which happens when someone applies knowledge and/or skills gained in one context to a new context. Some argue that the situation in which the learning takes place influences the subsequent use of the knowledge and skill, i.e. that learning is context-based (Brown, 1989). However, the issue relating to transfer is not how knowledge and skills are transported 'whole' from one setting to another, but how learning and performance in one setting prepares an individual to learn the rules, habits and knowledge appropriate to a new setting (Resnick and Collins, 1994). It is the knowledge of patterns, general principles and procedures that become the elements for transfer. So, if an individual gains new knowledge and skills relating to communication in one occupational area, then they should be able to draw upon that new knowledge and skills when moving to a different occupational area. This presumes that they understand the principles and procedures, and that the learning was not gained superficially – for example through rote learning – as then there will be less likelihood of transfer. Consider the Kolb Learning Cycle in Chapter 3. If the principles and procedures have been recognised, and analysed in relation to your own situation, then you are better able to carry that learning through to a new situation.

Whatever the strategy for personal development, whether through a formal training programme or informal learning, the learning outcomes relating to key skills need to be clearly articulated. Individuals need to be able to use unambiguous language to label their actions, their learning, knowledge and achievements so that they can identify how skill development occurs (Holman, 1995). There can then be ownership and action planning by the individual, and relevance to their education, work and their future.

Externally provided training programmes

For some staff, an externally provided training programme may be the most appropriate strategy. External programmes could include:

- Short, one-day sessions, addressing specific skills.
- Externally accredited programmes such as:
  - NVQs – Case Study 4.2 gives details of a member of staff on an NVQ programme.
  - Modern Apprenticeships, where part of the programme is delivered at a local further education college.
  - First degree, or masters, undertaken part-time – or through distance learning – with a university. Case Study 4.3 includes details of key skills that are integrated into a Diploma.

There is a growing requirement for key skills to be incorporated into accredited programmes designed to support people at work, for example:

- **Modern Apprenticeships.** From 2001 there was an obligation on all providers of Modern Apprenticeships to ensure that all trainees have the opportunity to gain a National Key Skill qualification in addition to the relevant NVQ.
- **Graduate Apprenticeships.** There is a requirement in the design of frameworks for either the inclusion of National Key Skill qualifications, or – where integrated – a mapping against the standards.
- **Foundation Degrees.** Key skills are an integral feature in this intermediate higher education qualification, underpinned by PDPs.

Case Study 4.3: *Citizens Support Bureau*

The organisation has not identified specific key skills that its staff must acquire. However, there is considerable emphasis in the organisation on personal reflection as part of any staff development and training.

For those members of staff who are on the Diploma in Advisory Services course, there are specific key skills integrated into each module that makes up the programme. These key skills for the diploma are recommended by the professional body, and by the level descriptors developed by the Southern England Consortium for Credit Accumulation and Transfer (SEEC). These include:

- management of information
- critical analysis
- evaluation
- self-evaluation, and development of own learning
- group working
- communication
- problem-solving
- ethical behaviour.

Work-based projects are negotiated with the course tutor so that any project undertaken will enable the member of staff to meet the learning outcomes for specific modules, but also meet personal and organisational objectives. These learning outcomes include key skills.

All learners complete a Project Agreement for each module that details the following, and is discussed with their line manager at the CSB:

- rationale for the project
- organisational objectives and success criteria
- personal development objectives and success criteria
- module learning outcomes.

This provides a tripartite agreement (CSB learner, university tutor, line manager) to the project, and to the personal and organisational objectives.

By undertaking the project – whether it is developing an initiative within their organisation or conducting an evaluation – the key skills are overt in the learning outcomes, as well as in the organisational and personal development objectives. The member of staff can also identify additional key skills that they feel need addressing for their professional context, as well as personal development. These could include time management, use of IT, and development of interpersonal skills.

One strategy that a member of staff, Jill, used was that of recording specific events and reflecting on these. She kept a logbook, and focused particularly on critical incidents. There had been a specific incident – over a period of time – when she had had to deal with a particularly difficult client who had been verbally aggressive and had threatened legal action. Jill:

- kept notes over the period of the episode
- analysed the way in which she dealt with the client and the actions she had taken
- identified what she did well and what she could have done better
- identified strategies to use should a similar circumstance arise again.

She was able to analyse the episode in depth as she had kept notes, including how she felt when confronted with someone who would not listen, became upset easily and talked about going to the local papers. Jill was able to learn from the experience and to take that learning forward. She identified personal development in the key skills of negotiation, problem-solving, communication, critical analysis, and dealing with difficult people. Throughout she maintained an ethical approach to the handling of the situation.

If resources are being used to enable a member of staff to attend an external course, is there the opportunity to use the knowledge and skills gained on return to work to consolidate the learning? Hattie *et al.* (1997) and Eraut *et al.* (1998) both suggest through their research that this rarely happens. Has there been a monitoring of the effectiveness of the training? Would you recommend the programme to others? Has there been an improvement in the skills of those who attended the programme?

A number of companies provide 'placements' for students from an educational establishment, and these students may have been asked by the relevant college or university to develop a portfolio of evidence to prove they have achieved specific key skills. They may ask for an endorsement stating that these have been achieved. The achievement of specific key skills may be mandatory for the achievement of their award. Their portfolio of evidence may be also be linked to Progress Files in which the student identifies the key skills they already have, and those they wish to target for development within the placement. These are likely to be identified within their PDP. It could be useful to take time to ask the students to describe the key skills they are targeting.

The Training Standards Council inspectors, whose duties are now carried out by the Adult Learning Inspectorate, investigated externally provided training programmes for trainees (which would include modern apprentices). Where they found strengths in key skills it was most often a result of close integration of key skills training and assessment in a trainee's vocational training. One of the challenges for training providers, whether a college or private training provider, is to get the commitment and support of employers. The report commented that employers could help by:

- giving trainees the right message – that key skills are important and worthwhile
- motivating trainees to improve their skills
- helping to identify opportunities for trainees to develop and demonstrate their skills at work
- providing time for trainees to develop their skills, either on or off the job
- giving trainees opportunities outside their normal work to develop skills that don't fall naturally inside their job roles.

These same principles could apply to staff, as well as students and trainees.

In-house programmes and strategies

Individuals construct knowledge through participation in normal workplace activities, and research by Eraut *et al.* (1998) confirmed that the challenges of work interactions were very important. Key skills are best learned, developed and internalised by individuals through normal work-based and everyday activities (Department for Education and Employment, 1998). These could include shadowing, collaborative teamwork and coaching. Further examples of informal learning can be seen in the case studies and in Chapters 6 and 8.

In addition to strategies that occur as part of everyday work, individuals may also be involved in more formal in-house strategies, such as:

- In-house training programmes to address specific issues that staff need to develop, which could be brief sessions of up to an hour, or may be part of a much longer training programme.
- One-to-one coaching sessions.
- Observation by colleagues, with feedback.
- Simulation and feedback.

ACTIVITY 4.5

Consider the following three scenarios. Imagine the people are staff within your own organisation and identify two possible strategies to support the development of each person.

A Dan has been promoted to have responsibility for client accounts and will be working more closely with clients. He has expressed the wish to develop his personal effectiveness and communication skills, particularly his negotiation skills.

B Sam needs to be more competent in the knowledge and use of IT as he wants to develop a database for his section.

C Les is already a very able manager of a small department within the company. Senior management has decided that Les has the potential to manage a larger department, and eventually take a strategic role within the organisation. During an appraisal it is agreed that she should further develop her skills of leadership and strategic problem-solving.

Assessing key skills

Whether supporting a member of staff to target their development through undertaking their normal work, devising more formal in-house programmes, or sponsoring attendance on an external programme, there needs to be some form of assessment. Assessment can:

- help the individual monitor their progress and plan future learning experiences
- provide an authoritative statement of attainment at relevant stages of development
- provide motivation to continue development.

No one comes with a blank sheet, and so it is logical that there is some form of initial assessment to identify the key skills an individual already has, so enabling target setting for further developments. It is important to identify assessment tools that can be seen as non-threatening, as well as consistent across the organisation. These can help identify useful trends that can aid future planning. If psychometric tests are used there needs to be training in the use of these. Tools could include papers, diagnostic tests, self-assessment, feedback from others, and/or the appraisal process. You may need to decide whether you are measuring attainment and/or potential, as different tools will be needed.

Although you don't always need staff to gain external key skill qualifications, you do need a process for the member of staff to demonstrate achievement of skills and for these to be recognised in some way. One way is through a professional portfolio, and Chapter 7 discusses portfolios relating to CPD. A portfolio approach to assessment of key skills can be effective, as it enables an individual to show development of a skill over time. The outcomes of research into effective portfolio building to demonstrate the achievement of key skills can be seen in Box 4.5. Restricted assessment tools, such as tests, do not always relate to the way in which key skills are usually defined, or need to be demonstrated. For example, it would be difficult to judge the ability of a member of staff to manage a team through a written assignment – observation, and feedback from team members, would be more appropriate.

Box 4.5: Assessing National Key Skills

A portfolio is one of the mandatory forms of assessment for achievement of the National Key Skills, and research by QCA indicates that for this to be effective:

- Candidates need to understand the role and importance of key skills.
- Line managers and senior management need to recognise its importance.
- Candidates need to see the relationship between key skills, personal progression, and the work they are undertaking.
- They need to start building the portfolio as soon as possible as it is very difficult to catch up later.
- Candidates need ownership of the evidence in the portfolio, and to avoid it being over-managed by tutors.
- Evidence needs to be accessible – many portfolios lack indexing or any method for tracking evidence.
- Volume is not a measure of quality. Many portfolios tend to be bulky – often because evidence had been inserted indiscriminately.

Note: To gain certification relating to the National Key Skills, individuals also need to take tests in the individual key skills of communication, application of number and IT in addition to the presentation of a portfolio. Evidence of achievement of the other three National Key Skills of problem-solving, working with others and managing own learning is based on the portfolio alone.

Box 4.6: Web sites providing support for development of key skills

- QCA web site at http://www.qca.org.uk. Details can be found of the latest information relating to key skills, together with key skill specifications and guidance that can be downloaded. Quite a lot is aimed at teachers, but there is information that could be of use to employers and trainers.
- www.keyskillssupport.net/about provides:
  - Information about the QCA key skills, together with details of the Key Skills Support Programme, which offers training to employers as well as leaflets and seminars.
  - Useful details of publications to help training providers encourage employers to get involved with key skills.
- There are assessment tools on the key skills support web site, http://www.keyskillssupport.net/assessment, but many of these are geared towards students on educational courses in colleges. However, they may provide ideas.
- A selection of information and services can be accessed via www.investorsinpeople.co.uk
- If further information is needed on basic skills, the Basic Skills Agency is at www.basic-skills.co.uk

Whatever the assessment tool used, it is important that feedback is given to the member of staff in a way that is appropriate to the person, acknowledging where there has been improvement, and – if appropriate – where further development may be needed. It is useful for any decision to be supported by reference to evidence from their work. This will help avoid accusations of subjectivity rather than objectivity.

Further details relating to the assessment of key skills, and evidence to demonstrate achievement, can be seen in the three case studies. There is also generic information relating to assessment in Chapter 5.

ACTIVITY 4.6

A member of staff has decided to include evidence of development and achievement of key skills in a portfolio to be presented for a professional qualification. They wish to demonstrate that they can delegate effectively, and plan and implement a course of action. What advice would you give them about the evidence they could include in their portfolio?

SUMMARY

- There should be identification of the key skills needed by staff within an organisation, the component parts, and the different levels.
- Key skills are important for:
  - an individual, so they can improve their productivity and employability
  - an organisation, so it can compete in global markets, be more productive, and harness the potential of all staff
  - the national economy, as skills levels are an important factor in determining UK competitiveness.
- Organisational culture, and structure, will affect the way in which key skills are developed in staff.
- It is important that there is overt support from senior management for the development of key skills, and individual members of staff are made aware of their significance as part of recruitment, appraisal, internal promotion and CPD.
- There is a variety of different strategies for organisations and individuals to use to develop key skills that should be appropriate for the individual and the skill to be developed, within the constraints of the resources available.
- Assessment helps individuals monitor their progress and plan future learning experiences, provides an authoritative statement of attainment at relevant stages of development, and can provide motivation to continue development.

REFERENCES

Association of Graduate Recruiters (1998) *Roles for Graduates in the Twenty First Century*, AGR, Cambridge.

Bennett, N., Dunne, E. and Carre, C. (2000) *Skills Development in Higher Education and Employment*, Society for Research into HE and Open University Press, Buckingham.

Brown, A. (1999) Going Dutch? Changing the focus from core skills to core problems in vocational higher education. In: *The Learning Society: International Perspectives on Core Skills in Higher Education* (ed. Dunne, E.), Kogan Page, London.

Dearden, L., Reed, H. and van Reenen, J. (2000) *Who Gains when Workers Train? Training and corporate productivity in a panel of British Industries*, No. WOO/04 in Working Papers from Institute for Fiscal Studies, London.

Dearing, R. (1997) *Higher Education in the Learning Society (Report of the National Committee of Inquiry into Higher Education)*, HMSO, London.

Department for Education and Employment (1988) *The Learning Age: a Renaissance for a New*

Britain, The Stationery Office (Command Paper Cmd 3790), London.

Department for Education and Employment (2000) *Skills for All: Research Report from the National Skills Task Force*, DfEE, London.

DfEE *Mapping Key/Core Skills in NVQs/SVQs* (1998) DfEE, London.

DTI/CBI (1997) *Competitiveness – How the Best UK Companies are Winning*, City and Guilds of London Institute, London.

Eraut, M., Alderton, J., Cole, G. and Senker, P. (1998) *Development of Knowledge and Skills in Employment*, Final Report of a Research Project funded by the 'Learning Society' Programme of the Economic and Social Research Council, University of Sussex Institute of Education.

Fallows, S. and Steven, C. (2000) *Integrating Key Skills in Higher Education: Employability, Transferable Skills and Learning for Life*, Kogan Page, London.

Felstead, A., Gallie, D. and Green, F. (2002) *Work Skills in Britain 2001*, Department for Education and Skills, London.

Green, F., Ashton, D., Burchell, B., Felstead, A. and Davies, B. (1998) Are British workers getting more skilled? In: Atkinson, A.B. and Hills, J. (eds) *Exclusion, Employment and Opportunity*, London School of Economics, London.

Harvey, L., Moon, S. and Geall, V. (1997), *Organisational Change and Students' Attributes*, Centre for Research into Quality, University of Central England, Birmingham.

Hattie, J., Marsh, H.W., Neill, J.T. and Richards, G.E. (1997) Adventure Education and Outward Bound: out-of-class experiences that make a lasting difference. *Review of Educational Research* 67, 43–87.

Holman, D. (1995) The experience of skill development in first-year undergraduates: a comparison of three courses. *Assessment and Evaluation in Higher Education*, **20**(3), 261–272.

Lester, S. (1998) Key Skills and Employers: The Wiltshire Study. *Capability*.

LSDA and Learning for Work (1999) Important findings from the Pilot of the Key Skills Qualification. In: *Key Skills Work*, No. 1 (December), Key Skills Support Programme, London.

National Skills Task Force (1999) *Anticipating Future Skills Needs: Can it be Done? Should it be Done?* Department for Education and Employment, London.

National Skills Task Force (2001) *Employers Skills Survey*, Department for Education and Employment, London.

Performance and Innovation Unit Report (2001) *In Demand: Adult Skills in the 21st Century*, Cabinet Office, London.

Proudfoot Consulting (2001) *Lost Time – the Global Productivity Study – An In-depth Analysis into the Current Levels of Productivity in Business* (contained in Skills Insight 2002).

QCA (1999a) *Key skills Units Levels 1–3 in Communication, Application of Number and Information Technology* – Qualifications & Curriculum Authority, London.

QCA (1999b) *Key skills Units Levels 1–3 in Working with others, improving own learning and performance and problem solving* – Qualifications & Curriculum Authority, London.

QCA (1999c) *Key skills Units Levels 4–5 in communication, application of number, information technology, working with others, improving own learning and performance and problem solving* – Qualifications & Curriculum Authority, London.

QCA (1999d) *Developing national occupational standards: signposting key and core skills* – Qualifications & Curriculum Authority, London.

QCA (2000) *Guidance on the key skill units: Communication, application of number and information technology (levels 1–3)* – Qualifications & Curriculum Authority, London.

QCA (2001) *Guidance on the wider key skills. Working with others, improving own learning and performance and problem solving (levels 1–4)* – Qualifications & Curriculum Authority, London.

QCA (2002) *The key skills qualifications specifications and guidance: communication, application of number and problem solving* – Qualifications & Curriculum Authority, London.

Resnick, L. and Collins, A. (1994) Cognition and learning. In: Husen, T. and Postlethwaite, T. (eds) *The International Encyclopaedia of Education*, 2nd edn, Elsevier/Pergamon, Oxford.
Skills Insight (2002) *Annual Skills Review 2002*, Skills-Insight/SEEDA, Guildford.

APPENDIX 4.1: EXTRACT FROM NATIONAL KEY SKILLS SPECIFICATIONS PUBLISHED BY QCA (1999C)

Level 4: Communication

Details are given of what you need to know in terms of developing a strategy, in monitoring progress, and in evaluation strategy and presenting outcomes.

What must be done	Evidence to demonstrate
Develop a strategy for using communication skills over an extended period of time	Evidence to show that you can • Establish opportunities for using communication skills and clearly identify the outcomes you hope to achieve • Identify relevant sources and research the information needed for planning purposes • Plan your use of communication skills, and make a reasoned selection of methods for achieving the quality of outcomes required
Monitor progress and adapt your strategy, as necessary, to achieve the quality of outcomes required in work involving: • One group discussion about a complex subject • One extended written communication about a complex subject	• Evaluate and synthesise information from difference sources • Communicate relevant information with accuracy, effectively using a form, structure and style that suits your purpose, and respond perceptively to contributions from others • Monitor and critically reflect on your use of communication skills, adapting your strategy as necessary to produce the quality of outcomes required
Evaluate your overall strategy and present the outcomes from your work, using at least one formal oral presentation, including the use of two images to illustrate complex points	• Organise and clearly present relevant information, illustrating what you say in ways that suit your purpose, subject and audience • Vary use of vocabulary and grammatical expression to convey particular effects, enable fine distinctions to be made, achieve emphasis and engage the audience • Assess the effectiveness of your strategy, including factors that had an impact on the outcomes, and identify ways of further developing your communication skills

Level 4: Working with others

What must be done	Evidence to demonstrate
Develop a strategy for using skills in working with others over an extended period of time	Evidence to show that you can • Establish opportunities for using skills in working with others and clearly identify the outcomes you hope to achieve • Identify relevant sources and research the information needed for planning purposes • Plan how you will work with others, negotiating responsibilities, methods and working arrangements for achieving the quality of outcomes required
Monitor progress and adapt your strategy, as necessary, to achieve the quality of outcomes required in taking a leading role in managing at least one complex group activity	• Take a leading role in managing an activity in ways that help you and others to be effective and efficient in meeting your responsibilities • Establish and effectively maintain cooperative working relationships, exchanging feedback and agreeing ways to resolve any difficulties • Monitor and critically reflect on your use of skills in working with others, adapting your strategy as necessary to produce the quality of outcomes required
Evaluate your overall strategy and present the outcomes from your work in at least one group situation	• Negotiate and develop effective ways of presenting the outcomes from your work, agreeing refinements with those involved • Use the skills of those involved to clearly present information that suits your purpose • Assess the effectiveness of your strategy, including factors that had an impact on the outcomes, and identify ways of further developing your skills in working with others

APPENDIX 4.2: EXTRACT FROM SPECIFICATIONS FOR MANAGEMENT NVQs AT LEVELS 3 AND 4

NVQ Level 3 Management	NVQ Level 4 Management
Unit 3 Manage yourself *Element 3.2 Manage your time to meet* *your objectives*	*Unit 3 Manage your own resources* *Element 3.2 Manage your own time and* *resources to meet your objectives*
Performance criteria: 1. Your objectives are specific, measurable and achievable 2. You prioritise your objectives in line with organisational objectives and policies 3. You plan activities that are consistent with your objectives and your personal resources 4. Your estimates of the time you need for activities are realistic and allow for unforeseen circumstances 5. You take decisions as soon as you have sufficient information 6. You minimise unhelpful interruptions to, and digressions from, planned work 7. You regularly review progress and reschedule activities to help achieve your planned objectives	Performance criteria: 1. Your objectives are specific, measurable and achievable within organisational constraints 2. You prioritise your objectives in line with organisational objectives and policies 3. You plan your work activities so that they are consistent with your objectives and your personal resources 4. Your estimates of the time you need for activities are realistic and allow for unforeseen circumstances 5. You delegate work to others in a way that makes the most efficient use of available time and resources 6. You take decisions as soon as you have sufficient information 7. When you need further information to take decisions, you take prompt and efficient measures to obtain it 8. You minimise unhelpful interruptions to, and digressions from, planned work 9. You regularly review progress and reschedule activities to help achieve your planned objectives

Appendix 4.2 continued

NVQ Level 3 Management	NVQ Level 4 Management
Unit 8 Lead the work of teams and individuals to achieve their objectives *Element 8.3 Provide feedback to teams and individuals on their work*	*Unit 10 Manage the performance of teams and individuals* *Element 10.4 Provide feedback to teams and individuals on their performance*
Performance criteria: 1. You provide feedback to your team in a situation and in a form and manner most likely to maintain and improve performance 2. The feedback you give is clear and is based on an objective assessment of your team members' work 3. Your feedback recognises team members' achievements and provides constructive suggestions and encouragement for improving their work 4. The way you give feedback shows respect for the individuals involved 5. You treat all feedback to individuals and teams confidentially 6. You give opportunities to team members to respond to feedback and recommend how they could improve their work	Performance criteria: 1. You provide feedback to team and individuals in a situation and in a form and manner most likely to maintain and improve their performance 2. The feedback you provide is clear, and is based on your objective assessment of their performance against agreed objectives 3. Your feedback acknowledges your team members' achievement 4. Your feedback provides your team members with constructive suggestions and encouragement for improving future performance against their work and development objectives 5. The way in which you provide feedback shows respect for individuals and the need for confidentiality 6. You give opportunities to teams and individuals to respond to feedback, and to recommend how they could improve their performance in the future

5 ASSESSMENT

Objectives

After reading this chapter, you will be able to:

- Describe some of the key issues in the assessment of work-based learning.
- Explain the differences between formative and summative assessments, criteria and some references tests and the variety of assessment methods used in work-based learning.
- Apply a taxonomy of learning objectives in the design of assessment activities.
- Plan and implement a variety of assessment strategies both for yourself and for others.

INTRODUCTION

Assessment is an integral part of the learning process. Being able to learn means both being able to assess what it is you do not know and what you already do. It is not enough to be engaged in some form of learning without regularly discovering first what and how much learning has taken place. This is true both so that individuals can be sure for themselves that what they are doing is effective, meaningful learning (see Chapter 3), but also so that they can demonstrate their achievement by means of attaining recognisable goals. Nevertheless, the workplace for most of us is not an academic institution such as a college or university. Although many think of assessment in terms of exams and tests, such approaches to assessment will be dealt with only briefly in this chapter. Instead, we will deal with the notion of assessment in the context of learning in and learning from the workplace. It is aimed at both learners and those who have responsibility for the learning of others. Above all, this chapter emphasises the importance of integrated and contextualised assessment. Assessment should not be an 'add on' that comes only at the end of a learning programme – it should be part of the process itself, supporting and encouraging learning through measurement. Achieving almost any goal at work involves assessment of some kind or another. Formal managerial responsibility usually requires periodic assessment of both the performance and development of others. Good management also involves the self-assessment and development of one's own abilities as a manager or worker. Learning new technical skills similarly requires assessment in different forms: first, assessment of what should be learnt and how; and second, assessment of what has been eventually achieved. Furthermore, assessment, evaluation and reflection are all essential components of the learning process (see Chapter 3).

The first part of this chapter deals with the various definitions of assessment and is an introduction to some of the principles of assessment. It then aims to show how a taxonomy of learning objectives can be used to specify course content and the assessment of achievement. This chapter focuses only briefly on assessment methods and issues in assessment such as fairness and equality, confidentiality and communication. These themes are covered in more detail in Chapters 7 and 8 of this book.

WHAT IS ASSESSMENT? QUESTIONS OF DEFINITION

In order to understand the nature and purpose of assessment, it is perhaps useful to begin by asking who assessment is for. The nature of assessment may be different, for example, if it is for oneself, for a teacher, for a mentor or employer or for a university exam board.

The purpose of assessment

Exactly how and when an assessment is done will depend upon its purpose. Assessment that is carried out to provide a student with feedback in the course of their learning (formative assessment) will be done during a learning programme. Formal assessment designed to 'sum up' the learning achievement (summative assessment) will inevitably come at the end (see Box 5.1). In fact, Rowntree (1987) distinguishes between some six different reasons for assessment (Box 5.2) and suggests that different methods and approaches may be used for these different purposes. Briefly, assessment may be done for many different people or organisations (for students, for teachers and facilitators, for employers, for university, school or college authorities, for professional and trades standards organisations, etc.) and these different audiences may require quite different things to be measured. Often these measurements need to be taken at different times.

The forms of reliability, validity, timing and comparison of results, for example, may all differ depending on the precise needs of the target audience. Thus the *specification* of any assessment is crucial. Careful and deliberate attempts must be made, first, to specify the purpose of any assessment and, second, to design the assessment strategy and methodology to meet the specific purpose for which it is intended.

Box 5.1: Formative and summative assessment

The terms 'formative' and 'summative' assessment were introduced by Bloom (1971) to distinguish between two fundamentally different approaches to assessment. Summative assessment produces a measure (or a 'summing up') of a person's achievement, and it is usually done at the end of a course. Formative assessment, however, is a more integral part of the learning process and is designed to guide and support the student in the course of a learning programme rather than to contribute to a final grade. Sometimes tensions arise between the goals of formative and summative assessment. On the one hand, formative approaches encourage students to treat assessment as an opportunity to learn and to take risks with what they do. On the other hand, summative assessment encourages conservatism. Risk-taking in exams is out, where everything depends on the outcome of the exam and there is no opportunity to learn from the exam process itself. Although the approaches can be combined, the effect usually comprises the formative aspects of the exercise because the learner generally focuses more on the outcome than on the learning process itself. Finally, summative assessment usually requires greater rigour of reliability and validity testing, although this does not mean to say that formative assessment should be done without quality assurance.

Box 5.2: The six purposes of assessment

Rowntree (1987) suggests that there are six important reasons for assessment:

1. Selection	Assessment is done to choose from among a number of applicants for entry to a course or profession.
2. Maintaining standards	Assessment is done to ensure that the reputation for quality is maintained by a profession or a college, etc.
3. Motivation	Assessment is done in order to provide an underlying motivation for study on a particular course or mode of professional practice.
4. Feedback to learners	Assessment is done so that peers may provide learners with feedback that will help them learn better or more appropriately in the future.
5. Feedback to teachers and facilitators	Assessment is done so that teachers and facilitators can adjust their approaches and the coverage of material in order to best meet the needs of learners.
6. Preparedness	Assessment is done at the end of a course so that awards may be given that will help the learner record and demonstrate their achievement.

The way in which an assessment is reported can also have considerable impact on the utility of a test and it is important that an appropriate method is used for each different purpose. Assessments can be judged, for example, by reference to specific and defined standards of achievement (criterion-referenced assessment) or by reference to others (norm-referenced assessment) (Box 5.3). When criterion-referenced assessments are used, it is feasible that all or none of the individuals in a test population can 'pass' the necessary standard benchmark. When norm-referenced methods are used, a given proportion will 'pass' regardless of how well or poorly the test population has done as a whole. This does not mean that one method is better than another, only that they are different and must be used appropriately. Norm-referenced testing is useful, for example, when assessments are done as part of the process of selective entry onto a course or programme where places are limited. In this case, it simply does not matter how difficult the test is (as long as it stretches the test group sufficiently to separate the high and low achievers). Norm-referenced tests do not necessarily need any predetermined pass mark, and can simply be used as a means of selecting the 'best' candidates. Criterion-referenced testing, however, is most appropriate where it is necessary to report whether specific standards or competencies have been achieved – as in the case of the driving test, NVQs or vocational A-level assessment systems (see Chapter 7).

Box 5.3: Criterion- and norm-referenced assessments

Making sense of any assessment inevitably involves comparisons of one type or another. The UK national driving test and Management Charter Status, for example, involve a comparison of performance against a set of standards (or pass criteria). Only if the standards are met or exceeded will the tester pass the driver. This is called criterion-referenced assessment because the outcome is measured against specific (and fixed) criteria.

The results of some tests are best reported by comparisons with the rest of the population. The IQ test, for example, is designed to measure the intelligence of a subject by comparison with what is known about the intelligence of the population as a whole. This type of assessment, where achievement is reported in relation to others (and not in relation to specific criteria), is called norm-referenced assessment. The purpose of the norm-referenced test is to compare one candidate with another and this can be done without reference to an external benchmark or standard. Selective tests that are designed to 'find the best' from among a bunch of potential candidates are usually of this type.

ACTIVITY 5.1

Think about some of the tests that you have done in the past. Can you decide which of these were formative and which were summative tests? Were these criterion- or norm-referenced tests? Now think of a test that you might design for your colleagues in the future. Try to decide what sort of test this should be and how the results should be presented. What are the benefits of each particular strategy and what is the best approach for the case you have in mind?

Validity

The validity of a test is a description of how well that test actually measures what it is supposed to. Gray (2001) states that 'to ensure validity an assessment instrument must measure what it is intended to measure, and although this is an obvious statement, it is not difficult, in designing assessment tools, to stray away from this central goal'. Most well-planned courses have a series of pre-stated learning outcomes that are set out in advance of the course (much like the statements that we have put at the front of each chapter in this book). This means that the things a learner will be expected to know or be able to do when the course is done are clearly identified. As long as the test that is designed to measure achievement on the course does indeed measure ability in all the learning outcomes that have been specified by the course, and no others, then the test can be said to be valid. However, some of a course's learning outcomes may be neglected by the test (creating a 'zone of neglect'), while other parts of a test may actually measure outcomes that are not directly related to the course of learning at all (a 'zone of invalidity') (Figure 5.1(a)). To achieve validity, a test instrument must exactly match the operationally defined subject (Figure 5.1(b)).

This definition of 'validity' is particularly important because it serves to emphasise the fact that assessment ought to be an integral part of learning-programme design. When assessment is 'bolted on' to a programme of learning as an afterthought, it is all too easy

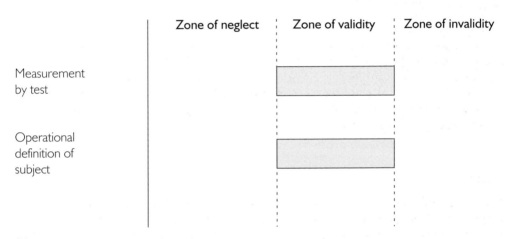

Figure 5.1 *(a) If a test instrument fails to measure traits that are described by the operational definition of a subject, a 'zone of neglect' is created; and if the instrument measures traits outside the operational definition of a subject, this creates a 'zone of invalidity'. (b) If the test instrument subject area and the operationally defined subject exactly match, the assessment may be considered entirely valid. (Adapted from Gray, 2001)*

to create zones of neglect or invalidity by testing subjects or contexts outside the specific frame of reference of the learning, or by simply failing to test important aspects of the programme. When a programme of learning is planned in conjunction with the planning of assessment, however, it is usually much more likely that an exact match between the test and the operational definition of the subject can be achieved.

Case Study 5.1: *A missed opportunity for valid assessment*

At Airsnack, members of the sales and marketing team are often invited to take part in a variety of short training courses available from a local training provider. These courses include topics such as The Principles of Marketing, Customer Accounts Management, Sales Techniques, and Customer Service. All of these short courses are assessed and those that complete the training are given a Certificate of Achievement when they pass the assessment. Unfortunately, these programmes are actually designed to cater for a second-year undergraduate market from local colleges and the assessment includes many tests that really rely on a prior understanding of market theory. This theory is not taught on the courses and it is not made clear that learners should only start the course when they have understood this theory themselves. The test is therefore lacking in validity because it measures ability in areas that are not actually specified or defined. As a consequence many Airsnack staff struggle with the course content and often do poorly in the end of course tests. Furthermore, experience has shown that several important items that are taught in the courses are not actually assessed at all. There have been several cases where learners have obtained their Certificate of Achievement but have clearly failed to learn all that was intended. Airsnack is now looking for an alternative training provider and is taking steps to make sure that the new provider has ensured the validity of all their assessment strategies and methods. In particular they will require any prospective provider to be able to demonstrate a detailed operational definition for the assessment and to be able to demonstrate that the assessment strategy is both reliable and valid.

Validity in the way we have described it so far is obviously important, but the issue of validity can be even more complex than this. In the context of work-based learning, Gray (2001) describes the importance of three specific types of validity: construct validity, content validity and predictive validity (Box 5.4).

Box 5.4: Construct, content and predictive validity

In principle, it is possible to measure any trait that can be defined. In practice, the operational definition of a subject is often hard to achieve. Management skill serves as a good example. Everyone has some concept of his or her own ability as a manager, but achieving a consensus on just how the traits of 'a good manager' should be defined (and thus measured) is far from easy. Before the trait of 'management skill' can be measured it must be defined operationally. The construct validity of a test relies on being able to ensure that the instrument measures what it is supposed to measure, and often this depends on how well it is operationally defined. Once the operational definition is established and there is at least broad agreement that construct validity is established, then the content validity of a test may be addressed. This refers to the degree to which the desired measurements are actually made by the test. Finally, the utility of a test is ultimately governed by its predictive validity. A test with high construct and content validity is actually of little use if it cannot be used to predict useful and meaningful outcomes in the future. A good test of a manager's ability should not just measure the traits of an individual at a given point in time, but it should actively predict who will go on to develop their abilities in the future. In effect, it should be able to distinguish those with most future promise.

Key reference: Benett (1993).

Briefly, construct validity refers to the measurement of abstract concepts and traits (such as ability, knowledge, attitudes, etc.), whereas content validity is an estimate of the extent to which the assessment tool measures the cognitive topics and behaviours described by the subject domain. Finally, the predictive validity of a test refers to its ability to forecast a future trait such as attainment or ability in work.

Figure 5.2 shows how concept and construct validity depend on the robustness of an operational definition. It is often this process of operational definition that is key to the development of a meaningful assessment programme.

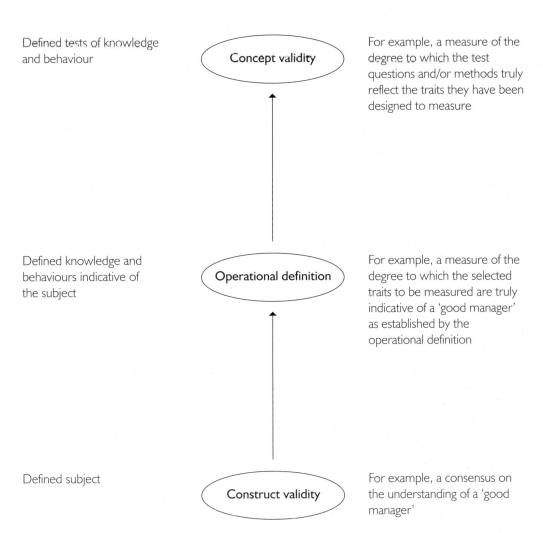

Figure 5.2 *The interdependence of concept and construct validity on the operational definition*

Case Study 5.2: *The design of teamwork training and assessment at Transglobal*

At Transglobal, the Human Resources Development Team (HRDT) has been charged with responsibility for the design and implementation of a three-day training programme to explore effective teamworking. After much debate it has been decided that this should be pitched at a 'middle tier' of managers in the organisation and that many of the potential participants would benefit from being able to claim university credit for successful completion of this course. Thus the HRDT has decided to take steps to ensure that rigour and quality, both of the learning and of the assessment, will be acceptable to a university exams board. In the long term they may seek accreditation for the programme with a university partner, and in the short term, individuals who have completed the course may be eligible for credit exemption when they join a university-based programme through APL or APEL systems.

The first step in the HRDT's learning programme design process then involves them in the operational definition of the subject. This includes specific statements about the level at which the subject will be taught and the subjects and competencies it will cover. In this case the Transglobal team decided that the operational definition should include Teamwork, Problem Solving and Target Setting. The team also decided that these three topics should be taught so as to cover the range of different common approaches and theories, an ability to evaluate the suitability of different approaches and an ability to reflect and assess one's own strengths and weaknesses. This definition then becomes a set of explicit learning outcomes or expectations of student ability at the end of the course, as follows.

At the end of the module, participants will be able to:

- Describe how team roles, styles and dynamics can be identified in theory and in practice.
- Describe the skills and attitudes necessary for effective teamworking.
- Identify strategies for the evaluation of successful teamwork.
- Evaluate a range of solutions with guidance, using appropriate techniques.
- Identify changes to be made to personal effectiveness in order for teamwork to be effective.
- Demonstrate how to plan and monitor behaviour, which will contribute to an effective team project.
- Demonstrate how to evaluate successful teamworking, including own ability.
- Begin to recognise own strengths and weaknesses in teamworking.

This list was used both as a detailed specification of what the programme should be designed to teach and a specific framework for the design of the assessment of the course.

From here the team began to plan both the content of the course and its assessment simultaneously. For example, to address the first expected outcome, it was decided that the programme should teach about the key psychological and group work theories of Schien, Douglas, Jacques, Tuckerman and others. It was decided that participants in the course could be tested on their understanding of these theories by making a brief (five minute) oral presentation to the rest of their learning group on the last day of the course. This would comprise only a small part of the overall assessment of the course. This method of assessment was to be assessed using the following criteria:

- Evidence of knowledge of the theories of chosen expert (5 marks).
- Evidence of an understanding of how this is different from other available theories (5 marks).
- Evidence of awareness of the strengths and weaknesses of chosen theory (5 marks).

- Evidence of suitable application of theory in given context (3 marks).
- Evidence of appropriate application of theory and conclusions to assess own (or group's) strengths and weaknesses (7 marks).

Total = 25

The rest of the assessment would be made up of a work-based project report (50 marks) and a learning diary (25 marks), both to be completed in the months following the course. For both of these assessments, specific marking criteria were also developed and explained to the learners.

To ensure the **construct validity** of the tests the team went over the operational definition of the subject repeatedly and tried to ensure there was consensus that this really was a good specification of what it meant to understand teamwork. This included agreement that this definition was appropriate to the level at which the learners could be expected to work. Ensuring construct validity in this way was done by probing the opinions of other managers and potential participants in the course, and also by reference to published literature on the subject. To ensure the **concept validity** of the tests the team repeatedly checked that indeed all that was specified by the definition of the course was tested in the assessment and that no marks were available in the test for anything that was not specified by the operational definition. Finally the team implemented a series of follow-up tests to determine the **predictive validity** of their tests. This was done by ensuring that the annual performance review of staff included assessment of their ability as team workers. The results were compared with the performance of individuals in their end of course assessment in order to determine exactly how well the training and its assessment could be used to identify 'team workers' and 'team leaders' with special potential.

Such an approach is obviously unsuited to all situations and assessment needs but in this case, Transglobal were able to develop a robust and highly effective training programme in which assessment was an integral part of the learning process as well as a means of demonstrating achievement.

ACTIVITY 5.2

Write a simple **operational definition** for some of your own skills. You could, for example, define a practical skill that you are required to put into practice routinely, or you could define your ability as a leader, your communication skills, or something else. Note that a definition for some topics may be much more difficult to achieve than it is for others. This definition should be a precise series of statements about what it means to be able to do the task in mind. Then review and define the knowledge and behaviours that you think you would have to demonstrate to prove your ability as specified by this operational definition. Discuss your definition and those specified traits with others (such as colleagues or a line manager) and ensure that construct validity can be established by an appropriate match between the two. Then plan a series of specific tests or means of demonstrating your ability in the areas of knowledge and behaviour you have identified. Review these 'test items' to ensure that they have good concept validity.

This is a difficult activity but it is very useful, both as a means of exploring the process of good assessment design and as a practical means of reflection on your own skills and learning needs. You may find that Case Study 5.2 helps to explain the processes involved in this activity.

In work-based learning practice the importance of establishing a sound basis for assessment validity cannot be over-emphasised. There are many cases where the responsibility for assessment design falls not to a tutor or supervisor, but is clearly the responsibility of the learner. In the process of learning contract negotiation, for example, the learner must be able to show how his or her work and evidence of achievement will demonstrate their ability and success. To do so requires a sound understanding of the test validity issues. There is little or no point in setting goals and outcomes that fail to achieve a valid demonstration of the desired abilities.

Reliability

The 'reliability' of a given test is a measure of its consistency. In the context of work-based learning, however, issues of reliability are often treated with less scrutiny than validity and here they are mentioned only briefly. This is because work-based learning tends to put a premium on the achievement of learners and appropriate (or valid) demonstration of this achievement. Issues of reliability such as consistent marking standards among examiners or different awarding bodies tend to be second to this. Of course this does not mean reliability can be neglected. Any organisation planning the assessment of others must ensure that the ways in which people are tested are reliable. Furthermore, if the organisation wishes to ensure that the assessments it does have credibility outside its own walls then issues of reliability become paramount. Providing training for staff in-house is valuable, but it is often of much greater benefit when the

---

Box 5.5: Guidelines for improving the reliability of marking assessments (adapted from Gray, 2001)

1. Take time to ensure that any specific marking criteria are broadly comparable with those from other programmes and assessment frameworks.
2. Make regular reference to assessment records from the past to ensure that marking standards remain consistent through time.
3. Randomise all papers to be marked so that the influence of good or bad papers is minimised.
4. Set and monitor precise completion dates so that work can be marked in batches when it is easier to check consistency in standards across the board.
5. Try to mark specific questions or phases of student work rather than marking everything from each student in turn. This helps to remove any bias of opinion that can be carried on from any one question to another.
6. Where possible and appropriate, anonymise work to be marked beforehand.
7. Use two independent markers or mark work on two independent occasions wherever possible.
8. Provide comments and reasons for the award of marks so that marks are easily justified and checked in terms of the standards of work they describe.

Key reference: Mehrens and Lehmann (1984).

---

standards of achievement can be reliably demonstrated to a third party – a university, a professional body or another employer, for example. Reliability is a particular issue where achievement standards must be comparable at national levels and/or by reference to professional standards or the standards of external awarding bodies. Standards of clinical practice in the NHS, usually tested at a variety of assessment stations in hospitals all over the country, are a good example. Parity here is vital because the NHS is subject to statutory requirements. Box 5.5 shows some simple things that can be done to improve a test's reliability.

Quality assurance

Workplace learning often puts more emphasis on process quality in assessment than on reliability issues per se. Most organisations already have comprehensive codes of practice that deal with issues of equity, equality and individual rights, particularly in the context of annual review, appraisal and performance-related pay. These represent important frameworks to ensure the quality (and reliability) of working practices. All of this must be used and developed to assure an appropriate approach to assessment in work-based learning and ethical keeping of learner attainment records. Firms that choose to use work-based learning as part of their programme of support for individuals and development of the company as a whole must do so in ways that are transparent and fair. Unfortunately, there are few national guidelines for the ways in which such quality assurance can be achieved. Of some 100 specific guidelines for quality assurance of learning in higher education in the UK (HEQC, 1995),] Brennan and Little (1996) report that only four are particularly relevant to work-based learning. These are:

- If an institution utilises placements, then such periods should carry the potential for the award of academic credit on the same basis as any other course or programme elements, provided there is appropriate, clearly defined and assessed learning to be achieved.
- It is vital that the quality assurance framework for the credit rating of off-campus provision relates in a systematic manner to the mainstream quality assurance mechanisms of the higher education institution.
- The learning achieved through work-based learning should include underpinning knowledge and understanding in order to attract the award of credit.
- Monitoring and review arrangements have to be clearly established – involving the students, the workplace and the higher education institution.

These talk more about the general approach to learning in the workplace, however, than about quality assurance in assessment practice. Those of us who are engaged in the processes and/or the assessment of work-based learning must therefore look more to the specific practices and codes of practice that represent the types of credit that will be awarded and the contexts in which recognition for learning is given. If, for example, your workplace seeks little or no formal and external recognition for the learning that takes place within it, then your own organisation's quality assurance procedures for supporting, developing and rewarding individuals are sufficient. Where university or college level credit, NVQs or professional body recognition is to be achieved, then inevitably the appropriate standards and codes of conduct must be applied. Nevertheless, some of these organisations provide very detailed guidance on their own quality assurance that may be adopted or modified by organisations that do not participate in such schemes directly. The Joint Awarding Body Guidance on Internal Verification of NVQs (QCA, 1998) and the NVQ Code of Practice (QCA, 2003) are useful examples.

ACTIVITY 5.3

List the ways in which your organisation seeks to give recognition for learning and achievement in the course of work. What are the quality assurance issues to this and how are they addressed in your organisation?

Box 5.6: Methods of assessment in work-based learning (from Brennan and Little, 1996, after Little and Nixon, 1995)

Method	Useful	Disadvantage	Comment
Direct observation of the student at work	Particularly used for assessing competence for NVQs Can provide evidence of teamwork, etc.	Expensive Disruptive to workplace	Important to have 'checklist' of what to observe
Assessment of student's logbook or work diary	Encourages self-reflection as a learner	Some doubt about validity	Needs to be combined with interview to establish validity
Interviewing/ interrogation at work	Obtaining evidence for knowledge and understanding needed for workplace tasks	Oral assessment can be subjective and less reliable	Sometimes workplace might need to be simulated
Surrogate assessment, i.e. the assessor obtains views of others (managers, peers, etc.)	Coverage of all workplace tasks and performance	May be doubts about reliability	Cheaper than trying to observe all tasks
Student prepares a final report and this is assessed	Encouraging reflection and communication skills	Needs to be combined with other methods	Report should contain reflection on what has been learnt
Written or oral tests of the intended learning outcomes from the work-based learning	Testing background knowledge and understanding	Lacks validity of direct observation	Some institutions will wish to include this method, if assessment leads to credit used for an academic award

LEARNING OBJECTIVES AND METHODS OF ASSESSMENT

So far in this chapter we have explored the general background to assessment – including its specification and design and the role and meaning of validity, reliability and quality assurance. Now we will explore assessment strategies and methods and the ways in which different types of assessment can be used to demonstrate different skills and knowledge.

Box 5.6 shows some of the most common methods for assessing work-based learning. Hevey (1993) also provides a framework for assessment methodologies in work-based learning that identifies a distinction between assessment tasks that are specifically done for the purpose of assessment and those that are 'naturally occurring evidence of work in progress'.

Evidence of achievement can include (a) written or oral assessment that demonstrates evidence of knowledge and understanding, (b) traditional skills tests or assessor-based tests of performance (naturally occurring evidence can be included), (c) samples or plans of work drawn from the workplace, or (d) observations or tests done in the normal course of work. The spectrum of such approaches is shown in Box 5.7.

Box 5.7: Distinct types of work-based assessment

Source 1: 'Specially elicited evidence'

Type (a): Written and oral exams

- Examination of relevant theory and underlying principles
- Written simulations
- Projects requiring independent planning and research

Type (b): Performance tests

- Skills and proficiency tests
- Direct observation of performance in simulated work situations
- Examining performance on relevant tasks and multi-skill functions

Source 2: 'Naturally occurring evidence of work in progress'

Type (a): Predetermined samples set in the workplace

- Samples of relevant work products
- Plans and evidence of preparation
- Evaluations of work outcomes and personal effectiveness
- Assignments and reflective accounts for work practices and procedures

Type (b): Ongoing work

- Direct observation of normal performance in real work situations
- Logbooks or diaries of day-to-day practice
- Oral questions about ongoing work
- Interrogation of rationale for work activities
- Peer assessment and reports

Key reference: Hevey (1993), cited in Brennan and Little (1996).

A TAXONOMY OF LEARNING OBJECTIVES

The list of assessment strategies and methods shown in Box 5.7 appears to be comprehensive. Unfortunately, there are few books or papers that specifically explain the application of a rigorous educational approach to the use of appropriate assessment methodologies. In order to attempt to do so, the following section of this chapter explores Bloom's Taxonomy of Learning and explains how such a framework can be used to specify assessment tasks.

Throughout the 1950s and 1960s, B.S. Bloom published a series of works that have had an enormous impact on teaching and learning methods, assessment strategies and curriculum design. In particular, Bloom argued that the 'intended behaviour' of learners (the ways in which learners act, think and feel) could be classified into general and specific categories, and that this 'classification' could be used both to specify the

Box 5.8: The six categories of Bloom's taxonomy for the cognitive domain

Level and description	Behavioural examples	Terms
Knowledge		
Remembering facts, definitions, lists, theories, rules, etc., from previous learning. This does not imply any understanding and is the lowest level of learning in the cognitive domain	Recalls terms, specific facts, principles, definitions, descriptions, events, dates; states rules and regulations; describes procedures and processes	States, describes, names, identifies, chooses, tells, selects, labels
Comprehension		
The lowest level of understanding, including such activities as translating written material from one form to another, interpreting, predicting, identifying examples of concepts	Interprets a graph, summarises a passage; uses a concept, extrapolates or interpolates, identifies examples of a concept in a list of items	Selects, chooses, identifies, infers, predicts, explains, paraphrases, rewrites
Application		
Using learned material in new situations, including solving problems using rules, principles, methods, laws and theories. This requires a much higher level of understanding than that required at the comprehension level	Applies rules or laws to solve a real problem; uses a process or procedure to correct a fault; constructs a graph from a set of data; finds the solution to a mathematical problem	Solves, predicts, selects procedure, finds errors, sets out pages, assembles apparatus, modifies process

Analysis		
Showing some creative ability in critical analysis of a situation or written material by such activities as breaking it down to identify implied meanings, distinguishing fact from opinion, identifying relationships among parts, and recognising the organisational structure of the material	Recognises unstated assumptions, logical fallacies and incon-sistencies; distinguishes between fact and inference, fact and opinion; analyses organisational structure of literary, musical or artwork	Discriminates, identifies, infers, selects parts, illustrates, differentiates, outlines
Synthesis		
Creatively putting ideas, concepts, rules together in a new way to produce such results as a unique communication (for example an essay), an original process or procedure, or new classification scheme	Writes a well-organised essay or report; devises a new process or procedure; integrates learning from different areas to produce a new solution to a problem	Creates, designs, makes, produces, plans, composes, reorganises, develops, writes
Evaluation		
Judging the value of written material (such as a process, project report, essay, novel), including justifying any judgements using definite criteria, either external (such as relevance) or internal (organisationally based). This is considered the highest level because it contains elements of all the other categories plus value judgements	Determines logical consistency of arguments presented, adequacy of support for conclusions; judges literary quality of a novel based on aesthetics or external criteria	Selects, justifies, criticises, contrasts, assesses, profiles, adjudicates

Key references: Bloom (1956) and Gronlund (1970), reprinted from Black (2000).

objectives of learning and to change the way the educational process was managed. Bloom identified three major divisions (or domains) of activity: the cognitive domain, the affective domain and the psychomotor domain. In each domain he identified five or six major categories of activity. Box 5.8 shows the six categories that Bloom attributed to the cognitive domain, and Box 5.9 shows Bloom's descriptions of the affective and psychomotor domains.

Since its conception, Bloom's approach has formed the basis for many approaches to curriculum design and it facilitates the use of specific learning objectives that both define what a programme should teach and how the learning should be assessed. As an example, Curzon (2001) uses an economics course to illustrate examples of both the general and specific instructional objectives that can be specified and measured in this way:

Box 5.9: Bloom's taxonomy of the affective and psychomotor domains

A. Affective domain. This domain deals with a variety of activities ranging from simple reception of stimuli to complex ability to characterise by the use of value concepts.

1. <u>Receiving</u> – attending to or heeding messages or other stimuli. This heading subsumes awareness, willingness to attend and controlled attention.
2. <u>Responding</u> – the arousal of curiosity and the acceptance of responsibility in relation to the response.
3. <u>Valuing</u> – the recognition of the value of a work situation so that motivation is lightened and beliefs emerge.
4. <u>Organising and conceptualising</u> – the partnering of responses on the basis of investigation attitudes and values, and the beginning of the building of an internally consistent value system.
5. <u>Characterising by value or value concept</u> – the ability to see as a coherent whole matters involving ideas, attitudes and benefits.

B. Psychomotor domain. This deals with motor skills and although no specific framework has been explained here, Simpson (1969) has developed the following approach:

1. <u>Perception</u> – the use of a learner's sense organs to obtain those cues essential for the guidance of motor activity, i.e. sensory stimulation, cue selection and translation (of sensory cases into motor activity).
2. <u>Set</u> – the state of readiness for the performance of a certain action.
3. <u>Guided response</u> – invitation, trial and error, etc. in order to perform the given operation under guidance.
4. <u>Mechanism</u> – the ability to perform the task repeatedly and with acceptable proficiency.
5. <u>Complex, overt response</u> – the performance of a task with a high degree of proficiency.
6. <u>Adaptation</u> – the use of previously acquired skills to perform novel tasks.
7. <u>Origination</u> – the creation of a new style of performance of the task after the development of new skills.

Key reference: Curzon (2001), adapted from various sources.

1. **(COGNITIVE DOMAIN) Category: Knowledge**

(General objective) At the end of the period of instruction the student will know the principal function of cheques.

(Specific objectives) The student will:

1. Define a cheque.
2. State to which class of documents it belongs.
3. List the parties to a cheque ...

2. **(COGNITIVE DOMAIN) Category: Comprehension**

(General objective) At the end of the period of instruction the student will understand the principle of diminishing utility.

(Specific objectives) The student will:

1. Explain the principle in their own words.
2. Illustrate the principle by means of a graph ...

ACTIVITY 5.4

Classify each of the following objectives by their domain (cognitive, affective or psychomotor), and categorise accordingly. The first has been completed as an example.

Cognitive/comprehension	At the end of this IT training course, the learner will be able to explain the principle of mail merge in their own words
(a) _____/_____	The trainee must demonstrate to the trainer that they have mentally prepared themselves for the task they are about to perform and have all the necessary tools to hand
(b) _____/_____	The final exam will require the participant to produce a written account of modern theories of leadership that compares and contrasts the four major themes taught in the course
(c) _____/_____	Finally, the group will be required to judge the project reports of each individual and decide which one should be recommended to the board. Their recommendation should be based on explained reasoning and the use of explicit criteria
(d) _____/_____	Given an electronic circuit specification, the engineer should be able to design and build a working prototype
(e) _____/_____	The individual must be able to listen attentively and show evidence of attending to the explanation
(f) _____/_____	Design a simple mathematical model to explain the relationship between the following sets of data for wage rates and unemployment

Suggested answers: (a) Psychomotor/set; (b) Cognitive/analysis; (c) Cognitive/evaluation; (d) Psychomotor/adaptation; (e) Affective/receiving; (f) Cognitive/synthesis

Such an approach provides a powerful and systematic method for the definition of assessment strategies that clearly test the outcomes of learning. Once defined in this way the test (or method of assessment) need only be selected to best determine performance in the learnt trait at the appropriate level.

Of course, Bloom's approach is not without its critics. Some argue that it is akin to a production line approach to learning and that by specifying precisely what is to be learnt and how this learning is to be demonstrated, it inhibits the freedom to learn in its broadest sense. Unexpected or unplanned learning, for example, may be marginalised, and the facilitation of learning from peer group exchange may be particularly difficult to prescribe in the manner suggested by Bloom. Nevertheless, if the objective of learning is to produce desirable goals, then these goals should be specified as clearly as possible at the outset and charted with precision. Bloom's approach is useful for this and related approaches have been developed by others such as Tyler (1964) and Ebel (1979).

ISSUES IN ASSESSMENT

Who should do the assessing?

In the general practice of work-based learning it is usually true to say that the learner has much greater involvement in (and hence responsibility for) the process of assessment than is the case in, say, traditional classroom-based education. The methods used in work-based learning are also almost uniquely variable and diverse. Learners and assessors should be aware of all the different methods of assessment that they can use and also of just how and why particular methods are more or less useful in different contexts or to demonstrate achievement in different areas. Each method of assessment is also likely to place more or less burden of effort on the shoulders of the learner or the assessor and this must be taken into account beforehand. Self-assessment, for example, is not onerous for tutors because the burden of responsibility lies clearly with the learner (although tutors may still play a role in helping students to self-assess with reliability and validity). The marking of a student dissertation, on the other hand, requires considerable time and a great deal of expert knowledge on the part of the assessor. These and related issues are further explored in Chapters 7 and 8 of this book.

Self-assessment

Self-assessment should, of course, be an integral part of the development of any learner. It is difficult to succeed in any new area of study or professional practice if the skills of self-assessment are not developed.

Generally, there are two distinct approaches to self-assessment (although in practice these are often combined). The first is an evaluative process of judgement in which a learner is encouraged (and hopefully supported) to reflect on what and how they have learnt in order to learn more. The second form of self-assessment is perhaps more appropriately termed self-grading, where the learner must use a set of criteria to judge their work. These criteria may be predetermined by a tutor or mentor, set by a professional organisation, or developed individually by the student themselves, or sometimes agreed by a process of negotiation between two or more parties. The care with which self-assessments must be treated depends largely upon the purpose of the assessment in the first place, but there is good research literature that demonstrates the correspondence (or sometimes the lack of it) between self-assessment marks and marks attributed independently by tutors. Boud and Falchikov (1989), for example, report that on balance most published comparisons of this type suggest that students tend to award themselves higher grades than their independent assessors, but that higher achievers more commonly underrate their work. However, other researchers have suggested opposite trends to these, and Brown and Knight (1994) suggest that there is no consistent pattern of under- or over-grading in self-assessment. Despite these concerns, there is no doubt that there is an important place for self-assessment in work-based learning because it is so important in making students aware of their own abilities and needs. Furthermore, in most organisations, individuals are frequently called upon to assess others and an ability in self-assessment is key to understanding the practice and application of assessment for others.

Self-assessment, however, requires support and development. Many people first report that they lack the knowledge and confidence to assess themselves. Furthermore, overburdening learners with the responsibilities of assessment can eat into their own reflective study time and ultimately it is a dereliction of duty if pushed to the extreme. More often than not, requiring that learners complete their own evaluation sheets to accompany submitted work is sufficient practice. This allows an assessor to help the student understand their achievement and progress objectively, but they can also be given feedback on how well they are able to self-assess their achievements.

Finally, care must be taken if the results of a self-assessment are to be used to present achievement records to third parties such as exam boards or professional bodies. Here rigorous explanations of the quality assurance procedure are usually needed in addition to other forms of evidence of achievement.

Group or peer assessment

Peer assessment is judged by many as an effective means of developing assessment skills in a more general context. It is, in effect, an excellent learning process, both for those being assessed, and for those doing the assessing. Like self-assessment records, the concerns over using peer assessment grades in any formal sense are considerable (although not insurmountable and sometimes valuable). Gray (2001) suggests that peers tend to be lenient to their colleagues and tend to over-grade their work and he also emphasises the need to control for possible collusion. Brown and Knight (1994) suggest that one particularly appropriate use of peer assessment methods is in formative assessment and that the presentation of work to peers prior to formal submission is an important means of securing advice and feedback.

As individuals become more experienced in peer assessment it is common for them to develop many of the subtle skills they will need as an assessor themselves, and often the skills they will need more generally in their place of work. Distinguishing extrovert presentations of poor quality content from less demonstrative but more worthwhile ones is one such subtle skill. Furthermore, the ability to identify (and deal with) instances where individuals shirk their responsibilities in a group context is another.

Feedback in assessment

In another variation on the theme of 'deep' versus 'surface' learning, Entwistle (1993; cited in Brown and Knight, 1994), expands the approach to students' expectations of assessment and identifies four styles of students – the deep learner, the surface learner, the strategic learner and the apathetic learner. How each of these students' learning styles corresponds with their expectation of feedback in assessment is explained by Brown and Knight (1994) and is shown in Table 5.1.

Table 5.1 *Learner's approaches and the expectations of assessment feedback (after Brown and Knight, 1994)*

Learning approach	Appropriate feedback
Deep	Detailed comments on the ideas, evidence and techniques. The goal is understanding and feedback should reflect this.
Surface	General comments. The relevance of detailed comments will not be seen.
Strategic	Mark-related comments, cueing students into what they need to do to get better marks. Detailed comments on ideas not welcome.
Apathetic	Encouraging comments needed – but 'boot in the rear' comments might 'kick start' the learner. Confidence building, however, is generally preferred.

ACTIVITY 5.5

Produce an outline plan for a short programme of learning and assessment using all that you have learnt in this chapter. Ensure that you pay appropriate attention to the issues of reliability and validity and the learning outcomes for the learning. Be sure that you are clear about the *level* at which the programme will be taught and the level at which the learners will be required to demonstrate their ability. Also be sure that you make an appropriate choice from the assessment methods available to you – this should include reference to the time and cost of implementing the assessment. Decide whether norm- or criterion-referenced tests should be used and decide on the methods of assessment that should be used. Try to make sure that you could justify these decisions.

SUMMARY

- Assessment is an integral part of learning and teaching and it should be planned carefully as part of the design of any programme of learning.
- Issues of validity and reliability are important if assessment is to be 'fit for purpose'.
- Writing learning outcomes provides a powerful means of specifying course content and assessment for any programme of learning that is planned in advance.
- This chapter has explained the variety of assessment methods that are commonly used in work-based learning. It has also discussed the strengths and weaknesses of most of these methods and reviewed their costs and staff time implications.

REFERENCES

Benett, Y. (1993) The validity and reliability of assessment and self-assessment of work based learning. *Assessment & Evaluation in Higher Education* 18(2), 83–93.

Black, T. (2000) *Assessment, Evaluation and Educational Measurement – Study Guide*, The University of Surrey, Guildford.

Bloom, B.S. (ed) (1956) *Taxonomy of Educational Objectives: Handbook I. The Cognitive Domain*, Longman, Harlow.

Bloom, B. S. (1971) Learning for mastery. In: *Handbook on Formative and Summative Evaluation of Student Learning* (eds Bloom, B.S., Hastings, J.T. and Madaus, G.F.), McGraw-Hill, London.

Brennan, J. and Little, B. (1996) *A Review of Work Based Learning in Higher Education.* HEQE. http://www.dfes.gov.uk/dfee/heqe/wblindex.htm. The Quality Support Centre of the Open University, October 1996.

Brown, S. and Knight, P. (1994) *Assessing Learning in Higher Education*, Kogan Page, London.

Curzon, L. B. (2001) *Teaching in Further Education*, 5th edn, Continium, London and New York.

Ebel, R. (1979) *Essentials of Educational Measurement*, 3rd edn, Prentice-Hall, Englewood Cliffs, NJ.

Gray, D. (2001) *Learning & Teaching Support Network Assessment Series No.11 A Briefing on Work-based Learning*, Learning and Teaching Support Network, York.

Gronlund, N. (1970) *Stating Behavioural Objectives for Classroom Instruction*, Corrier-Macmillan, New York.

HEQC (1995) *Guidelines on the Quality Assurance of Credit Based Learning*, QUA/HEQC, London.

Hevey, D. (1993) *Issues in the Design of Competence-Based Assessment Strategies*, The Open University Press, Vocational Qualifications Centre, Milton Keynes. (http://www.ltsn.ac.uk/application.asp?app=resources.asp&process=full_record&section=generic&id=11).

Little, B. and Nixon, N. (1995) *Assessment Strategies for Work Based Learning*: QSC Briefing Papers. Quality Support Centre, London.

Mehrens, W.A. and Lehmann, I.J. (1984) *Measurements and Evaluation in Education and Psychology*, 3rd edn, Holt, Reinhart and Winston, New York.

QCA (1998) *Joint Awarding Body Guidance on Internal verification of NVQs*. Qualification and Curriculums Authority, London.

QCA (2003) *NVQ Code of Practice*. Qualification and Curriculums Authority, London.

Rowntree, D. (1987) *Assessing Students: How Shall We Know Them?* Kogan Page, London.

Tyler, R.W. (1964) *Basic Principles of Curriculum and Instruction – Syllabus for Education 360.* Chicago University Press, Chicago.

6 RECOGNISING PRIOR LEARNING AND MAKING IT COUNT

Objectives

After reading this chapter, you will be able to:

- Identify the knowledge, skills and understanding you have gained through work.
- Understand the role of professional reflection and so form principles for future action.
- Use the process of Assessment of Prior Learning (APL) to enable you to gain access to an award-bearing course, access to a specific job, and/or credit towards an award.

INTRODUCTION

Most people learn throughout their lives. This learning may be gained through formal education and training, for which a certificate demonstrating achievement is awarded, but many people also learn a great deal through the experience of doing their job, or through self-study.

We will be examining the nature of learning that is gained from experience. This may be through deliberate planned experiences, or everyday, unplanned experiences. We will also look at where learning can occur in the workplace, how it can be recognised, and how it contributes to self-development. We will also consider how the knowledge and skills you have gained through learning from experience, and your achievements, can be used in gaining credit towards qualifications.

APL, APA, RPL – WHAT IS IT ALL ABOUT?

Different organisations have different acronyms for a similar process. A number of them can be seen in Table 6.1, and you will meet others. Where you see the use of 'accreditation', such as in the 'accreditation of prior learning', there is the presumption that there has been a process of assessment of evidence of the learning involved to enable accreditation.

We are going to focus on the assessment, and recognition, of experiential learning (APEL) for which you do not have a certificate of achievement as evidence. However, if you wish to know more about APL, there is an overview in Appendix 6.1.

WHAT IS EXPERIENTIAL LEARNING?

Experiential learning is a meaningful encounter, i.e. an active engagement where there is analysis not just of the subject matter but often analysis of our own reaction – including implications for future work. Sometimes this is done unconsciously. In this chapter we use a broad definition of the term 'experiential learning' to include learning from:

Table 6.1   *Acronyms relating to recognition of prior learning*

Acronym	Meaning
RPL	Recognition of prior learning. This is an overarching term that includes learning for which you have a certificate demonstrating achievement; learning from courses that only give a certificate of attendance; learning gained from experience
APCL	Assessment (or accreditation) of prior certificated learning. You have a certificate that provides proof of achievement, not just attendance
APL	Similar to APCL – prior certificated learning. However, a number of organisations use this as a generic term to include both certificated as well as experiential learning
APEL	Assessment/accreditation of prior experiential learning for which you do not have a formal certificate of achievement
AP(E)L	Assessment/accreditation of both certified and experiential learning
AP(E/C)L	As above
APA	Assessment/accreditation of prior achievement
LOFT	Learning outside of formal teaching

- Everyday experiences where learning is informal and unplanned and where knowledge and skills are gained through the experience of undertaking a job, discussions with colleagues or knowledgeable others, etc. This is very much experience-based learning.
- Deliberate experiences where learning is planned. These could include coaching, attendance at in-house programmes or external programmes, or self-study. There may be a certificate, but not one that provides evidence of achievement – more a certificate of attendance. Frequently it is expected that the knowledge and skills gained from the experience of being on the course, or coached, will be used within the job role and built upon – and so learning from deliberate experiences is then built upon through everyday experiences.

You need to be aware that other writers may have a narrower, or slightly different, definition of experiential learning. Many will focus on the first definition above, and the main focus of this chapter will also be around the process of capturing and recording informal, unplanned learning from everyday experiences.

The responsibility for the learning is on the learner, and experience alone is not sufficient to count as learning. Individuals can go through experiences without learning anything. You must consciously realise the value of the experience (Barkatoolah, 1985) and identify the learning that you have gained.

Learning is not just involvement with a body of knowledge to be learnt, or skills to be gained – you may also be dealing with complex problems and engaging with others. There can be the involvement of emotions and feelings as well as the influence of context and culture. The learning gained often has a personal meaning for those involved, and each person can have a unique 'take' on an experience. In some instances you may need to present others with evidence of learning for the purposes of assessment, and some of these assessment processes are designed to enable individuals gain:

- access to an award-bearing course
- access to a specific job
- credit towards an award
- promotion and/or a pay rise.

Other processes are based on the notion of informal self-assessment and focused planning for improved performance. There are links here to the concept of lifelong learning, where an individual is expected to reflect constructively on their experience and learning, record the results of such reflections, and use these to plan their future actions (Fryer, 1997).

Where the process of assessment is involved, whether by self and/or others, then the term we will use will be APEL – Assessment of Prior Experiential Learning. It is one of the terms contained in Table 6.1, and one that you will meet frequently in the literature.

WHY RECOGNISE PRIOR EXPERIENTIAL LEARNING

Identifying knowledge, skills and understanding gained through experience and the evidence that could 'prove' this learning can be time-consuming. So why should anyone wish to go through this process? The following benefits have been gleaned from a number of sources, including personal interviews.

An employee's perspective

Recognising prior experiential learning can:

- support access to an award-bearing course
- gain credit towards a specific qualification, with a saving in time and money
- support negotiations with your employer for career development
- generate self-esteem
- raise confidence
- support personal growth and development
- increase self-awareness
- build on previous experience rather than replicating learning.

An employer's perspective

Many of the benefits for the employee are also benefits for the employer, as there is value in having an employee with confidence and self-esteem. The benefits of APEL also include:

- Avoidance of wasting time and resources in repetitious learning for knowledge and skills already gained.
- A process that helps the employee to take responsibility for their own learning, and is motivational.
- Support for the process of appraisal.

There are now more demands on individuals to possess the necessary capabilities to move and adapt to modern and changing times. Stephenson (1992) identified the valuable members of the workforce to be those individuals who:

- had justified confidence in their ability to take effective appropriate action
- could explain what they were about
- continued to learn from their experiences as individuals and as valuable members of the workforce.

He argued that capability is focused more specifically on the capacity to manage one's own learning – which is a crucial element in the process of APEL.

WHERE LEARNING CAN TAKE PLACE – WHERE AND HOW WE GAIN KNOWLEDGE AND SKILLS IN THE WORKPLACE

Learning from experience can be far more indirect that we realise – certainly when we are learning from everyday experiences. It is useful to identify where and how you have gained your knowledge, skills and understanding, as this can help you focus on the actual learning you have gained, and also the way you like to learn. Some people prefer to learn:

- by going to resources such as books, papers and the Internet
- through discussion with people
- through watching others
- by experimenting.

We often underestimate what we learn from others – such as from teamwork, one-to-one coaching, mentoring, or attendance at in-house programmes. It is easy to forget how much you may have learnt from those informal discussions with friends and colleagues over coffee, or by the photocopier. You may have had one of those conversations where you 'took your mind for a walk' with a friend or colleague (or a stranger) to try to identify all the possible solutions there could be to something that was bothering you. We can be very creative in our problem-solving – particularly in informal situations where we feel secure and where we can bounce ideas off others. We learn a great deal from these experiences.

ACTIVITY 6.1

Think of the new knowledge, skills and understanding you have gained in the last six months. How have you done this? Make a personal list of all of the different ways including how you have learnt by yourself, and how you have learnt from others.

The list below, which details different ways of learning in the workplace, was compiled from contributions from mature students on a work-based degree programme who were wishing to gain academic credit for the learning gained through the workplace. They were considering all the ways in which they gained knowledge, skills and understanding needed to do their jobs, deal with problems, and to complete specific projects. Some are deliberate experiences of learning, others everyday experiences. The list is not exclusive and is only a sample of what came from the group:

- team meetings
- working with others
- feedback from performance appraisal process

- mentoring
- coaching
- observation of others
- shadowing
- being challenged
- informal meetings, e.g. coffee with colleagues, friends
- alternating roles
- simulation exercise and feedback
- being a member of a professional network
- information from suppliers
- attending in-house programmes and putting new ideas into practice
- Internet, books, magazines, articles
- thinking about how a particular aspect of a job, project, incident or situation was dealt with; considering where it went well, where it did not go well and where it could be improved.

You may wish to review your response to Activity 6.1 and add additional strategies to your list of how you learn in the workplace.

REFLECTION AS A DEVELOPMENT EXPERIENCE

A great deal of learning also happens in the process of thinking about how a particular aspect of a job, project, incident or situation was dealt with – whether it went well, where it did not go well, where it could have been improved. This reflection may have been done on your own or with others. This process reflects the cycle of experiential learning met in Chapter 3 when you were introduced to models of learning, including that of Kolb (1984).

In Kolb's Experiential Learning Cycle, the cyclical approach facilitates the analysis of learning from the processes of assessment, planning, implementation and evaluation. He emphasised the four basic stages of reflection:

1. Concrete action: you may have recently been involved in a specific situation that required some action or response. This may have been a presentation at a team meeting, dealing with a difficult situation or person, demonstrating a new product to a client, creating a new database.
2. After the event you then thought about the experience – what went well, what could be improved.
3. By 'reflecting' on the experience you possibly identified what you would do if it occurred again, and so you formed principles for future actions.
4. When the situation arises again, or something similar, then you can put into practice what you have learnt from the first time you undertook the action, e.g. how you would improve the presentation at a team meeting, or deal more effectively with a difficult situation or person.

Your knowledge, skills and understanding are steadily built up through different experiences, and reflection is the active engagement with the experience and plays a special role in drawing meaning from experience. It is in the process of reflection that we recognise what we have learnt in terms of knowledge, skills and understanding, and how we have learnt this (Boud *et al.*, 1996). It involves thinking about, and critically analysing, our actions, with the goal of improving our professional practice.

Kolb's cycle of learning from experience is reflected in the work of Schön (1987), who wrote about the 'reflective practitioner' and identified two kinds of reflection:

1. **Reflection-on-action** – this occurs either following an activity, or by taking time-out during an activity. It can be described as a 'cognitive post-mortem'. Full attention can be given to analysis without the necessity for immediate action, and when there is opportunity for you – as the professional – to receive assistance from others in analysing the event. For example, you may have been involved in negotiating a complex deal with a prospective client. After a particularly challenging meeting – or during a coffee break – you think about how the meeting went, how you dealt with the issues and the person, and the implications for future action. You may then modify your approach next time you meet with the prospective client.

2. **Reflection-in-action** – this occurs during (without interrupting) an activity by thinking about how to reshape the activity while it is under way. It is sometimes called 'thinking on our feet' and happens as we work, influencing our decisions as a situation unfolds. If we take the above example, you do not have the opportunity to withdraw to think about how the negotiation is going. If the prospective client raises an issue during the negotiation that you have not met before, or acts in a way that is unexpected and new, you deal with it, drawing on the knowledge and skills you already have. It becomes an online experiment as you adjust and improve actions in response to the issues raised.

However, in skilful action – where we often do make changes based on already held knowledge and skills – it can be difficult to say exactly what we do know. In other words, professionals are not always able to describe what they do to accomplish an activity: they just do it. Osterman (1990) maintains that an important part of reflective practice is developing the ability to articulate that tacit knowledge in order to share professional skills, enhance the body of professional knowledge within the organisation, and to develop one's own practices. We will look further at strategies for identifying what we know, and can do, later in this chapter.

Below is a model of structured reflection taken from an article by Gray (2003) – adapted from Johns (1993) and Carper (1978) – which consists of a series of questions that can help you focus on an experience in a structured and meaningful way. This model, or similar, is used frequently by healthcare professionals, but its potential for application is much wider. Basically, it consists of a core question: 'What information do I need to access in order to learn from this experience?' followed by the seven cue questions:

1. **Describe the experience**: what was special about it, what essential and significant background factors contribute to this experience?
2. **Reflection**: what are you feelings about this experience and what are the feelings of the patient (other person)? Why did you act the way you did and what were the consequences of those actions?
3. **What factors**, both internal and external, influenced the choices you made? What knowledge helped you make those choices and what other choices could have been taken? What would the outcome of alternative actions have been?

4. **What have you learnt** from this experience? How has this experience changed your knowledge? How will it affect your future choices and decisions? How does it relate to past experiences and potential future experiences?
5. **Analysis**: can you make any sense out of this experience?
6. **Conclusion**: could you have done anything else?
7. **Plan**: should the situation arise again what, if anything, would you do differently?

It must be admitted that some people may never reflect on their actions – either consciously or unconsciously – and so may never learn and move forward. This may be because there are barriers that prevent them from learning from experience. Reflection does not automatically accompany work. Some barriers are external, such as from other people, the larger personal situation, the context of the learner, and social forces. Internal barriers can include previous negative experiences or established patterns of behaviour. A number of individuals may find it difficult to reflect as they find it intrusive, particularly if the results of their deliberations are to be in the public domain – such as in their CPD portfolio, as part of their organisation's appraisal system, or in a narrative accompanying evidence presented to a college or university to claim credit.

TIME, SELF AND THE SITUATION

Much experience is multi-faceted, multi-layered and so inextricably connected with other experiences that it is impossible to locate temporally or spatially. It almost defies analysis, as the act of analysis inevitably alters the experience and the learning that comes from it (Boud *et al.*, 1996).

Learning always relates, in some way, to what has gone before – we do not begin with a clean slate. In some instances there may be immediate learning and an immediate gain of knowledge and skills – such as in an example of observing someone else undertake a particular task and realising how it is done. However, it does not have to be recent; it can occur over time, and learning may take a number of months – or even years – before it is apparent.

Emotions and feelings are sometimes neglected in our society. There is a cultural bias in favour of the intellectual and practical – but acknowledgement of your emotions and feelings in a situation can help or hinder learning as it will affect the way you perceive an experience and learn from it. If the experience just undergone was painful, then there may be no wish to reflect on the situation and identify issues, to explore what happened so as to learn from the experience, and so possibly act in a different way in the future.

Do not underestimate the impact of the environment in which your learning takes place. You construct your own experience in the context of a particular setting and range of cultural values that you, and others, hold. Your environment can both inhibit and encourage you to learn from the experiences you meet. For example, is your organisation supportive and conducive to learning? Does it encourage its staff to develop both personally and professionally? How are individuals dealt with? Learning takes place best when you have confidence and self-esteem. If you feel under threat at work, or suffer from a lack of confidence, this may reinforce negative images of yourself and prevent you learning from your experiences. You may believe you are incapable of learning and if you think this it will in fact handicap you, therefore you don't learn from the situations you find yourself in. The way in which we interpret experience is intimately connected with how we view ourselves (Boud *et al.*, 1996). The extent to which we can change is affected by the supportiveness of the workplace – we need support, trust and challenge from others. We need diversity and difference of experience, and we need challenges and opportunities to be available.

IDENTIFYING WHAT YOU HAVE LEARNT

We have considered where and how you may have gained knowledge, skills and understanding, and now you need to identify more specifically exactly what you have learnt. The problem is that the very nature of experiential learning means that what you have learned almost becomes a part of you. This can mean that the learning is difficult to recognise and 'pick out' from your overall experience. Often it is hard to remember a time when you did not know, or could not do, something that has become part of your life, particularly your professional life.

You will have learnt a great deal by just undertaking your job, or a specific project, and thinking through how you will meet your objectives/targets. You will have:

- learnt new skills so that you can undertake specific tasks you have to do
- faced problems and identified ways to solve these by analysing the issues and coming to a solution
- developed new ways of doing things – usually through reviewing different strategies, and seeing more appropriate ways of going forward
- worked with people to come to conclusions
- investigated issues that have needed solutions, and have found these in different places – through thinking it through by yourself, from colleagues, family, the Internet, books, visitors.

What follows are three possible approaches to help you identify knowledge, skills and understanding that you have gained through:

- undertaking your usual job role/s
- undertaking a specific project/initiative
- dealing with a specific incident or situation – such as a difficult client/colleague, a challenging meeting, or an emergency situation.

You may not wish to tackle all of Activities 6.2–6.4; you may find that only Activity 6.2 is relevant. However, going through the activity may help you identify the knowledge and skills you already have, and possibly had not realised. It helps make the tacit knowledge more overt so that you can discuss your knowledge, skills and achievements in appraisal sessions, when applying for a career move, or when applying for a course.

Learning from your job

When you consider the job you do, think about all the tasks you have to undertake, and the areas of responsibility, such as:

- managing individuals and/or teams
- training staff

- marketing
- managing finance
- recruitment
- dealing with customer complaints
- contract management
- computing/IT
- creating products such as software programs, engineering items
- health and safety.

Don't forget areas of responsibility that occur in more than one situation. For example, you may:

- manage finance for a specific project, and deal with finance for your department
- manage individuals in your section, as well as those within a project team
- have responsibility for training new staff that arrive at the organisation, as well as implementing IiP.

ACTIVITY 6.2

Think about your job role, your tasks, responsibilities and major accomplishments and make brief notes on the following:

- The responsibilities you have in your job.
- What you actually have to do.
- The major things you have achieved – for yourself and/or for your organisation.

Now take just one of your tasks/areas of responsibility that emerge and make notes under the following headings:

- Brief description of the task/responsibility.
- Three things you have to know, and how you gained this knowledge.
- Three things you need to be able to do, and how you gained these skills.
- If someone asked you to prove the above, how could you do this? Is there a product? Can someone confirm your knowledge and skills – such as a line manager, colleague? Are you the only one who knows about your knowledge and skills?

Learning from undertaking specific projects

Let us consider the knowledge, skills and understanding you may have gained through undertaking a specific project such as:

- developing a new software program
- investigating and creating new procedures for the care of specific patients
- developing policy relating to how the organisation deals with complaints
- setting up a system for inducting new recruits into the organisation
- planning and delivering a specific training programme
- reviewing health and safety and making recommendations for improvement.

In some cases you may have had to gain specific knowledge and skills before you could complete the project; this may have been gained from other people, from going on a course, or from the Internet.

ACTIVITY 6.3

Think about the projects you have been involved in, and/or managed. If there is more than one, then make a list of these. Choose one of the projects from the list and make brief notes on the following:

- An overview of the project.
- The responsibilities you had: were you a member of a team with a specific task? Did you have a management role? Were you the only one undertaking the project?
- The major things you achieved – for yourself and/or your organisation.
- Three things you had to know, and how you gained this knowledge.
- Three things you needed to be able to do, and how you gained these skills.
- If someone asked you to prove the above, how could you do this? Is there a product? Can someone confirm your knowledge and skills – such as a line manager, a colleague?

Learning from specific incidents or situations

As part of your work you may have had to deal with a specific incident or situation through which you have learnt a considerable amount. This may have been an unusual event or the first time you had met such a situation.

Learners on a work-based course identified the following when considering incidents or situations through which they had gained knowledge and skills:

- Dealing with a difficult person such as a client not happy with the service provided; a member of a team who is not contributing to a team project; someone who is bullying other staff.
- Dealing with a difficult situation such as discovering someone had broken the law; having to give a formal warning to a member of staff.
- Going through the process of making someone redundant.
- Dealing with an accident, or other emergency in the workplace.
- Dealing with an inspection or auditing visit, e.g. IiP, ISO 2000, Health and Safety, financial auditors.

These are only a few ideas – you will have other experiences to draw upon. Through these events you will have gained new knowledge, skills and understanding – particularly an understanding of yourself. Some situations may have only lasted a short period of time, such as dealing with an emergency. Other situations may have involved actions over a period of time – such as the process of making someone redundant. It may be that, by reflecting on the incident or situation whilst it was under way, you identified knowledge or skills that you personally needed to resolve the situation – either the current one or any future similar situation.

ACTIVITY 6.4

Think about the incidents and situations you have been involved in. Make a list of those that have happened in the last two years. Choose just one from your list and make brief notes on the following:

- An overview of the incident or situation, including what led up to the incident and how it was resolved.
- Three things you learnt from the event.
- Three things that went well, and why.
- Three things you would do differently if you met a similar incident or situation, and why you would do these differently.

It is unlikely that there will be nice neat evidence of your learning and achievements from the incident or situation, particularly if you had to deal with a difficult person or confidential situation. If needed, there may be a colleague who could confirm it occurred and that it was resolved appropriately.

If you are identifying the knowledge, skills and understanding you have gained for the purposes of appraisal, or for purposes of self-development, then you may just wish to record the learning gained. However, it can also be useful to identify the 'evidence' in case this may be needed, e.g. in your professional portfolio, for appraisal, or for a promotion interview. If you are looking to use the process of APEL to gain access to a course, or a grant of credit towards a qualification, you will certainly have to provide evidence of this learning. You may also be asked to write a narrative relating to the learning gained in the workplace. Activities 6.2–6.4 can provide you with the basis for your professional narrative, and we will come back to these later. They can help jog your memory. The seven cue questions on pages 115–16 can also help you focus on what you learnt.

USING APEL FOR PERSONAL PLANNING FOR IMPROVED PERFORMANCE

In later sections we will consider using APEL to gain access to courses as well as gaining grants of credit towards qualifications. However, not all people wish to go through a formal assessment process, but want to identify for themselves what they have learnt so as to plan for further CPD in the workplace. You may wish to reflect on your experience and take stock of knowledge and skills so as to:

- construct an individual development plan
- prepare yourself for an interview – for promotion, or change of career
- be ready for an appraisal meeting.

In these situations there may also be a requirement that you provide evidence of your learning. For example, in a CPD portfolio for Chartered Engineering status, you may have to include samples of evidence, or details of where the evidence could be found. At a promotion interview, or for an appraisal, you may be asked for product evidence that proves your knowledge and skills. The process of reflection on your learning, identification of the knowledge and skills you have gained in the workplace – often through everyday, unplanned activities – can raise your self-awareness, and can be empowering. It demonstrates your capacity to manage your own learning and development over time.

Activities 6.2–6.4 can help you identify the knowledge and skills you have, as well as the cue questions on pages 115–16. You may also find it useful to complete some form of audit. This may be one devised by your organisation that identifies specific levels of knowledge and skills, or one from elsewhere. For example, the e-skills National Training Organisation has developed a Skills Framework for the Information Age that provides a common reference model for the identification of the skills needed to develop effective information systems, and making use of information communications technologies (http://www.e-skills.com/sfia). The Skills Framework is a matrix of levels of responsibility and accountability on one axis and areas of work on the other.

Remember that there are general/transferable skills you may have gained in addition to vocationally specific ones, such as time management, working with people, using initiative and problem-solving. These are detailed in Chapter 4 and can help to jog your memory and identify knowledge and skills you did not realise you had learnt, and in some cases provide a benchmark against which you can assess your knowledge and skills – and the evidence to demonstrate these. By being aware of the knowledge and skills you have gained, and becoming a reflective practitioner, there is greater likelihood of you reinvesting any new knowledge and understanding gained back into your work.

In Case Study 6.1, Les uses her company's core competency framework to judge how much she has learnt about presentation skills in preparation for a promotion interview and is looking to identify what knowledge and skills she has gained are relevant for a new post she is applying for within her company.

Case Study 6.1: *Transglobal*

Les was an administrator and had responsibility for three other members of staff. A vacancy had arisen in another section, and it would mean a promotion if she was successful in her application. Her interview was in a few days, and she was aware that she needed to focus on the knowledge and skills she had which were relevant for the new post, and where she had demonstrated these.

The company was performance-driven, and on the corporate web site were details of the core competencies that formed the competence framework. Those interviewing her would use these core competencies as a benchmark as these formed the basis of appraisal, promotion and reward system within the organisation.

Les had been through the appraisal system about a year ago, and through the web could access her appraisal records, as well as her Personal Development Plan.

In the new job there would be a strong emphasis on the ability to communicate ideas and information effectively – including the ability to give presentations to staff as well as visitors to the organisation. If she were successful in her application, she would be much more involved in the marketing side of the operation. When she looked at her last appraisal it had been noted that she could communicate effectively with colleagues. Since her appraisal, she had:

- accessed web-based training programmes to find out how to use PowerPoint in presentations
- been on a one-day in-house course on presentation skills
- observed a colleague making a presentation, using PowerPoint, to a prospective client.

Les had recently given a presentation to a group of visitors from abroad and had received feedback from a colleague who was present which had been positive – she had been congratulated on her performance. She now considered she met the core competence relating to communication at Level 3, and was beginning to move towards achieving Level 4. She felt she was able to speak clearly and adapt her style of presentation to suit her purpose, subject, audience and situation. She could structure what she said so that the sequence of information and ideas could be easily followed, and used a range of techniques to engage the audience. If evidence was needed by the interview panel she could discuss the recent presentation, and provide a copy of the observation feedback from her colleague and of her PowerPoint presentation.

Feeling more confident, she then went on to look at other core competencies, including managing time, using initiative, and being customer-orientated.

Learning outcomes

You may be asked to identify personal learning outcomes – statements of what you know, understand and can do. In Activities 6.2–6.4 you identified the knowledge, understanding and skills gained – or needed – in undertaking your job, undertaking a project, or dealing with a specific incident. Look back at your notes on these. What if you were then asked to put this into the form of learning outcomes?

Learning outcomes usually start with the phrase "I am able to . . .". They usually contain three elements:

- A verb that indicates what you were able to do at the end of a period of learning, and possibly action.
- Words that indicate on what, or with what, you are dealing. If the outcome is about skills then the words may describe the way the skill is performed.
- Words that indicate the nature of the performance required: the complexity and/or significance of the situation.

You need to identify the level at which you are operating, and the level of your knowledge, understanding and skills. Look at the following learning outcomes, which all relate to finance, but are at very different levels:

- I am able to formulate a budget for my section, working competently under supervision.
- I am able to formulate a budget for my section, working competently and independently and seeking assistance or supervision where appropriate.
- I am able to formulate a budget for my section, working autonomously and accepting accountability.

Box 6.1 gives further examples from staff who have identified what they have learnt at work.

Box 6.1: Examples of personal learning outcomes

Area: Meeting health and safety requirements in a small business
I am able to:

- understand the legislation relating to health and safety, particularly in relation to the operation of my own company
- identify the implication for my company
- develop, and implement, strategies to monitor health and safety – in liaison with my line manager – to ensure that staff are keeping to the regulations.

Area: Leadership and team-building
I am able to:

- recognise the importance of teamwork to improving the competitiveness of the company
- create a working environment where teamworking can thrive
- encourage initiatives from my team members
- develop structures to enable us to complete tasks in a way that minimises pain and maintains good working relationships.

Area: Designing a database
I am able to:

- analyse the information gained from research to identify a structure for a database appropriate to meet the needs of the organisation
- design a database, with only minimal help, to meet the needs of the organisation
- produce a plan of action for integrated data flow for the medium term
- set up rules and procedures relating to the database
- convince potential users, at a variety of levels within the organisation, of the benefits of the database.

Area: From role as divisional customer relationship manager
I am able to:

- understand and evaluate the varying priorities of both customer and internal organisations with a view to achieving a common understanding of standards of service expectations
- develop and maintain methods and processes for monitoring and improving customer relationships
- understand the importance of teamwork and effective communication in the provision of customer service
- resolve conflict through negotiation, promoting the concept of a win:win solution
- acknowledge and consider the impact of continuous organisational change in terms of both customer service and customer perception.

Using APEL to gain access to awards/qualifications

You may be considering enrolling on a course that will lead to a qualification, but you may find that a specific formal qualification is usually needed to get onto the course. Look closely at any details relating to entry requirements. For example, typical entry requirements to a BTEC Higher National Diploma may be a National Diploma or A-levels. Typical entry requirements to a first degree may include A-levels, BTEC National Diploma or European/International Baccalaureate. Entry to a postgraduate award may ask for a good first degree or a relevant professional qualification at an equivalent level.

However, some courses may include one of the following phrases, or similar, under their entry requirements, indicating that access for those without formal qualifications will be supported where appropriate:

- Mature candidates without formal entry qualifications will be considered on an individual basis.
- Candidates with equivalent professional experience are also eligible.

Therefore, you may not have the stated formal qualifications but you may feel that the learning you have gained from undertaking your job may be equivalent to that expected from someone who has achieved the formal qualification. In this case, contact the admission tutor, explain the position and they can advise you further.

Different organisations have different entry procedures. Some admission tutors may invite you to an interview, ask for references, and ask for evidence of your prior learning. It will vary according to the nature of the course and the qualification. In all cases the admission tutors want to ensure that your learning is at the right level and that you will be able to cope with the requirements of the course – they do not want you to fail. APEL for the purposes of access to a course is likely to focus on specific areas of knowledge and/or skills, the quality and effect of your everyday and planned experiential learning, the level of your knowledge and skills, and the capacity to gain from further education and training. You may therefore be asked to 'prove' that you have learnt from everyday experiences, and from planned experiences, and that the knowledge and skills you have are at the same level as someone with formal qualifications.

Previous activities (6.2–6.4) will help you to identify where you have learnt, and what you have learnt. Another issue is the level of your learning. Are your knowledge and skills at a high enough level to gain access to your target course? In the next section we are looking at levels, but if you go to Appendix 6.2 you can see a framework containing examples of current national qualifications and the relationship between these. A further aid to identifying level may be Appendix 6.3, which gives:

- Eight Summary Credit Level Descriptors that have been adopted as a basis for many awards in further and higher education, as well as training courses.
- Five levels of attainment relating to NVQs. These cover all levels of occupational performance and all areas of employment. Therefore, an NVQ Level 3 in Management should require the same level of operation as an NVQ Level 3 in Customer Service or Engineering.

These are generic and give an overview of the level of complexity, relative demand and autonomy expected of someone completing a unit or programme of learning at these levels. They are only guidelines – but they may help you identify the approximate level of your knowledge and skills and so better equip you when you apply for a course. It is worth remembering that the knowledge and skills required in the workplace may be at different levels. For example, your knowledge and skills relating to IT may only be at Level 2, whereas your ability to manage people, and your knowledge and skills in this area, may be at Level 3 or even 4 in the Summary Credit Level Descriptors. It will depend upon the requirements for your job role and responsibilities.

IDENTIFYING PERSONAL LEVELS OF KNOWLEDGE, SKILLS AND UNDERSTANDING

If you are looking to gain access to a course, gain a grant of credit towards a qualification or gain exemption from specific course modules, you need to look in more detail at the differences in complexity, demand and autonomy of your work, responsibilities and achievements. Take the example of team management, a responsibility that many staff have in their workplace. To manage a team you need:

- knowledge of how a team works, and the different roles within a team
- to be able to analyse and evaluate the operations of your team, and the interaction of the team members
- to be able to work effectively with others, communicate clearly and solve problems
- the practical skills of being able to manage people, and delegate tasks.

Now consider the different levels of operation in the following examples:

A Dan manages a fairly small team who have been together for some time, know what is expected of them, work fairly harmoniously, and reach their minimum targets. They attend a weekly briefing where there is a general exchange on what has been achieved the previous week, and what will be done the next week. Dan knows the general theory of teamwork, is a conscientious team manager, but has never challenged the team to look at how it could be more effective.

B Jo has been asked to put together a new team of people to delivery a major project. Jo, with a line manager, will select the team members, identify with the new team how they will operate, the team targets and the individual targets to be met. There will be one or two people who do not easily operate in a team environment but they have the necessary skills for the project. Jo has acquired additional knowledge and skills (from an in-house programme) to deal with any potential problems that could arise with some of the more difficult members of the team.

C Sam manages a team of managers who in turn manage teams of their own. A number do not wish to be involved in strategic decision-making, and one or two have caused problems in team meetings, attempting to undermine Sam's authority. Sam has a great deal of knowledge of how different teams operate, gathered over several years of experience with different journals and in-house courses. Sam has also developed the skills required to deal with difficult members, of enabling all team members to take part, and of reaching relevant decisions. Many of these skills have been developed through analysis of previous actions in similar circumstances, identifying what did and what did not work, and learning from these everyday experiences.

These are very simplistic examples, but Dan is able to work effectively with support from a line manager; has a knowledge of the subject area; can identify solutions to a variety of problems; can communicate effectively; and can operate in the predictable context of the team. Jo, however, is working more independently. The situation is more complex and so requires the application of a wider range of team skills, a greater knowledge of teamworking, together with the skills of evaluation and target setting. Sam is working effectively at a strategic level as a team leader, and is able to clarify tasks and make appropriate use of the capabilities of each member. There are highly complex and unpredictable issues that have to be faced and Sam has the knowledge and skills to deal with these, as well as being able to exercise initiative and take personal responsibility.

Based on the simplistic examples of Dan, Jo and Sam – and using the Summary Credit Level Descriptors in Appendix 6.3 – an initial view would be that Dan could provide evidence of knowledge, skills and understanding at Level 3 or 4, Jo at Levels 5 or 6, and Sam at Level 7. This is a simplistic interpretation and other factors would affect any decision on level. However, it will give you an idea of level of operation and the knowledge and skills gained through the different experiences of Dan, Jo and Sam.

As you will have seen from the framework of qualifications in Appendix 6.2, the 'numbering' system currently used is not helpful. You will often find that Level 4 is called Higher Education Level 1, and Level 5 is called Higher Education Level 2 – the numbering beginning all over again at higher education level. However, there are initiatives that promote the use of Levels 1–8, something we will do in the rest of this chapter. A further issue is the NVQ framework – which only has five levels. Don't get hung up over these – institutions will give information on the requirements of courses. The overview details in Appendices 6.2 and 6.3 are for guidance only.

ACTIVITY 6.5

Look back at Activities 6.2–6.4 and at the knowledge, understanding and skills required for, and gained through:

- undertaking your job
- undertaking a specific project
- dealing with a specific incident or situation.

How complex was the situation? How much knowledge was required (and/or learnt)? How much originality was required in the problem-solving? How much personal responsibility did you have? What level/s do you feel you were operating at based on the Summary Credit Level Descriptors?

GAINING CREDIT TOWARDS QUALIFICATIONS THROUGH THE PROCESS OF APEL

You may have enrolled on a course leading towards a specific qualification. However, when you look at the components of the course, and qualification – such as the units – you realise that you have already gained the specific knowledge, skills and understanding detailed in these units, or in the course programme. Therefore you decide to ask a course tutor about the process through which you can either claim exemption from specific units, and so avoid having to go over the learning again, or claim a grant of credit towards a qualification because, although your learning may not match specific units, you have gained knowledge and skill relating to the area of study and the educational institution will allow you to submit evidence that reflects the outcomes for the programme.

A number of qualifications are based on accumulation of credits at specific levels – such as higher education degrees and BTEC awards. For example, a Certificate of Higher Education usually consists of 120 credits at Level 4, and an Honours degree usually consists of 360 credits (approximately 120 credits each from Levels 4, 5 and 6). The units that make up these awards have a specific number of credits attached to them, and if a learner successfully completes a unit these are credited to them. The learner accumulates credits towards the number needed for the full award. If they leave a programme before they gain enough credits for the award, then the institution will usually let them have a transcript that details the units they have achieved, and the credits they have accumulated.

The usual process for gaining formal recognition, and credit, for experiential learning includes:

1. Advice and guidance from the institution on:
   - whether your claim for credit, or unit exemption, has potential, e.g. your knowledge and skills are at the appropriate level
   - the type of evidence required
   - how the evidence is to be presented, e.g. a portfolio.
2. Presentation of the evidence by you.
3. Assessment by the institution – college, university, or similar.
4. Moderation/verification by a second person who can confirm that criteria have been met.
5. Receipt by you of the results of the assessment.

An important aspect is the benchmark that is to be used to judge your claim. For example, if you are making a claim relating to:

- NVQ units. Each unit of competence describes what you need to do, what you need to know and understand, what evidence you need to provide to meet all of the NVQ requirements (some evidence is mandatory), and examples of evidence you could provide to meet the NVQ requirements. Each unit contains a number of elements, and an assessor will use the detailed performance criteria for each element in the assessment of your claim. NVQ units do not have credits attached. To achieve the full NVQ you need to achieve a specific number of units: mandatory and optional.
- BTEC First, National or Higher units. The detail in the units will give you the number of credits attributed to the unit, the level, and the learning outcomes that have to be met. These tell a learner beginning the unit what they must do. An assessor will use these as the benchmark against which to assess your evidence. The content of the unit can give you an idea of the breadth of knowledge and skills expected.
- Higher education.
  - Claim relating to units (often called modules). These usually contain learning outcomes – statements that indicate what you should know, understand and be able to do after a period of learning – similar to BTEC units. These will be used by an assessor.

– Claim relating to programme outcomes. Some university courses allow you to put in a claim for a grant of credit where your learning matches the general outcomes of a specific award, but not necessarily the exact learning outcomes contained in a specific unit. For example, you may be registered for a part-time degree related to the management of people. You have a great deal of knowledge, skills and understanding in the area of mentoring, but there is no specific module relating to this. Therefore, you may be able to write a reflective narrative about the knowledge and skills you have, produce relevant evidence to support the claims in your narrative, identify exactly what knowledge and skills you do have (your own personal learning outcomes) and present this for assessment. If the institution does allow you to 'write your own learning outcomes', they will give you guidance on this. Not all higher education programmes permit this type of claim – they only allow claims against specific units.

What is important is that you obtain details so that you know what is expected in terms of level of knowledge and skills, and any specific evidence requirements – you need to know the benchmark against which you will be assessed.

USING APEL FOR COMPETENCE-BASED AWARDS

There are different courses leading to qualifications that are different in nature. NVQs are competence-based awards, and competence here is defined as the ability to apply knowledge, understanding and skills in performing to the standards required in employment, including solving problems and meeting changing demands (Beaumont, 1996).

When you look through the individual units that make up the qualification, you may feel you have already demonstrated (in your place of work) the ability to apply the knowledge, understanding and skills described in a number of the units. Remember that there is an emphasis on 'the ability to apply' and so you will be looking to provide proof of this ability to meet the criteria for a unit. Have a look at the example of Bill in Case Study 6.2.

As mentioned in the previous section, the detail in NVQ units gives a great deal of information should you wish to prove you have met the requirements of the unit through everyday, or planned, experiences. Evidence of your achievements must match the elements and performance criteria. Evidence of just one situation where you demonstrated you could apply your knowledge and skills may be insufficient – frequently you will need proof of two or more situations in which you demonstrated your skills, knowledge and understanding. If you are unable to produce the mandatory evidence for a specific unit, it may be necessary for you to gain further evidence that does match the mandatory requirement. Look closely at the relevant units.

Some NVQs also have external assessment associated with selected units – these units cannot be accredited via the process of APEL. You may be able to submit evidence, but you will also be asked to take the external assessment.

It is most likely that you will be asked to produce a portfolio of evidence for assessment that matches the criteria of all, or part, of a unit – and the evidence submitted must be authentic, current, relevant and sufficient. Edexcel, one of the main awarding bodies for NVQs, suggests that most portfolios will require:

- a statement of the claim for accreditation
- a statement of authenticity
- a CV
- a summary of the claim – which units, or parts of units, you are claiming you already have the evidence for
- a commentary that identifies prior achievement against assessment criteria and requirements
- a list of evidence for each unit demonstrating achievement against each assessment criteria and requirement claimed.

Edexcel also suggests that separate evidence is not required for each assessment criterion. Wherever possible, claimants should be encouraged to present a small number of complex pieces of evidence that demonstrate the achievement of a number of assessment criteria and requirements.

When you are putting together your portfolio of evidence drawn from everyday, and planned, experiences, one problem could be how to provide evidence from past performances – such as dealing with a difficult client. Unless someone is there watching you, this could be a problem. In some instances a narrative/case study with an endorsement from a line manager may be sufficient. Another problem could be gaining documented evidence, because many organisations are actively attempting to reduce the amount of paper in circulation. When you register for the NVQ, explain that you wish to produce a portfolio demonstrating achievement of specific unit/s through prior learning, and someone will advise you on evidence. The QCA – who oversee NVQs – has suggested that the term 'collecting evidence' may have been interpreted too literally in the past and this has led to too much 'paper' being collected. The presentation of evidence need not be confined to paper-based portfolios – consider portfolios that contain products, videotapes, or are IT-based.

If you do submit a portfolio, but the evidence for a unit is unconvincing yet nevertheless substantial – or you are unable to produce the evidence as it no longer exists and your employer fails to respond to a request for an endorsement/testimony – it will be necessary for you to take an assessment appropriate to the element being claimed. As this is a competence-based award, then the evidence may come from you being observed in the workplace. This was an option available to Bill in Case Study 6.2.

Physical products such as manufactured objects, drawings and documents need a statement of authenticity. Where it was created in the past for another purpose, you will need to obtain proof it is your work. Verification may sometimes be needed from an appropriate third party, such as a colleague. The endorser should make a statement that describes the role of the learner with respect to the evidence – and this is particularly important if it was part of a group project.

Case study 6.2: *Airsnack*

As Airsnack grew, the directors decided that someone should be appointed to take responsibility for customer service and liaison with clients. Bill was interviewed for, and given, this position. He had been sent on a number of external one-day courses that gave an overview of the knowledge and skills needed.

Over the previous two years Bill had learnt a great deal from undertaking his job: primarily dealing with the airlines for which they provided in-flight food. There had been a number of specific occasions when he had had to draw upon all of the knowledge and skills he had gained in order to deal with problems that had arisen between Airsnack and their clients. Virtually all of the problems had been resolved amicably, and to the benefit of both sides.

Bill felt that he would benefit from gaining a qualification in customer service. The company agreed to sponsor him, and Bill obtained details – initially from the web site of an awarding body – of NVQs in Customer Service at both Level 2 and Level 3. He felt that Level 3 would be more appropriate, and this was confirmed when he spoke to a tutor at the local college. When he received the candidate guidance and logbook relating to the NVQ he realised that he already had the knowledge and skills – as well as virtually all of the evidence – for two of the units: 'Organise, Deliver and Maintain Reliable Customer Service' and 'Monitor and Solve Customer Service Problems'. He was somewhat daunted by the criteria and evidence requirements but – in discussion with his tutor – realised that he did in fact already have the relevant product evidence, such as copies of minutes of meetings and correspondence. He could easily obtain witness statements from his line manager and clients, as well as provide case study narratives – personal statements – detailing how he had dealt with specific incidents in the last two years. If there was not quite sufficient evidence of prior learning and achievements to meet the requirements of the unit, then it was agreed the tutor could be an observer at the next meeting with a client.

USING APEL FOR OTHER AWARDS

If you are registering for awards such as BTEC Firsts, Nationals or Higher Nationals, there will be a requirement to produce evidence that meets specific learning outcomes. Some awards, as with NVQs, may be subject to specific evidence requirements and required external assessments may have to be completed. Contextual unit grading is also an integral part of some qualifications, and when producing evidence from prior learning you need to be aware of these specifications, as well as the unit specifications.

If there is insufficient evidence in your portfolio, you may be asked to undergo an oral assessment, complete an appropriate assignment, complete a written test, or carry out a demonstration.

So what about registering for a degree or other higher education award? Are universities any different in their requirements? The principles remain the same. You need to identify the units, or modules, you are looking for exemption from and then provide evidence of achievement from everyday, or planned, experiences that meet these. Higher education is looking for evidence of high levels of knowledge and skills, formulation of clear arguments, analysis, evaluation and synthesis. An assessor of your evidence will be interested in why you took certain actions and made certain decisions – and therefore is likely to ask you to write a professional, reflective narrative to accompany the evidence that allows you to explain the process and the implications for the organisation. Much of the evidence of your learning will be captured in the narrative and not (as with most competence-based courses) on the amount of evidence that can be collected with reference to the experience. Jill, in Case Study 6.3, is an example of someone applying for credit towards a degree.

Be warned, however, different universities, and courses, will have varying procedures and requirements relating to APEL. The role of the professional bodies may also determine the procedures, and the maximum amount of credit that can be allowed. Therefore it is important to speak to the relevant course tutor.

A typical APEL portfolio for higher education is likely to contain a summary of the amount of credit being claimed through the process of APEL, a CV, professional narrative/account of learning, and supporting evidence. As mentioned, you will be given guidance – so check with the appropriate institution, whether a college or university.

Case Study 6.3: *Citizens Support Bureau*

Jill decided that she wanted to study for a degree. She contacted her local university and registered for a BA (Honours) in Management Studies. She already had a Diploma in Advisory Services, but she had achieved this over 10 years ago and since then had moved into a management role within the CSB.

She met with a tutor and discussed the possibility of gaining credit based on the assessment of her prior experiential learning. During this discussion she discovered she could gain a grant of credit that could either be through matching the outcomes from her own learning with the learning outcomes of a specific module, and/or matching the programme outcomes. Up to two-thirds of the award could be through the process of APL (240 of the 360 credits).

She was a manager of a team of four staff. She had also had responsibility for recruiting and selecting new staff, as well as recruiting and selecting volunteers to work within the CSB. There were two modules whose learning outcomes she felt she matched in terms of her knowledge, skills and understanding: Selecting Staff (20 credits at Level 4 (HE Level 1)) and Team Management (20 credits at Level 5 (HE Level 2)).

Jill had also introduced a mentoring scheme for new staff. As there was no module within the Management Studies programme relating to mentoring, she obtained permission to 'write her own module'. First of all she made notes on the process of introducing the scheme and this helped her to identify what she had learnt through the process. Not only had she researched the concept of mentoring, she had drafted an overview of the scheme, taken on board feedback from colleagues, and written the policy as well as the support documents for the mentors and mentees. She then went on to develop and deliver a training programme to both mentors and mentees. Her portfolio of evidence included narratives, extracts from a sample of documents, details of a training programme and evaluations from those on the course, and endorsements from colleagues confirming her role in the development of the scheme. Thirty credits at Level 5 (HE Level 4) were awarded through the APEL process.

When she considered the evidence for the module on Selecting Staff, she decided to take a case study of the recruitment and selection for a specific post. To preserve confidentiality she removed names from all product evidence, such as on the form used during the interview process. Her line manager confirmed the lead role she had taken in the process.

It was more difficult to provide product evidence relating to team management. There were records relating to meetings, and the names of team members could be changed. Her line manager could confirm the authenticity of these. However, a number of the learning outcomes related to dealing with different types of team member, and strategies used to encourage collaborative working. Her narrative for this area was longer than that for Selecting Staff or Mentoring as there was less evidence she could produce. She also had to demonstrate her ability to analyse and problem-solve. She wrote about the factors that influenced the decisions she made, the actions she took, and the implications for the people involved and the organisation.

CREATING PORTFOLIOS OF EVIDENCE OF EXPERIENTIAL LEARNING

We have mentioned portfolios a number of times, and the suggested content for a portfolio for assessment against NVQs. A portfolio is not exclusive to APEL. You can find out more about different types of portfolio in Chapter 7. In some instances you may be asked to provide just one item of evidence to demonstrate your learning through experience. This could be an essay, a report or an artefact. Therefore, in this situation, a portfolio – a collection of evidence – will not be required.

Evidence

The purpose of providing evidence in an APEL portfolio is to support and verify the claim you are making. Evidence will be varied and will reflect your organisation and the role you play in it – wherever you have gained knowledge, skills and understanding. Some evidence will be direct: evidence that is of your own making, or for which you have been primarily responsible as part of a team. This could include:

- action plans – objectives and results
- budgets or financial forecasts
- procedures you have been responsible for designing
- monthly or annual reports
- articles you have written
- a training plan
- a questionnaire you have designed, administered and analysed
- a handbook or manual you have contributed to
- photographic, audio, video or other electronic recording of your activity
- artefacts.

Some evidence will be more indirect and will be information gathered from others about you. Examples might include:

- statements from employer/clients/colleagues
- certificates of attendance at in-house programmes
- observation report
- awards.

The supporting product evidence you include in the portfolio may be written documentation for a particular audience and has not been written to be assessed as part of an APEL portfolio. Therefore, a brief explanation within the narrative is helpful for the assessor. If any further explanation is needed, then this can be attached to the actual product evidence.

Witness statements and endorsements can be cost-effective and in many cases are the most appropriate evidence to support your claim. Written statements and endorsements should feature on headed notepaper or be stamped with your organisation's stamp. Remember to give each item of product evidence a number or code and use this when referring to the item in the narrative. This 'coding' can be useful when you are asked to compile a 'matrix' relating to NVQs and then match your knowledge and skills against the unit assessment criteria; it saves you time as all you need do is record the code number of each piece of evidence rather than write out the full title!

Narratives

As mentioned above, you may be asked to write a professional narrative that will be an account of how your learning was achieved, the evidence, and guiding the assessor through the claim. However, this narrative can also be evidence in its own right as it can show your ability to reflect on learning, analyse, evaluate, and problem solve – this is particularly important if you are presenting your portfolio to higher education. The narrative may be a case study, such as managing a team or dealing with a difficult situation. It may focus on a specific project that you had responsibility for, or contributed to, such as investigating, designing and implementing a new software system. The length of the narrative really depends on what you are recounting, and what you are claiming. You need to remember that higher education is looking for evidence of analysis and critical thinking that is often greater than is required in many workplace situations. It is particularly interested in:

- Why you may have taken a particular action, and the implications of taking such an action for you and/or the organisation.
- Why you may have made certain recommendations, and the implications of these.

Advice and guidance will be available – you need to ask. If you are asked to write a narrative, then Activities 6.2–6.4 may help you identify what you have learnt and the evidence, and the cue questions on pages 115–16 can help in the writing of the narrative.

Quantity of evidence

What about quantity of evidence? It is likely you will need to produce evidence for competence-based programmes that proves you have met the assessment criteria at least twice – certainly for NVQ units. It will be different for most higher education programmes. Here you are likely to be asked to select samples of your work that you believe best demonstrate your knowledge and skills as they relate to the unit criteria.

Confidentiality

Make sure you respect the confidentiality of your organisation's data or information, and the details of individuals. For example, you could:

- present a confidential report, such as the appraisal of a member of your team, and delete the information that identifies the individual
- ask your line manager, or other significant person, to confirm that a specific action, and learning, has taken place.

If in doubt, check with your manager, and/or the relevant assessor of your claim, before including the evidence. In some instances you may wish to show an assessor specific product evidence – such as a confidential report or details of the development of a new product – but not wish to let the evidence out of your sight. Ask the assessor if you can present the evidence for assessment and then take it away again. The assessor can confirm that they have seen the appropriate evidence.

WHAT ARE EXTERNAL ASSESSORS OF EXPERIENTIAL LEARNING LOOKING FOR?

There will be a few differences between awards, but most assessors will be using the following criteria:

- **Authenticity**. Is the evidence genuine, and clearly your own achievement and no one else's?
- **Relevance**. Is your learning demonstrated by the evidence relevant to the target qualification? Is it at the right level and covers a similar knowledge and skills base?
- **Validity**. Does the evidence support your claim? Does it match the criteria?
- **Standards**. Are the learning, knowledge, skills and achievements demonstrated through the evidence at an acceptable level?
- **Sufficiency**. Is there sufficient evidence to support your claim?
- **Currency**. Is your learning current, or if not, is there evidence of appropriate updating? There is often a limit to the age of the evidence you are producing and you should be advised of this. Some subjects age more quickly than others, such as IT.

If the assessor has any doubts about any of the above, then you may be asked to produce further evidence in support of your claim. However, if there are any queries, these will usually be discussed with you. What is important is that:

- Educational institutions need to be seen as upholding standards – academic and vocational – as well as responding to the individual needs of students.
- Students need to be clear about what is involved, and what can be expected.
- Employers and professional bodies need to be assured that credit achieved through the process of APEL meets the same standards as that achieved through traditional modes.

SUMMARY

- Many people learn a great deal through the workplace: through the experience of doing their job, undertaking specific projects, and/or dealing with specific incidents.
- The process of recognising and assessing prior experiential learning (APEL) can enable people to make the most of appraisal schemes, support career opportunities, gain access onto award-bearing courses, and gain credit towards awards.
- The process of APEL benefits the employer as it avoids wasting time and resources in repetitive learning for knowledge and skills already gained, helps employees take responsibility for their own learning, and can be motivational.
- Structured, and professional, reflection enables people to identify exactly what they have gained through experience, the implications for self and the organisation, and how it will affect future actions and decisions.

- When submitting evidence for APL to an external institution, such as a college or university, assessors will be looking for authenticity, relevance, validity, standard/appropriateness of level, sufficiency and currency.

REFERENCES

Barkatoolah, A. (1985) Some critical issues related to assessment and accreditation of adults' prior experiential learning. In: Warner Weil, S. and McGill, I. (eds) *Making Sense of Experiential Learning: Diversity in Theory and Practice*, Society for Research into Higher Education, Open University, Oxford.

Beaumont, G. (1996) *Review of Top 100 NVQs and SVQs*. Department of Education and Employment London.

Boud, D., Cohen, R. and Walker, D. (eds) (1993/1996) *Using Experience for Learning*, Society for Research into Higher Education/Open University Press, Buckingham.

Carper, B. (1978) Fundamental ways of knowing in Nursing. *Advances in Nursing Science* **1**, 13–23.

Eraut, M. (1994) *Developing Professional Knowledge and Competence*, Falmer, London.

Fryer, R.H. (1997) *Learning for the Twenty-first Century: First Report of the National Advisory Group for Continuing Education and Lifelong Learning*, DfEE Publications, Sudbury.

Gray, C. (2003) *Reflective Practice*. Article in 'Theories and Models' published on 'Nurses Network' http://www.nursesnetwork.co.uk (accessed 23 July 2003).

Johns, C.C. (1993) Professional supervision. *Journal of Nursing Management* **1**, 9–18.

Kolb, D. (1984*) Experiential Learning: Experience as the Source of Learning and Development*, Prentice Hall, Englewood Cliffs, NJ.

Mulligan, J. and Griffin, C. (eds) (1992) *Empowerment through Experiential Learning: Explorations of Good Practice*, Kogan Page, London.

Nyatanga, L., Forman, D. and Fox, J. (1998) *Good Practice in the Accreditation of Prior Learning*, Cassell, London.

Osterman, K.F. (1990) Reflective practice: a new agenda for education. *Education and Urban Society* **22** (2), 133–152.

QCA (2002) *NVQ Code of Practice*, Qualifications and Curriculum Authority, London.

Schön, D. (1987) *Educating the Reflective Practitioner: Toward a New Design for Teaching and Learning in the Professions*, 1st edn, Jossey-Bass, San Francisco.

Simosko, S. and Cook, C. (1991/1996) *Applying APL: Principles in Flexible Assessment: A Practical Guide*, Kogan Page, London.

Stephenson, J. (1992) The concept of capability and its importance in higher education. In: *Capability and Quality in Higher Education* (eds Stephenson, J. and York, M.), Kogan Page, London.

Stephenson, J. (1998) Capability and quality in higher education. In: *A Capability Approach to Higher Education* (eds Stephenson, J. and Weil, S.), Kogan Page, London.

APPENDIX 6.1: RECOGNISING PRIOR CERTIFICATED LEARNING

In order to gain recognition for prior certificated learning – certainly from an educational establishment – you must have completed, in whole or in part, a formally assessed course or programme of study for which you have an official certificate, diploma or transcript. Usually this document will be from an educational institution, a professional body, or a national examining body. A certificate of attendance on a course is not sufficient – it needs to be a certificate demonstrating achievement of learning. In addition to the certificate, you are likely to be asked for details of the syllabus and assessment. If appropriate, you may be asked to bring in one of the assignments you did.

National awards tend to have a 'currency' as organisations have an approximate understanding of the level of these awards and are aware that such awards have gone through a rigorous checking system to ensure the quality and validity of the end award. These awards include NVQs, higher education degrees, BTEC First, National and Higher National awards and other awards that are used as examples in Appendix 6.2. If any of the certificates are awarded by a local organisation for a small local group of candidates, these are unlikely to have the standing that national awards have. Therefore, if you decide you wish for formal recognition of these awards – such as exemption from part of a programme you are studying – a tutor may want additional evidence over and above the certificate and details of the syllabus. They may want details of the nature of assessment and the awarding body's quality assurance systems.

Whoever assesses your certificate will make a judgement based on whether it meets the following criteria:

- Authenticity. Is it your certificate?
- Relevance. For example, is the learning gained relevant to a programme of study you intend to undertake, or – in the case of applying for a rise in pay – is it relevant to your job role?
- Standard. Is the learning, knowledge and expertise demonstrated through the certificate at an acceptable level?
- Currency. Is the date of the award recent? The definition of currency may vary from subject to subject and some areas 'age' much faster than others, e.g. IT.

You may sometimes hear the phrase 'credit accumulation and transfer' (in some educational literature this is abbreviated to CATs). For example, you may have been on a course at a college or university and have successfully completed a number of units. Each of these units may attract a number of credits at a specific level of study. You may then have to move to another part of the country and wish to complete the course (or similar) at another college or university. If you register on a similar programme at the new institution, the institution may recognise all or some of the credits you bring with you – the evidence being either a transcript or a certificate. You can therefore 'hand in' these credits towards the award at this second institution – you do not have to begin all over again. This can be very useful when you consider, for an example, an Honours degree is usually 360 credits and can take a number of years if you are studying on a part-time basis. More and more educational institutions are now recognising the credit gained at another college or university and allow you to transfer those credits to the new award.

You need to be aware that you will not necessarily gain the number of credits that may be on your transcript. It will depend upon the match of the learning outcomes of your previous programme with those of your target qualification. For example, you may have a transcript from another educational institution that confirms achievement of three modules amounting to 60 credits overall. However, the assessor may decide that only two of these modules are relevant, and so only 40 credits may be credited to your target qualification.

APPENDIX 6.2: EXAMPLES OF QUALIFICATIONS FRAMEWORK

Levels	General qualifications, including higher education awards	Vocationally-related qualifications	Occupational qualifications
8	Doctorate		
7	Masters Postgraduate Diplomas Postgraduate Certificates		NVQ Level 5
6	Honours degree Some Ordinary degrees (to be phased out at this level)	Graduate Apprenticeship	
5	Diploma of Higher Education Foundation degree Some Ordinary degrees	Edexcel (BTEC) Higher National Diploma	NVQ Level 4
4	Certificate of Higher Education	Edexcel (BTEC) Higher National Certificate RSA/OCR and CGLI/AQA Higher Awards	
3	A/AS levels (including vocational As/GNVQ Advanced) Access to higher education courses	Edexcel (BTEC) National Diplomas Modern Apprenticeship – Advanced level OCR Diploma in Administrative and Secretarial Procedures	NVQ Level 3
2	GCSE grades A–C (including vocational GCSEs/GNVQ Intermediate)	Edexcel (BTEC) First Diplomas Modern Apprenticeship – Foundation level	NVQ Level 2
1	GCSE grades D–G (including vocational GCSEs/GNVQ Foundation)	CLAIT RSA Word Processing Stage 1	NVQ Level 1
Entry qualifications (pre-level 1), e.g. certificate of (educational) achievement; basic skills certificates; entry level certificates			

APPENDIX 6.3: SUMMARY CREDIT LEVEL DESCRIPTORS DEVELOPED WITHIN A HIGHER EDUCATION PROJECT

Learning accredited at the following levels will reflect the ability to:

Entry level – employ recall and demonstrate elementary comprehension in a narrow range of areas, exercise basic skills within highly structured contexts, and carry out directed activity under close supervision.

Level 1 – employ a narrow range of applied knowledge, skills and basic comprehension within a limited range of predictable and structured contexts, including working with others under direct supervision but with a very limited degree of discretion and judgement about possible action.

Level 2 – apply knowledge with underpinning comprehension in a number of areas and employ a range of skills within a number of contexts, some of which may be non-routine; and undertake directed activities, with a degree of autonomy, within time constraints.

Level 3 – apply knowledge and skills in a range of complex activities demonstrating comprehension of relevant theories; access and analyse information independently and make reasoned judgements, selecting from a considerable choice of procedures, in familiar and unfamiliar contexts; and direct own activities, with some responsibility for the output of others.

Level 4 – develop a rigorous approach to the acquisition of a broad knowledge base; employ a range of specialised skills; evaluate information, using it to plan and develop investigative strategies and to determine solutions to a variety of unpredictable problems; and operate in a range of varied and specific contexts, taking responsibility for the nature and quality of outputs.

Level 5 – generate ideas through the analysis of concepts at an abstract level, with a command of specialised skills and the formulation of responses to well defined and abstract problems; analyse and evaluate information; exercise significant judgement across a broad range of functions; and accept responsibility for determining and achieving personal and/or group outcomes.

Level 6 – critically review, consolidate and extend a systematic and coherent body of knowledge, utilising specialised skills across an area of study; critically evaluate new concepts and evidence from a range of sources; transfer and apply diagnostic and creative skills and exercise significant judgement in a range of situations; and accept accountability for determining and achieving personal and/or group outcomes.

Level 7 – display mastery of a complex and specialised area of knowledge and skills, employing advanced skills to conduct research, or advanced technical or professional activity, accepting accountability for related decision-making, including use of supervision.

Level 8 – make a significant and original contribution to a specialised field of inquiry, demonstrating a command of methodological issues and engaging in critical dialogue with peers; accepting full accountability for outcomes.

(Source: *Credit and HE Qualifications: Credit Guidelines for HE Qualifications in England, Wales and Northern Ireland 2001*. Guidelines jointly prepared by CGFW, NICATS, NUCCAT and SEEC.)

NVQ Framework

The five levels of attainment in the NVQ Framework cover all levels of occupational performance and all areas of employment. The framework reflects progressive levels of achievement for candidates as follows:

1. Competences that involve the application of knowledge and skills in the performance of a range of varied work activities, most of which may be routine and predictable.

2. Competences that involve the application of knowledge and skills in a significant range of varied work activities, performed in a variety of contexts. At this level, there must be activities that are complex or non-routine and some individual responsibility and autonomy. Collaboration with others, perhaps through membership of a work group or a team, may often be a requirement.

3. Competences that involve the application of knowledge and skills in a broad range of varied work activities performed in a wide variety of contexts, most of which are complex and non-routine. Considerable responsibility and autonomy and control or guidance of others are often required.

4. Competences that involve the application of knowledge and skills in a broad range of complex, technical or professional work activities performed in a wide variety of contexts and with a substantial degree of personal responsibility and autonomy. Responsibility for the work of others and the allocation of resources is often present.

5. Competences that involve the application of skills and a significant range of fundamental principles across a wide and often unpredictable variety of contexts. Very substantial personal autonomy and often significant responsibility for the work of others and for the allocation of substantial resources feature strongly, as do personal accountabilities for analysis and diagnosis, design, planning, execution and evaluation.

7 PORTFOLIO BUILDING – PRESENTING ACHIEVEMENT, REVIEWING PROGRESS AND SETTING GOALS

Objectives

After reading this chapter, you will be able to:

- Compare and contrast various ways of building a portfolio.
- Decide on personal approaches to recording knowledge, competence and skills.
- Construct a portfolio that can be added to regularly in order to keep pace with CPD.

HISTORICAL CONTEXT

Mention the word 'portfolio' today, and many people conjure up a picture of a large lever arch file bulging with documents. This view has its roots in the early days of the operation of NVQs in the 1980s. Companies and businesses had begun to see that the exam system alone was an ineffective tool for measuring the knowledge, competence and skills that would enable effective performance in the workplace. Of course, in addition to national exams, tests of particular skills and knowledge had been in operation before, but there was a huge number of different schemes and types of awards, and people had no clear framework for progression. The Department for Education and Skills explains clearly on their website (http://www.dfes.gov.uk/nvq/history.shtml) the context of education and training at the time NVQs were introduced:

> Up to the late 1970s, the UK had a rigid system of schooling and training. Young people would enter the education system at about 5 years of age and change schools at about 11 years of age. The type of secondary school very much rested on the outcome of one single examination. Those who passed this examination would normally be expected to eventually go on to universities and colleges at the age of 18. For those that did not pass the exam it was assumed that, after a few years more schooling, they would leave and go straight into work ...
>
> However, there were millions who left school with few, if any, qualifications, entering a world of work that would offer little or no training, no opportunity to develop themselves and no recognition for any competencies they did develop.

On the other hand, the cry from some industries and organisations was that they needed to retrain highly qualified graduates before they could be effective in their job role, so radical changes were needed. In addition to NVQs there were other approaches to demonstrating achievement. Records of Achievement (ROAs) had been introduced in schools and encouraged self-selection of items to put together in a portfolio. In this way, school students were encouraged to reflect upon their work, and select from it what they could defend as their best achievements – not drawing solely from exams, but from coursework, school, and out of school activities. The purpose of this portfolio was for school-leavers to be able to demonstrate knowledge and skills to employers. Following

Sir Ron Dearing's review of qualifications for 16–19-year-olds in 1997, the then National Record of Achievement (NRA) was reviewed and plans made to introduce a new record of achievement. These Progress Files are described later in the chapter. Clearly the last 15–20 years have marked a period of rapid evolution within education (some might say revolution!), which has meant that achievement is no longer measured by exams alone, but by an ongoing assessment in which the learner plays a vital part. Changes in school exams have reflected this and have moved towards a combination of formative and summative assessment.

Importantly, NVQs, from their earliest days, have been brought about by a partnership between the education system and employers. The awards are offered in both educational institutions and in the workplace. Companies and organisations train their own assessors and internal verifiers. Estimation of excellence is no longer solely in the hands of the educational institutions, although it continues to be measured against national criteria. Learners of all ages take charge of part of the process, and become involved in their own development. In addition, contributions from peers, tutors and colleagues validate claims by an individual, and often add in their own perspectives of the learner's achievements.

Although 'the portfolio' became the tool for demonstrating knowledge, skills and competence within NVQs, it is now used by many other people in the workplace. Portfolio building is part of an exciting change that provides a way for the learner to take the initiative in their development. The weighty bulging document file has given way to a variety of different portfolios for different purposes, compiled by learners of all ages.

Reflection and review

Reflection upon learning is a common thread in this chapter as the development of a portfolio involves a process of reflection and review. Friedman and Watts (2002: 2) clarify the issue in this way:

> *The professional acts as a kind of practical scientist drawing on their repertoire (i.e. knowledge of previous experience) and reframing the current problem to fit with it.*

This drawing upon the repertoire of 'professional acts' and examining current practice in the light of them enables people to learn from their work experience. As we saw in Chapter 1, the evolution of this approach in work-based learning was influenced by theory stemming from the work of Schön (1983). In discussing the 'reflective practitioner' he saw that professionals operate in three different ways in respect to learning at work. He termed these 'knowing in action', 'reflection in action' and 'reflection on action'. Much debate has ensued on the issues surrounding Schön's assumptions. Eraut (1994) challenged the issue of how much time for reflection was possible in the process of action. Friedman and Watts (2002: 2–3) argue that:

> *Schön did not argue that reflection occurs in action. Instead it occurs in what he termed an 'action present' (Schön, 1987: 26) 'a stretch of time within which it is still possible to make a difference to the outcomes of action' (1992:58). This indicates that Schön was aware of the importance of time and the fact that reflection and action are not carried out simultaneously.*

Kolb (1984) added to the debate. His model of experiential learning is useful in considering Schön's three key concepts. Integrating the two, Schön's reflection on action needs to lead to Kolb's abstract conceptualisation stage, if the learning from reflection on action is to be internalised, and therefore be useful to the professional in future circumstances. It is this abstract conceptualisation stage that needs support in the process of learning from experience. Dennison and Kirk's cycle (1990), 'Do, Plan, Review, Learn, Apply', is also relevant here. For the stage 'Learn' they comment on the need for the tutor to introduce theory or suggest generalisation before moving on to applying the knowledge. The issue of the enabling or facilitation role of 'supporters' of various kinds is discussed later in this chapter. The learning from reflection upon action and review of practice is a vital ingredient in the process of portfolio building. How else can best practice be identified, and learning from experience be presented to others?

Activity 7.1 suggests a starting point for the process of reflection and review.

ACTIVITY 7.1

Review your CV. Identify your strengths and weaknesses, then list the five aspects of your knowledge, competence and skills that you are most proud of. Ask a colleague to do the same (from their experience of you, not from your CV), and then reconsider your list. How would you present these strengths to prospective employers or colleagues?

Note: Throughout the rest of this chapter, there will be references to a web site where examples from current portfolios or related material are stored. Names are fictitious (except where people are happy to be identified) but the material is not.

WHAT THEN *IS* A PORTFOLIO?

In spite of the fact that the range of portfolios and the variety of their uses are changing and developing rapidly, there are common threads running through definitions. *Longman's Dictionary of English Language Usage* (1990) defines a portfolio as:

1. A hinged cover or flexible case for carrying documents, drawings, paintings etc – **also** [our emphasis] the contents of such a case.
2. The office and functions of a government minister or member of a cabinet (was given the portfolio of Northern Ireland).
3. The securities held by an investor (an individual or a bank).

Definitions 2 and 3 do add to the picture of the portfolio in the way that we are dealing with it in this chapter. Many portfolios describe job roles and responsibilities, and all present a range of proofs of valuable personal assets. The first definition, however, highlights the essentials of a portfolio (in the way it is being addressed in this chapter) – it is simply a container, a way of carrying documents and other materials. Importantly, the second half of the definition points out that 'portfolio' is also used to refer simply to the contents of the container.

The nature of the portfolio, therefore, is defined by the purpose it serves, and the focus of this chapter is accordingly on the portfolio as 'contents'. It will demonstrate that portfolios can be valuable tools for recording, tracking, monitoring, reflecting upon self-development and feedback, and in action planning for future development. Portfolios today are being developed by children, young people and adults, and cover knowledge and experience from a wide range of education, training and experience in, and out of, work.

An important issue to remember with all portfolios is that many have a shelf life – the evidence becomes out of date, and this is why *continuous* professional development is increasingly encouraged both in educational institutions and in the workplace. The NVQ framework has built into it the requirement for teachers and trainers, assessors and verifiers to continually update their competencies, and many other organisations have strategies for checking on the updating of skills. It is not always a question of new skills being developed, but it may be to check that previously acquired skills are still being demonstrated, or that new theory, changes in the law, or changes in company procedures or organisation are being considered and allowed to impact on previously acquired skills.

What are the common features of a portfolio?

In setting out guidelines for the assessment of portfolios, Kemp and Toperoff (1998) highlight the 'living growing nature' of a portfolio, and the fact that it is a tool to enable people to demonstrate their achievement to others – they describe a portfolio on their website (http://www.etni.org/ministry/portfolio/default.html) as:

> *A living growing collection of student's work – each addition is carefully selected by the student for a specific reason s/he will explain. The overall purpose of the portfolio is to enable the student to demonstrate to others, learning and progress. The greatest value of portfolios is that, in building them, students become active participants in the learning process and in its assessment.*

Day (2002: 72) similarly identifies the active participation aspect in discussing how portfolio building enables people to take ownership of their own development, and be able to communicate that to others:

> *The portfolio process draws upon the strengths of peer learning as well as individual analysis. It often involves a series of activities and exercises designed to help learners identify, describe, and provide evidence of what they know and can do.*

An example of this can be seen in the development of the European Language Portfolio (ELP). The Council of Europe (Language Policy Division) promoted the ELP as a means of supporting 'the development of plurilingualism and pluriculturalism'. There are portfolios for both adults and children, and people are encouraged to reflect upon their language learning, and to record it, either within an education system, or outside of it. Further details of this portfolio are developed later in this chapter (see page 148).

Portfolios very frequently involve feedback from peers, line managers, advisers and assessors, enabling the holder of the portfolio to critically evaluate their strengths and weaknesses. The regular practice of reflection and review facilitates both self-development and team-building, as people begin to build on their strengths and work to deal with areas of weakness. Of course the process requires honesty and motivation, and this is sometimes painful. Bacal (1999: 153) discusses what he calls 'bi-directional evaluation', in other words a two-way feedback between manager and employee:

> *Just like everyone else, to better support and improve performance of their staff, they (managers) need to know what they should change …*

> *In fact if employee feedback is considered part of the managers formal evaluations, it resembles a variation of 360 degree feedback.*

This may be a worthy aim, but perhaps the more traditional 360° feedback is easier to handle, as feedback is given from a range of people, as compared with a two-way exchange with your manager!
To summarise:

- The portfolio is owned by the individual, and the contents chosen by them.
- It is a growing, changing record of best practice.
- It encourages a variety of ways of presenting evidence.
- It encourages feedback or input from others.
- Individuals learn from the process of portfolio building and increase in confidence.
- It facilitates the development of reflection, analysis and criticism.
- It enables the individual to communicate their best practice.

HOW ARE PORTFOLIOS DEVELOPED AND ASSESSED?

Support for developing a portfolio

The essence of portfolio building is selection, not collection. The process of selection itself is an empowering one, as it requires criticism, analysis and honesty. These characteristics, if developed, are strengths that are clear to an assessor, committee or employer when portfolios are presented. Haphazard collections of evidence often lead to bulky portfolios that are not focused on targets, and this, in turn, affects presentations and conveys negative messages.

If the portfolio is also to be a growing, changing record of best practice, then the holder needs to reject outdated material, and replace evidence from time to time with better quality or more focused evidence. This is a process that needs support. It is impossible to view your own development totally objectively, so feedback and review processes are vital to the quality of the portfolio.

In most situations, there will be a range of people who, to a greater or lesser extent, and depending on the purpose of the portfolio, aid the process of building a portfolio. For example, NVQs may have advisers and mentors. Many higher education work-based learning programmes have assessors and internal moderators, subject-specific tutors and external examiners. Many companies and organisations provide coaches, mentors and trainers who are part of their support system. The word 'supporter' is being used in this chapter to express a number of similar or overlapping roles – mentors, coaches, advisers, teachers or trainers. Supporters therefore are there to enable, facilitate and guide through a variety of approaches (see Activity 7.2). This facilitation may include encouraging the planning of 'the next step' when one award is completed, and mentoring the candidate into the next award. With the evolution of a national framework of qualifications the movement of people across the range has begun – for example, people with degrees taking NVQs to demonstrate current practice and knowledge, or to gain new expertise, and people who have gained NVQ awards in management moving into undergraduate and postgraduate degrees.

ACTIVITY 7.2

Go to the web site http://www.som.surrey.ac.uk/learnatwork and click on Planning the Next Step 1 to 6 for examples of exit interviews for candidates who have achieved NVQ Levels 4 or 5 in addition to a degree, and others who have targeted degrees as their next step. See also Planning the Next Step 1 for an example of a mentoring report for one of those candidates, who moved across from NVQ 5 into a Masters programme.

Contributions to the portfolio can also be made from a wide range of 'others', who are able to evaluate or confirm knowledge, competence and skills. Many workplaces are environments where learning takes place every day, but needs to be 'tapped' to provide evidence of personal learning and development. Some companies encourage this with in-house company systems, but others leave it to the individual to analyse their own learning and plan further development.

Assessment

Assessors could be individuals, boards or committees, again depending on the purpose of the portfolio. The role of the assessor is to ensure that the contents of the portfolio meet the requirements of an organisation, awarding body or professional body. In fulfilling that role, assessors give formative feedback and are involved in planning and guiding the selection and presentation of evidence against standards. The summative assessment given by assessors is the first step towards accreditation or acceptance into a professional association. In judging evidence, many assessors also have to bear in mind the NVQ criteria of validity, sufficiency and authenticity (NVQ Code of Practice 2001). In addition, many people operate an extra criterion, that of 'currency'. Some universities, for example, only accept evidence that has been demonstrated in the last seven years, others go back much further. Discretion needs to be applied to currency, as it is sometimes absolutely crucial how old the evidence is. For example, evidence focused on IT skills and knowledge is certain to be out of date in seven years.

In the case of NVQs, assessors are required to be qualified in assessment practice to national standards, and their work is sampled by internal and external verifiers who are similarly required to be qualified to national standards. This provides a structured framework for an audit trail from the candidate to the awarding body. In other areas, for example higher education, assessors do not need a specific qualification in assessment, but there are a variety of models of assessment. In addition to assignment, group assessment, observation of professional placement or performance, portfolio, and exam, there are also models of assessment where presentations are assessed by self-evaluation plus peer group and tutor feedback. Since the Disability Equality Act (2002), inclusive practice of assessment has been discussed more widely than before. Implementing inclusive practice is not just a question of developing a policy and offering some specialist equipment to students with impairments, it will require educational institutions and companies to look at their practice of assessment. As far as this relates to portfolio building, this may mean being prepared to deal with contributions written by a 'writer', audio or video taped material, and may involve giving more time for work to be completed.

Many portfolios will include questioning to clarify the evidence or to test related or underpinning knowledge. NVQs often have banks of questions, while other awards ask questions as and when required. Whatever the case for this type of testing of knowledge, the outcome of the questioning is normally recorded in the portfolio. There is also an element of questioning in professional discussions and in feedback sessions, and these too can be included in the portfolio as evidence of knowledge and understanding. In terms of entry into professional bodies, part of the assessment may be conducted through interview, the only record of success being the membership or charter being granted.

ACTIVITY 7.3

Examine your own situation. Identify the people who support your learning and development at work. Draw a line from the supporter to the mode of support they offer. Some people may offer a range of support, and you are likely to identify gaps in support as well. This exercise will be useful preparation for performance planning and review meetings. It will also be a useful tool for reviewing company practice if you are responsible for training and developing others.

Mentors	Questioning
Advisers	Feedback
Teachers and trainers	Observation
Assessors	Witness statements
Supervisors	Endorsements
Employers	Training
Colleagues	Professional discussion
Clients	Work shadowing
Managers	Reports
Technical experts	Guidance
Peers	Performance planning and review
Coaches	Target setting
External auditors	Appraisals

What will the portfolio look like?

It is appropriate at this point to reconsider the portfolio as a container. Some people are still very prescriptive about the format – an extreme example of this is proposed by Hansen (2003), who advises (http://www.quintcareers.com/job_search_portfolio.html):

Most experts agree that the portfolio should be kept in a professional three ring binder (zipper closure optional).

This description does not convey the message of a flexible, living, growing portfolio.

In reality, the way evidence is stored will vary tremendously from individual to individual, even if developed for the same purpose. It will certainly need to be clearly indexed, but the contents could be presented in a variety of ways. Some NVQ portfolios have summaries for each set of evidence, and some portfolios for claiming APEL have narratives that not only give an overview of the learning outcomes being claimed, but are also cross-referenced to relevant theory. Activity 7.4 gives you access to examples of indexes of portfolios, and to narratives within portfolios set up to claim APEL.

ACTIVITY 7.4

Go to the web site http://www.som.surrey.ac.uk/learnatwork and click on Building Portfolios for examples of indexes and narratives.

If a number of documents are drawn upon in portfolio building they could be included, or a list of them could be drawn up with reference to where they are stored. Audio tapes and video clips provide a useful medium for many of the types of evidence, and photographs, slides, charts and diagrams all have their uses in building up a portfolio. Alternatively, the 'container' could simply be the computer, CD or diskette.

It is important to bear in mind that not all types of evidence or ways of recording evidence are appropriate in every situation; for example:

- Observation/videoing when someone's privacy would be invaded (e.g. to assess someone blanket bathing a client as part of their evidence towards an NVQ in Care).
- Observation/videoing of senior management meetings when confidential issues are being discussed.
- Observation/videoing in a secure area (nuclear plants, some military situations).

Because a wide range of individuals could be referred to in the evidence, it needs to be clear that permission has been gained and that the Data Protection Act has also been observed.

WHAT ARE THE TYPES AND USES OF PORTFOLIOS?

Although the list in Table 7.1 is by no means exhaustive, and the categories overlap, it does illustrate the increasing variety and types of portfolios, and how they are currently used. Each type of portfolio is discussed in detail in the pages following.

Portfolio Type 1 – Demonstration of achievement in previous or current work

Traditionally, previous and current achievements were summarised in a curriculum vitae (CV). Up until about 15 years ago, the CV would have probably focused on the historical picture and started with school exams and grades. Because exams were the only way of measuring or assessing knowledge, little would have been said about personal skills or what had been learned from experience. These issues might arise at interview, but often selection had already taken place by the time people were invited for interview.

Table 7.1   *Seven types and uses of portfolios*

Type of portfolio	Example of use
Portfolio Type 1 Demonstration of achievement in previous or current work	A portfolio for presenting yourself at interview to replace or add to the 'historical' CV National Records of Achievement Teaching portfolios (USA/Canada, UK) Job skills/career portfolios
Portfolio Type 2 A compilation of evidence of achievement of set targets (technical, key skills, personal, transferable skills)	NVQs Measured by Personal Development Plans and Reviews 360° review To meet Learning Outcomes set by educational institutions, companies or organisations
Portfolio Type 3 To claim credit against undergraduate or postgraduate degrees (advanced standing)	Assessment of Prior Learning (APL) or Assessment of Prior Experiential Learning (APEL)
Portfolio Type 4 To support an application for entry into a professional body	For example, to be a Chartered Engineer (Royal Aeronautical Society); to be a Chartered Manager (Chartered Management Institute)
Portfolio Type 5 Electronic or 'paperless' portfolios	An overarching approach, providing a network of references to where documents may be found, video clips, audio tapes, web pages, slide shows, etc.
Portfolio Type 6 Compilation of ongoing evidence of achievement and cultural experience	Euroean Language Portfolios Progress Files
Portfolio Type 7 Continuous Professional Development (CPD)	Portfolios held by individuals to give evidence of ongoing development and regular training in their expertise, subject or skill. Also a useful tool in reviewing and reflecting upon self-development, and strategies for setting targets for future development

The group of portfolios in this category range from what might be called a living, growing CV to a subject-specific portfolio. The process is informal in the sense that it is not generally structured to meet formal requirements by an awarding body or a professional body, but it is often targeted at meeting the needs of formal situations – interviews, presentations/reporting to line managers, or applications to job agencies.

If you are seeking work there is obviously a strong motivation to present a CV that highlights your strengths, but in some instances you may also need to be ready to put together a presentation portfolio for interview. If you are keeping a CPD portfolio (Portfolio Type 7), you will have ready resources to draw upon for interview.

ACTIVITY 7.5

Go to the web site http://www.som.surrey.ac.uk/learnatwork and click on CVs and Presentation Folder to view examples.

National Records of Achievement (NRAs) have been referred to briefly in this chapter. As stated in the Introduction, they served a clear purpose first as Records of Achievement, and then as NRAs. They involved the holder in selection of their own best practice and were targeted at 16-year-olds. In the light of the government's new emphasis on continuity from 14 to 19, NRAs are to be phased out in 2004, and replaced by Progress Files (which are already in operation). These will be discussed in Portfolio Type 3 as, although they are replacing NRAs, their purpose has a different focus.

The practice of compiling *teaching portfolios* in Canada and the USA is widespread and is sometimes parallel to the UK approach, where the portfolio is held by the student and teachers/trainers are the assessors. Teachers themselves also build portfolios in order to gain awards or demonstrate CPD. An interesting and different development has arisen where teachers in higher education are building the portfolios, as discussed by Seldin (1997). He suggests that faculty members might prepare a teaching portfolio to present to committees when seeking a new role or advancement within the university.

He then goes on to discuss whether there are other purposes for which professors might prepare a portfolio. Seldin arrives at six reasons for preparing a portfolio (http:/www.city.londonmet.ac.uk/deliberations/portfolios/):

> *They might do so in order to: (a) document for themselves how their teaching has evolved over time; (b) prepare materials about their teaching effectiveness when applying for a new position or for post-tenure review; (c) share their expertise and experience with younger faculty members; (d) provide teaching tips about a specific course for new or part time faculty; (e) seek teaching awards or grants relating to teaching; (f) leave a written legacy within the department so that future generations of teachers who will be taking over the courses of about-to-retire professors will have the benefit of their thinking and experience.*

Although this sounds quite revolutionary in terms of UK universities, Canada has used this type of portfolio (called a teaching dossier) for 20 years, and it is currently being piloted in US institutions. In 1990 there were thought to be ten institutions in the USA using this type of portfolio, and currently there are thought to be 1000.

In the UK, teacher training is competence-based, which lends itself to using portfolios as a tool. Portfolios are also compiled by teachers to meet the standards of accreditation of awarding bodies, a similar function to the portfolios described in the next section (Portfolio Type 2).

With regard to *job skills*, Hansen (2003) lists 16 possible inclusions in a portfolio of this kind. Most have characteristics in common with other records of achievement, but there are some new and interesting ones, which relate to personal skills (http://www.quintcareers.com/job_search_portfolio.html):

Professional Philosophy/Mission Statement: A short description of the guiding principles that drive you and give you purpose.

Skills, Abilities and Marketable Qualities: A detailed examination of your skills and experience.

List of Accomplishments: A detailed listing that highlights the major accomplishments in your career to date. Accomplishments are one of the most important elements of any good job-search.

These three areas of the portfolio will convey your personal drive, your awareness of your strengths in relation to a particular market, and will demonstrate your ability to see a project through to completion. These are all attributes that may not be clear from a traditional CV.

One of the benefits of a portfolio is that it can be used flexibly, taking out evidence as it becomes out of date, and replacing it with current or better quality evidence to suit a situation, or a job that is applied for. This makes it a very useful tool when looking for a new job or promotion in an existing career. For example, Case Study 7.1 demonstrates the need to encourage flexible portfolio development that can be used for job-seeking, for demonstration of CPD, or towards an accredited qualification.

Case Study 7.1: *Citizens Support Bureau*

In a Citizens Support Bureau (CSB) regional office, the management group have been looking at opportunities for development for all of their staff. They have a number of people working towards the Diploma in Advisory Services, and some have moved across to university degrees, gaining credit from APEL. All workers have gained a thorough knowledge of the way the CSB works through a central scheme of training using subject-specific handbooks. However, there are many people who are volunteers and get little recognition for the work they do. Many are not confident that they could achieve a Diploma in Advisory Services, in spite of the fact that they perform well at work. Many of the skills needed for work at the CSB are transferable personal skills (e.g. listening skills, dealing with conflict, advising, analysing, clarifying, monitoring). With this in mind, the CSB has decided to initiate a CPD scheme for all staff in the region. Each person is given their own portfolio and a handbook, which has a framework (in a diary format) for recording personal skills. There is also an additional section in the booklet for recording activities relating to specific skills (e.g. giving financial advice). Staff are encouraged to complete their diary on a weekly basis, and record work activities relating to specific skills as and when they happen. As there are many situations where staff work in pairs, for example in face-to-face interviews with families, the regional office has suggested that after the interview the two members of staff complete feedback sheets on each other's performance. Each month, a 'surgery' is held by consultants to support staff in identifying evidence of their learning and development for their CPD portfolios. Some of the evidence will come directly from the diaries, and some from feedback sheets, but the weekly review of their work may lead to other evidence. In this way the CSB regional office hopes to encourage the workforce to reflect and review their practice, and begin to recognise evidence of their knowledge and skills.

There are professional organisations who recommend strategies for presenting job skills. Designers, people working in marketing and artists have, for a number of years, used the concept of a portfolio of their work to demonstrate their creative skills. A job skills/career portfolio for other job-seekers is a more recent development. In many ways it is very similar to the living, growing CV.

Portfolio Type 2 – A compilation of evidence of achievement of set targets

All the examples listed in this category are to do with achievement against targets. These could be related to technical skills, key skills, personal skills or transferable skills.

The targets for *NVQs* and other awards are defined by national standards, and include a range of technical, personal and key skills. The range and type of evidence has to demonstrate various aspects of work practice, and its associated knowledge and skills.

ACTIVITY 7.6

Go to the web site http://www.som.surrey.ac.uk/learnatwork and click on Portfolios matched against Standards 1–3 for extracts taken from portfolios of NVQs delivered within a company. The extracts show samples of evidence cross-referenced to national standards.

In other situations the targets are driven by *personal development planning and review*. This can be very productive, as action planning for work and self-development become part of the same process. This process is two-way. Training and development can enable people to meet work objectives, and work experience can enable people to achieve a variety of awards.

In the case study below, Airsnack uses the positive experience gained through the building of NVQ portfolios to strengthen communication within teams, and to encourage the wider workforce to reflect on their own practice.

Case Study 7.2: *Airsnack*

Airsnack has already introduced NVQs into the company, so some employees have become familiar with that type of portfolio building. In addition, some groups have been encouraged to work on projects together, while others have experienced being coached and mentored through workplace activities. Two people have had specific input into staff meetings: John, who has made a presentation to colleagues as part of his development of the key skill of communication, and Bill, who is working towards an NVQ in Customer Service.

Much of this has begun to build the foundations of a strong communication system (a need identified earlier by Airsnack). Airsnack has decided to move forward on this foundation, and has organised an away day for the company. In preparation for the day, the workforce has been asked to complete a questionnaire entitled 'Strengths, Weaknesses, Opportunities and Threats in Airsnack's Communication Systems'. The questionnaire covers issues such as two-way communication and feedback, mentoring and coaching, involvement in the decision-making process, etc. The results of this questionnaire are collated on flip charts (one for each section of the questionnaire). This is done before the away day, and copies will be available for group discussion.

The morning of the away day has been set aside for a series of short presentations – by project teams, others involved in NVQs, managers reviewing their business plans, and the HR manager outlining the value of CPD files and the company support available in developing them. Each group or individual has been asked to summarise what they have learnt from this experience in terms of communicating with others.

In the first part of the afternoon, people meet in small groups to discuss the morning's presentations and to map the results against the SWOT analysis provided. Items can be added or crosses made against those questioned by the group. The last activity of the day is to pull together the feedback from these groups, in order to produce a final format of the SWOT analysis.

Following the away day everyone will receive the updated copy of the SWOT analysis, and the CPD material. People will be invited to bring their CPD portfolios to their next appraisal meeting.

In addition to the relationship between development and work performance, the above case study also highlights the value of feedback from others. Some companies have developed their own approach to what is termed a *360° review* – a tool that is used to appraise performance by eliciting feedback from peers, colleagues, managers, technical experts and by self-evaluation.

In the case of Lloyds TSB the 360° review is used in some regions as part of a personal development folder. In the case of BAESYSTEMS, the results are also targeted against the company's core values. In addition, PDPs and PDRs take account of 360° review. In this way the results are linked to work objectives, and a complementary part of the process leading to team planning of work objectives (plan on a page).

ACTIVITY 7.7

Go to the web site http://www.som.surrey.ac.uk/learnatwork and click on 5 1–2 for examples of 360° review, performance planning and review, plan on a page and index of CPD portfolio.

Many organisations, particularly those involved in training and education, encourage the identification of *learning outcomes*. The Southern England Consortium for Credit Accumulation and Transfer divides skills into four categories – knowledge and understanding, cognitive/intellectual skills, key/transferable skills and practical/subject-specific skills. Many people in higher education use this framework for writing learning outcomes. This is a type of target setting. It is written about here, but it also forms part of the next category of portfolio discussed. Some universities and colleges design their modules with set learning outcomes, and student work is assessed against related assessment criteria. It is a useful way to focus on the contents of assignments or projects, and for the students to have clear statements of their expected outcomes. It is also an excellent way of presenting yourself to others at interviews, in seeking internal promotion, or in preparing portfolios of evidence for professional bodies.

ACTIVITY 7.8

Decide which of the learning outcomes in the table below applies to you. Add in any others you think are relevant to you. Use this information to plan how you would present evidence to demonstrate them in the context of your work. Draw up a presentation for an interview based on these learning outcomes.

I am able to ...	Evidence
Contribute effectively at team meetings	
Encourage other team members to participate	
Complete written reports	
Deal with conflict	
Make presentations to my colleagues, my line managers and clients	
Communicate effectively with clients over the telephone	
Give feedback to others on their performance	
Represent the team's view to higher management	
Use email to keep in touch with my team	
Organise and chair meetings	
Participate in video or audio conferencing	
Motivate others when action planning	
Interact with others in problem-solving	
Brief others and deal with questions from them	
Draw out the quieter members of my team	

Portfolio Type 3 – To claim credit against undergraduate or postgraduate degrees

While Chapter 6 has dealt extensively with the operation of APL/APEL, this section will focus on the portfolio itself. In the majority of cases, *APL* does not need additional evidence, as it relates to previous certificated learning where the level of the award is stated, or can be clearly assessed. Occasionally, when it is not clear that the award is at a higher education level it may be necessary to provide further evidence. In some cases as part of an application, a candidate may be invited to talk through their evidence in a viva, which is recorded much as professional discussion is in NVQs.

In the case of *APEL*, the candidate has to demonstrate knowledge competence and skills in a particular area of their experience. This can be done by self-written modules. In some universities, modules of this kind are structured by the student, who identifies their own learning outcomes, writes a narrative to give an overview of the context at work, and selects sample evidence to endorse their claims. The narrative is cross-referenced to theory, reflects on practice, and identifies the learning gained (Figure 7.1).

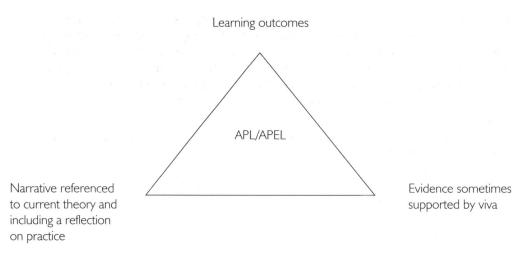

Learning outcomes

APL/APEL

Narrative referenced
to current theory and
including a reflection
on practice

Evidence sometimes
supported by viva

Figure 7.1 *Structuring an APEL module*

In some higher education institutions, there are two main approaches to writing APEL modules. The first is where the candidate matches their experience against taught modules, where the framework of learning outcomes and assessment criteria is already devised, and the second is where the candidate writes the learning outcomes themselves. The second requires much more of the candidate, and involves teaching and discussion before modules are written.

Activity 7.8 has laid some foundations for understanding this approach. It is important that the structure of APL/APEL is rigorous – experience cannot automatically be equated with learning. Many of us have a wealth of experiences that we have not learnt from! Reflection, analysis and engaging with relevant theory anchor the experience in the process of learning. This type of portfolio is a unique opportunity for people to demonstrate their learning in the workplace, and to gain credit towards a variety of qualifications.

ACTIVITY 7.9

Go to the web site http://www.som.surrey.ac.uk/learnatwork and click on Building Portfolios for examples of self-written modules (Managing Change and Teambuilding).

Portfolio Type 4 – To support an application for entry into a professional body

Presenting a type of portfolio of experience is part of the application for a number of professional bodies. The form this takes can vary, but the significance of this is that professional bodies are targeting entrepreneurs, looking at practice, problem-solving and continuous development.

For example, it is significant that the cover of the Royal Aeronautical Society's guidance notes on the society and its privileges of membership has the banner 'Recognising Potential'. Its headed notepaper has 'ENTER THE FUTURE OF AEROSPACE' written on it. A clear message is given of the value of living, growing, and developing skills.

There are many different routes to becoming a member, open to 'interested amateurs' through to people at the very top of their careers. Although the types of membership are different, the same theme of recognising potential runs through all membership. This theme is followed through in the sections of the guide, where innovation, being a catalyst in the workplace, and continuous development are highlighted. The quotations below (Royal Aeronautical Society, 2002) give a flavour of that theme:

- Influencing futures.
- By encouraging members to maximise their skills and abilities, the Society is an important catalyst between employees and employers.
- Influencing progress.
- The Society is a worldwide hub for the dissemination of specialist information, knowledge and innovative thought.
- Recognising professionalism.
- Recognising opportunities .

One of the society's primary functions is to support and encourage members in the continuous development of their skills and knowledge.

There is one route to becoming a chartered engineer where qualifications are required, and another route based on relevant experience. For the experienced or 'mature candidate' route, the central part of the application, the submission of a project, relates strongly to portfolio building as discussed in this chapter. People applying via this route need to demonstrate their understanding of the principles that underpin their project, and their reflection upon the learning achieved through the project that they are submitting.

The submission could be a critical exposition of an aspect of engineering practice, or it could be more evidence-based, with the candidate's commentary linking the evidence. Alternatively:

> *the bulk of the submission might consist of reports or design studies (published or unpublished), which may be accompanied by drawings and calculations. In this case the candidate's paper must provide a commentary, and connecting dialogue setting the material into the appropriate perspective and highlighting the candidate's understanding and application of engineering principles and knowledge.*
>
> Royal Aeronautical Society (2002)

Following submission of this evidence, there is an oral exam where the candidate can bring further evidence to support the claims made within their submission. The evidence may be:

> *A design study, notes, and/or drawings of original work, photographs or copies of published works, that he or she considers will be helpful in demonstrating that an appropriate standard of knowledge has been attained ... the candidate will be given every opportunity to demonstrate his or her technical knowledge in the chosen field, as it is the candidate's understanding of relevant engineering principles which is being tested.*
>
> Royal Aeronautical Society (2002)

These are the same principles that we have discussed for APL/APEL and there are many common features with other types of portfolios.

Similarly, the Chartered Management Institute (CMI) has a route for people to be accredited as a Chartered Manager. Candidates have to complete the CMI Continuous

Professional Development Record, which is online (see Portfolio Type 7), followed by a face-to-face interview. The CPD is a type of electronic portfolio, and the process of reassessment every three years ensures that competencies are updated. As with the Royal Aeronautical Society, there are entry qualifications for the Chartered Manager Scheme, but there are also routes through for candidates without those qualifications, but with relevant and consistent experience.

Portfolio Type 5 – Electronic or 'paperless' portfolios

Barrett (2000) defines electronic portfolios as follows:

> *My definition of an electronic portfolio involves the use of electronic technologies, allowing the portfolio developer to collect and organize portfolio artefacts in many media types (audio, video, graphics, text) and, in the case of standards-based portfolios, uses hypertext links to organize the material to connect this evidence to appropriate goals or standards. Often terms like electronic portfolio and digital portfolio are used interchangeably; I make the distinction: an electronic portfolio contains artefacts that may be in analog form; in a digital portfolio, all artefacts have been transformed into a computer readable form.*

The distinction is appreciated but in the short description below the term electronic has been used to cover both types. In a sense this type of portfolio is an overarching approach to all portfolios. With the use of digital cameras and scanners, people can shape, monitor and re-evaluate a portfolio with ease. The strengths of an online CPD 'portfolio' are discussed later in this chapter.

Increasingly, people are looking for creative and more effective ways of recording evidence, and experimenting with commercial software packages. Some packages on the market can record the portfolio itself, plus the assessment, internal verification and external verification processes. This is particularly useful where portfolios are built to meet National Standards and the reporting system is structured. The way that awarding bodies are moving will save time and provide a more efficient service but there are practical barriers that are to do with cost and availability of equipment. Other examples of paperless portfolios involve online businesses offering, for example, teacher training in languages. Open Learning International is an example of a worldwide provision for teacher training, delivered online (http://www.olionline.com).

In the case of Open Learning International too, the portfolio evidence, the assessment plus internal and external verification are online. Information stored on secure servers can be downloaded by assessors and verifiers for discussion or monitoring, and group discussions and observation of teaching sessions can all be correlated into the online record. There are still issues in many countries with regard to the expense of webcams and other equipment, but many people see these barriers as being simply a matter of time.

There are still situations where candidates themselves are not happy with a totally paper-free approach, and access to all the appropriate equipment is still an issue. There are also situations where the assessment team meet face-to-face but the portfolios, internal and external verification and the standards are online. This situation (or variations of it!) makes discussing the portfolios difficult. An office-sized computer monitor does not lend itself to round table discussions. Alternative provisions – rooms with digital projectors, or networked computers – are often a luxury. There is some discussion about the authenticity of testing online, but systems have already emerged to try to ensure 'safe assessment', and assessment of paper-based portfolios also needs monitoring for authenticity.

Portfolio Type 6 – Compilation of ongoing evidence against attainment targets

European Language Portfolios (ELPs) have been promoted by the Council of Europe and piloted in 15 European countries between 1998 and 2000. The portfolio has the overarching target of promoting plurilingualism and pluriculturalism. It has long-term aims of providing a framework for languages in Europe, which would facilitate the operation of a multilingual mobile workforce, and also bring some common benchmarking into language qualifications and levels. As part of this framework the portfolio has six levels (see Appendix 7.1).

Although portfolios in this category are closely related to other types of portfolios, they do have some very distinct features. The first is that the ELP has both quantitative and qualitative assessment. It is designed to record people's experiences of, and achievements in, language learning, and to develop cultural awareness. It has a mixture of self-evaluation and the recognition of formal certification with regard to language learning, and an encouragement to log cultural experiences, reflect upon them and evaluate them. Secondly, it is offered Europe-wide and invites people to participate whether they are in or out of an education system.

The portfolio has three sections – Language Passport, Language Biography and Dossier:

- The Language Passport combines self-evaluation, a résumé of language learning and intercultural experience, and a summary of certificates and diplomas.
- The Language Biography encourages the holder of the portfolio to reflect on their progress, state what they have achieved and to describe linguistic and cultural experiences they have had in and out of formal education.
- The Dossier is a selection of evidence to support the language biography.

ELPs have been designed for a wide range of the population, starting with primary age children, and many organisations have begun to implement them in their field of education.

It may seem strange to separate *Progress Files* from the forerunner to this type of portfolio – the NRA – but it is to emphasise the different nature of the two portfolios. Progress Files have some things in common with CPD portfolios, job skills portfolios and with ELPs. As with CPD files and job skills portfolios, Progress Files are not about past achievements, they are about moving on and planning future development:

> *They can help learners of all ages to develop skills to identify their achievements to date, consider career goals/key skills, plan next stages in learning and record and present achievements to others.*

http://www.dfes.gov.uk/progfile

As with the ELP, Progress Files have a structured framework that provides guidance and materials to encourage self-evaluation, recording achievement and setting goals. Both ELPs and Progress Files are also provided for a wide range of age groups (although Progress Files start at Year 9 in the UK system, and ELPs are offered to primary age children).

Portfolio Type 7 – Continuous Professional Development

Of all the portfolios, this can the most valuable, because if it is kept up to date it provides an ongoing resource for other portfolios, and also involves the individual in planning their future development. Keeping a record of CPD is an indication of strong motivation for self-development, which is not only personally satisfying, but is likely to increase a person's employability. With an increasingly mobile workforce it is important for people to be prepared to present their current skills and competencies. To do this, they must select evidence, reflect on its value, and see the cohesiveness of various aspects of the portfolio.

Case Study 7.3: *Transglobal*

Transglobal, as an international IT company, has online systems for recording performance development and review. The system is effective. Objectives are set annually and reviewed every six months. It also uses a training needs analysis tool to review and record key skills and core competencies, using the company Intranet. The company supports the virtual CoPs by funding face-to-face meetings twice a year. There are strong indications that Transglobal is a developed learning organisation. However, it has been recognised by a number of the workforce that the training and development, although very good, does not give them national or international qualifications. In the current climate of mobile workforces this has become very important. The company decides to work towards national/international accreditation in a two-stage action plan. First of all it will support any employee who wishes to develop a CPD portfolio. In this way each employee will begin to review their progress holistically and think about what direction their more formal training might take. It will mean that motivated people will be supported into the next part of the action plan. This will be that all those completing CPD portfolios will be offered an advice session where appropriate formal qualifications will be discussed.

In a move to add value to the training and development in an international company, Transglobal has also invited its employees to develop individual ELPs. This is particularly relevant in a global company that was formed by merging a French company with a UK-based one. It will also not only benefit the company in its contact with clients, but will give a further dimension to the CPD portfolios.

Systems will be set up with a framework for integrating the three aspects of development that are already online (the achievement of core skills and competencies, achievements in meeting targets within performance development and review, and company-organised training). Each employee will also have exclusive access to their own portfolio on the Intranet and can add data relating to achievement, training and experience inside or outside of the company. Transglobal have agreed that employees have the right to this portfolio if they leave the company.

The key to building CPD portfolios is motivation. People are willing to undergo CPD by attending courses, but keeping a portfolio of evidence may be a different matter. Some awarding bodies require their staff to provide, on an annual basis, evidence of CPD, for both their subject area and their role (e.g. assessor, internal verifier). However, if there is no requirement placed upon a person, they have to be strongly motivated in some other way to maintain a portfolio, which is more than a file of qualifications and certificates of attendance. This motivation could come from the individual's own desire to progress, or it could be built into the company's programme of training and development. The CMI has an online scheme for CPD (the *smart* Continuing Professional Development scheme, http://www.managers.org.uk/institute), which builds up a personal profile of planned self-development, and is free to its members. The CPD scheme:

- offers members an online Personal Development Profile (CPD Profile) to record all aspects of their learning and development
- tests their knowledge, understanding and ability in specific management skills and techniques
- scores how they assess themselves at these skills
- enables them to invite others to assess them at these skills
- provides individual and combined feedback on their score
- enables them to discover new learning opportunities
- assesses how they learn, how they apply that learning in the workplace and provides constructive feedback
- provides recognition of development through the award of a CPD Certificate
- recognises the results of significant CPD activity with the potential to become a Chartered Manager.

The CMI has therefore provided two motives. The first is that a CPD Certificate is awarded, and the second is that CPD is a prerequisite for people to be recognised as a Chartered Manager (Portfolio Type 4). The online system is probably motivating in itself, and the assessment is completed sequentially. It also facilitates analysis of, and reflection upon, personal development. The profile itself is divided into sections, which can be updated by the candidate as appropriate. However, this scheme is different to other CPD portfolios in that it is an assessed scheme. The results demonstrate 'best practice' within management and leadership, and are set against national standards. Other CPD portfolios are compiled by the individual who has judged their own best practice and will use the portfolio to defend their choice.

The process is of planning and review. Figure 7.2 provides a useful framework for the process of building a CPD portfolio and echoes the various cycles of learning discussed on pages 141–2. This cycle of planning departs from the other models in that it does not have a stage where learning is internalised, or conceptualised, and concentrates more on identification of learning opportunities being recorded rather than informing future actions.

A generic, current CPD portfolio would include all that an individual has identified as significant about their own practice and development, in a specific and recent period of time. (See Activity 7.7 for an example of a CPD portfolio index.) With such a portfolio, the holder could take out those elements that apply to a certain situation, and form a portfolio for a particular purpose. For example, someone who is a manager in an engineering company and also externally verifies for management NVQs may need one type of portfolio when applying for a lead verifier post in management, another to be

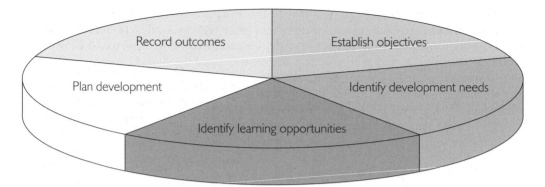

Figure 7.2 *Building a CPD portfolio (adapted from http://www.managers.org.uk/institute)*

accepted as an assessor for ISO 9001, and a third when applying for a post in another engineering company. The basic framework for each one may be the same, or similar, but the emphasis (and therefore the content) would be different, with more detail given to the targeted area.

One of the greatest advantages of portfolio building is its flexibility. This chapter has detailed seven types of portfolios, but it can be seen that many overlap in their use, and all could be used as a resource that can be drawn upon to illustrate other aspects of the person's development.

BARRIERS TO PORTFOLIO BUILDING

In Chapter 5 we looked at issues of assessment and measuring skills in the workplace. Work-based assessment using portfolios of evidence, although a radical change, has not been without its difficulties. It is clear that the move away from a strongly exam-led curriculum has dramatically changed approaches to assessment. Some of the changes relate to practice, in the sense of people learning to work in a different way, but a very great deal is to do with a mindset built up over previous years and relating to previous systems of education.

In addition, whilst many people have embraced the radical changes that new forms of assessment have brought, the rapid pace of change has made it difficult to internalise the whole approach. It has taken time to see the value of approaching assessment in a holistic way, and for assessors to look at the context, consistency and range of practice and knowledge, rather than being focused on exam results. To some degree or another, those of us from the education sector involved in the initial launch of NVQs still had the exam approach imprinted on our minds from our own schooling, and transferred this across into our practice within NVQ systems. The evidence for this was that in the early days of the implementation of NVQs there was a perceived need to provide a separate piece of evidence for each individual criterion of the standards, rather like a series of answers to an exam question – hence the evolution of the bulging lever arch file! The amount of time to accumulate evidence in this way, and for portfolios to be assessed, internally verified, and externally verified, was demotivating and made candidates feel that they were just paper-chasing. The security for assessors and candidates alike was based on something like a tick on the page of a test – it was proof of 'correct' performance as a correct answer would be in an exam. Of course this devalued NVQs and cast doubt on a system of assessment that is far more exciting than ticking boxes!

It has taken time for candidates, assessors and verifiers alike to see that this form of assessment is not to do with the performance of one aspect of practice on a particular day at a particular time, but is about developing and confirming consistent excellent practice across a range of subjects and situations. Another aspect of this exam imprint has been the vague unease that people felt in giving candidates time to develop a skill, or gain the knowledge. Compared with an exam where candidates have one chance to demonstrate their knowledge and skills, it seemed initially like 'cheating' to give them a chance to improve, albeit within a framework of time. Formative and summative assessments were not new, but only the summative assessment counted – in the new situation the *process* of acquisition of knowledge and skills is important. This process is illustrated by the thinking of Schön (1983), Kolb (1984), Dennison and Kirk (1990), Eraut (1994), Boud and Garrick (1999), and many others. In spite of this the academic/vocational divide (as those who think, and those who do) is still a common perception. NVQs have developed to higher levels but there is still scepticism in paralleling Levels 4 and 5 to undergraduate and postgraduate levels, although the national qualifications frameworks for Scotland, Ireland, Wales and England all place them (or their national equivalent) in that category. In spite of the initiatives to widen access to higher education, much of the current public debate centres around the accusation that widening access means lowering standards, rather than raising standards by recognising a wider range and types of knowledge. There is still some way to go, therefore, in the acceptance of different ways of assessing knowledge, competence and skills, and presenting achievement.

Box 7.1: Summary of barriers to the use of portfolios to review and assess knowledge

- A mindset that places exams as the only real form of assessment.
- A rapid change of practice, with limited time to assimilate the implications of those changes, leading to ...
- A lack of understanding of the nature of portfolios both as a tool for assessment and review, and also to present achievement.
- Traditional views about access to higher education.
- The perception of traditionally delivered degrees as the 'gold star' route to certain areas of employment.
- The slowness of change in systems and structures within higher education.
- The ranking of 'academic' and 'vocational' programmes of study.

BREAKING BARRIERS

What has been argued is that barriers to the use of portfolios in assessing and presenting achievement, reviewing progress and setting goals are largely related to valuing and managing change. The breaking of barriers therefore depends on the effectiveness of the change agents – governments/national assemblies, schools, colleges of further education, confederations of employers, universities, the quality and curriculum authorities in the four nations of Scotland, Ireland, Wales and England, the Department for Education and Skills (and their equivalent in the other three nations), and the Learning and Skills Councils. In addition there is an extensive range of quangos and committees who influence education, training and development. In some senses the lead taken by many of these groups in developing and reviewing policy, funding initiatives and putting the debate in the public forum has provided a strong foundation for a change of mindset, but that change needs to be worked through in practice.

The government's current Widening Participation Programme is causing academics to rethink their practice and take steps to increase access to higher education. Partnerships are being forged with further education colleges, schools and local communities. These initiatives are working across a wide region and involve more than one university. Partnerships between universities and industry have developed more widely, and there has been the emergence of work-based learning degrees at graduate and undergraduate level. Foundation degrees with a subject-specific (vocational) focus are emerging, and there is an increasing focus on cross-phase work in partnership.

There remain some difficult areas to tackle. Systems within universities are not all set up to cater for the different patterns of access that are emerging, and students are still categorised by the term 'traditional' and 'non-traditional', giving the impression that the latter are measured against the former.

In many ways companies and organisations have not had the same philosophical difficulties, as the relationship between knowledge and practice is often vital to success. Those with strong training programmes are expert in measuring performance (e.g. 360° appraisal) and are used to quality audits (e.g. ISO 9001) where requirements need to be met on an ongoing basis. The issue of consistency and range of practice is important commercially, and it is often normal practice to provide different types of evidence to demonstrate development. Some companies have virtual universities and/or open learning centres, and multimedia evidence and evidence stored electronically are common practice. Performance is often referenced and measured against company values (e.g. as in BAESYSTEMS). Highly developed training systems combine company training with national/international awards (e.g. Disneyland in Paris, where a 'package of training' for managers of boutiques is composed of NVQs in Languages, the team-building unit from an NVQ in Management and Disney's own company training). Others encourage their employees to develop their own CPD files (e.g. OCR), some in a more structured way (as in Lloyds TSB). Progress Files and ELPs combine a structured framework with the encouragement for people to reflect upon and evaluate practice. 'Living and growing' portfolios of professional development fit well into this context (Kemp and Toperoff, 1998).

What many companies and organisations often do not provide is a breadth of national/international accreditation and help with gaining chartered status and/or membership of professional bodies. Company training and development, even if it is excellent, gives credit to the individual within the company, but that individual does not take the credit with them when they move into a new company. In today's world of mobile workforces, this is important. Individuals can keep their own CPD files, but feedback from others, within and outside of the company, needs company support in terms of mentors advisers, and sometimes training. These portfolios are not only empowering for the individual, but will be valuable for the company in building team relationships, and may well affect retention of staff. Those reviewing and feeding back learn from the experience, as well!

The measurement of practice against theory also provides a wider context for best practice, and informs ongoing development. Work-based learning degrees, higher education diplomas and certificates, NVQs and a range of awarding body qualifications provide an opportunity to do this, many of them portfolio-based. The individual achieves an accredited award, and the company gains a better informed worker who reflects upon and reviews practice. The portfolio is an essential tool in the processes of change because it enables the individual to select and accumulate evidence that demonstrates achievement, and is conducive to the process of reflection and review.

SUMMARY

- Portfolios can be used as a tool to keep pace with continuous professional development (CPD).
- The portfolio approach is used for a variety of other purposes.
- The process of compiling a portfolio is a learning exercise for the holder in self-evaluation, analysis and forward planning.
- Compiling a portfolio is an empowering process.
- Demonstration of excellent practice is in the hands of the holder of the portfolio.
- Portfolio building has been an integral part of changes in assessment practice.

REFERENCES

Bacal, R. (1999) *Performance Management*, McGraw-Hill, New York.

Barrett, H.C. (2000) Create your own electronic portfolio (http://www.transition.alaska.edu/www/portfolios/toolsarticle.html) (accessed 10 July 2003).

Boud, D., Keogh, R. and Walker, D. (1985) *Reflection: Turning Experience into Learning*, Kogan Page, London.

Boud, D. and Garrick, J. (1999) *Understanding Learning at Work*, Routledge, London.

Day, M. (2002) *Assessment of Prior Learning – a Practitioner's Guide*, Nelson Thornes, Cheltenham.

Dearing, R. (1996) *Review of Qualifications for 16–19 year olds*, SCCA, London.

Dennison, B. and Kirk, R. (1990) *A Simple Guide to Experiential Learning*, Blackwell, Oxford.

Eraut, M. (1994) *Developing Professional Knowledge and Competence*, Falmer, London.

Friedman, A.L. and Watts, D.C.H. (2002) *Reflection in Work-Based Learning*, University of Wales Institute, Cardiff.

Hansen, R.S. *Your Job Skills Portfolio: Giving you the edge in the Marketplace* (www.quintcareers.com/job_search_portfolio.html) (accessed July 2003)

Kemp, J. and Toperoff, D. (1998) Guidelines for Portfolio Assessment in Teaching English ETNI (http://www.etni.org.il/ministry/portfolio/default.html) (accessed August 2003).

Kolb, D. (1984) *Experiential Learning: Experience as the Source of Learning and Development*. Prentice Hall, Englewood Cliffs, NJ.

QCA (2001) *NVQ Code of Practice 2001*, Qualifications and Curriculum Authority, Sudbury.

Royal Aeronautical Society (2002) *A guide to the Royal Aeronautical Society and the privilege of membership*, RAS, London.

Schön, D. (1983) *The Reflective Practitioner; How Professionals think in action,* Temple Smith, London.

SEEC (2004) *Credit Level Descriptors for Further and Higher Education,* SEEC Office University of East London, London.

Seldin, P. (1997) *The Teaching Portfolio,* 2nd edn, Anker Publishing Co. Inc., Bolton, MA http://www.coe.int/portfolio

APPENDIX 7.1: GLOBAL SCALE

Proficient user	C2	Can understand with ease virtually everything heard or read. Can summarise information from different spoken and written sources, reconstructing arguments and accounts in a coherent presentation. Can express him/herself spontaneously, very fluently and precisely, differentiating finer shades of meaning even in more complex situations.
	C1	Can understand a wide range of demanding, longer texts, and recognise implicit meaning. Can express him/herself fluently and spontaneously without much obvious searching for expressions. Can use language flexibly and effectively for social, academic and professional purposes. Can produce clear, well-structured, detailed text on complex subjects, showing controlled use of organisational patterns, connectors and cohesive devices.
Independent user	B2	Can understand the main ideas of complex text on both concrete and abstract topics, including technical discussions in his/her field of specialisation. Can interact with a degree of fluency and spontaneity that makes regular interaction with native speakers quite possible without strain for either party. Can produce clear, detailed text on a wide range of subjects and explain a viewpoint on a topical issue giving the advantages and disadvantages of various options.
	B1	Can understand the main points of clear standard input on familiar matters regularly encountered in work, school, leisure, etc. Can deal with most situations likely to arise whilst travelling in an area where the language is spoken. Can produce simple connected text on topics that are familiar or of personal interest. Can describe experiences and events, dreams, hopes and ambitions and briefly give reasons and explanations for opinions and plans.
Basic user	A2	Can understand sentences and frequently-used expressions related to areas of most immediate relevance (e.g. very basic personal and family information, shopping, local geography, employment). Can communicate in simple and routine tasks requiring a simple and direct exchange of information on familiar and routine matters. Can describe in simple terms aspects of his/her background, immediate environment and matters in areas of immediate need.
	A1	Can understand and use familiar everyday expressions and very basic phrases aimed at the satisfaction of needs of a concrete type. Can introduce him/herself and others and can ask and answer questions about personal details such as where he/she lives, people he/she knows and things he/she has. Can interact in a simple way provided the other person talks slowly and clearly and is prepared to help.

8 THE WORKPLACE AS A LEARNING ENVIRONMENT

Objectives

After reading this chapter, you will be able to:

- Identify a company culture that is conducive to learning.
- Discuss the variety of ways of learning in the workplace.
- Describe the network of support available in your workplace.
- Outline the strengths and weaknesses of the various forms of support.
- Draw up a personal plan for learning in your workplace.

INTRODUCTION

There has been a wealth of information and practical suggestions in previous chapters with respect to learning in the workplace. This chapter looks at how the culture of an organisation can affect such learning, and what factors influence or change that culture. We shall also consider the formal and informal opportunities that exist for learning in the workplace, and how such learning can be supported. Formal learning in the workplace is largely a recognised necessity, as it contributes to the development of company knowledge and expertise and, in some cases, also gives an individual a transferable qualification or award. On the other hand, there has been an increasing awareness over the last ten years of the value of informal learning, which has been heightened by research carried out by, amongst others, Eraut *et al.* (1998: 3). The research covered three fields of employment – engineering, business and healthcare – and their three main research questions were:

- What is being learned at work?
- How is learning taking place?
- What other factors affect the amount and direction of learning in the workplace?

This chapter will address these questions, particularly the last two, and will challenge the reader to be clear about the culture of their organisation, and to evaluate how far it has developed as a learning organisation. Informal learning, in particular, depends on the culture of the organisation, which can either be a rich resource for learning, or a restriction upon individual and team development. It seems appropriate then to begin with an examination of the culture of a company or an organisation, as the source of support for learning. We then move on to consider some of the factors affecting it, how to maintain a learning culture, how and what is being learned in the workplace, and finally we re-evaluate the culture of the organisation that we work for in the light of the issues raised in this chapter.

COMPANY CULTURE AND LEARNING IN THE WORKPLACE

Company culture is the biggest factor affecting learning in the workplace. Learning at work is shaped and characterised by the culture and environment of the organisation.

The nature of the learning that takes place will depend to some extent on how employees relate to one another and how they are supported in the process of developing themselves. Many of the ways of learning in the workplace need good communication systems, confidence in peers, and a desire to see others develop to their full potential. Systems of performance management and related support for staff development are radically affected by company culture and the environment people operate in. If the culture is hierarchical and combative, developing individual members of staff often amounts to training people to work harder at 'their job'. The effect of this is that the 'ripple' of control runs through the company, and the status quo is reinforced. Managers and leaders alike can create this culture. Managers with an overall operational role can create systems that perpetuate their control, and leaders can easily slip into developing people in their own image. This often creates a culture where people are 'watching their back', and not seeing themselves as part of a team. Much of this defensiveness is to do with the anxiety of maintaining power and control. Very often, individual managers are not aware of how their particular need to control has a widespread effect on the whole organisation, and that the result can easily be a controlling regime that deadens initiative and curtails learning in the workplace. Murrell and Meredith (2000: 6) suggest three possible perceptions of power within organisations:

- **Distribution**. Power is 'given'. This perspective implies that power is finite, that you lose power if you give it to someone else.
- **Creation**. Power is 'made'. This perspective implies that power is created when two or more individuals interact and share information, authority, and/or responsibility.
- **Creative distribution**. Power is 'unlimited'. This implies that when people are mutually influential, power grows exponentially.

Hierarchical management, then, depends on clear control. It also creates a fear of losing the 'edge' that is created by being the one person, or the group of people, holding on to important areas of knowledge. For this reason, 'distributing power' as defined above also creates fear, as it is perceived by some as losing power. To maintain power, a distance has to be preserved between the controller and the controlled – it is difficult, for example, to maintain that distance if you are in a bumper car with your colleagues on an away day, or playing on the football team with them! Clearly, social activities can be effective in supporting changes of culture. Sometimes, however, it really is true that if control is lost, the irrelevance of the top 'controller' is laid bare. More often than not, losing the need to control is the beginning of productive relationships that exploit the expertise of the team or company, becoming, in Murrell and Meredith terms, 'mutually influential'. This mutual influence in management leads to a creativity in teamworking, a point further developed by Kirby (2003) in outlining the attributes of effective entrepreneurial managers:

The most effective entrepreneurial managers are creative and skilful in handling conflicts, generating consensus decisions and sharing power and information. They:

- *are able to get people to open up and share their views*
- *get problems aired and identified*
- *acknowledge, without being defensive, the views of others*
- *are aware that high quality decisions require information flowing in all directions*
- *are comfortable with knowledge, competence, logic and evidence prevailing over official status or formal rank*

- *are able to get potential adversaries to be creative and to collaborate by reconciling viewpoints*
- *are constantly blending views, often risking their own vulnerability in the process of giving up their own power and resources.*

Kirby (2003: 187)

Can there be any doubt that entrepreneurial creative management, although more difficult to sustain than hierarchical management, is a rich environment for learning in the workplace? Yet, even if systems are set up to involve people in decision-making, they can be manipulated or bypassed, and this does not provide the context for learning in and from the workplace. Once a culture has developed along these lines it is often difficult to break the mould, and there are consequently missed opportunities for both formal and informal learning arising out of the day-to-day life of an organisation. We see examples of these missed opportunities in the situation detailed in Box 8.1. The fact that it was an organisation with a 'shallow' management structure gives an outward impression of devolved power, but it is clear that the organisation is operating in quite a different way. The process described is the devolution and accountability of budgets. This is a normal process for many organisations, but the culture is a controlling one, and this dynamically affects the development and operation of teams. The name of the company and of the section head have been changed, but all other details describe a real situation.

Box 8.1: Furbishing International, and the dangers of a controlling culture

Senior management team (heads of departments and others)

↓

Middle managers (section heads)

↓

Team leaders and teams

Furbishing International has the company structure outlined above and employs more than 5000 people. The senior management team (SMT) meet every Wednesday afternoon. Sometimes, when difficult issues arise, longstanding members of the SMT meet in the pub before the meeting to discuss the agenda items.

It is the responsibility of all senior managers to implement any actions from the meeting, and to inform their teams. Pierre has been a middle manager (section head) for a year. His head of department holds a meeting on Friday morning of each week for him and three other colleagues. Each section head has four or five team leaders who run teams of 10–30 full-time staff and a larger number of part-time staff. Frequently on a Friday morning, all the actions from the previous SMT meeting are divided up between the four section heads. It is up to them to organise their own teams. Finance is a regular issue on the agenda of meetings. In theory, the organisation has 'shallow management' (three levels only) with budgets devolved to teams. The budget presented to section heads is equally divided between the four. They then have to monitor their own budgets, and present accounts to

►

the head of department at the end of the financial year. The SMT budget will also be published and discussed at the same time.

Up to the time of Pierre's appointment, the section had been well resourced for three of his teams, but the fourth team had been terribly under-resourced. It was clear to Pierre at the beginning of the year that he needed to negotiate with his team leaders in order to redress the balance. In effect, three team leaders needed to be prepared to allow the fourth team leader to receive more money, and for them to receive less. It took a few meetings to thrash out the problems associated with this, and the team had worked together to build the section up. This had involved one team leader meeting per week throughout the year, which had been held at lunchtime. Fortunately, the team leaders were willing to give up their much valued lunchtimes to work together. By the middle of last year, things were going well, Pierre's accounts were on a database, and his team leaders were happily reviewing expenditure against their individual budgets. About this time, one of Pierre's team leaders, who knew the head of department personally, told him that her budget was inadequate. Unbeknown to Pierre, the head of department allocated her extra resources from his own budget, which gave her 25% more than Pierre had originally allocated to her team. Eventually, some weeks later, she told Pierre about it.

At the end of the financial year Pierre was the only section head to present accounts, and at that point he discovered that another section head had been given extra money from the head of department's budget. This same section also ended up the financial year in debt. The head of department made no comment about that section head's budgeting or Pierre's.

The section heads and their departmental manager discussed the SMT and departmental budgets at the end of the year, but these 'extra' payments did not feature in the discussion.

What can we learn from this way of operating? Details of what *could* have been learned by the company are listed in Table 8.1, together with suggestions for missed opportunities to develop a more open culture.

ACTIVITY 8.1

Can you identify opportunities for learning and development that you, or your team, have missed this year? What were the opportunities for formal and informal learning?

FACTORS AFFECTING CULTURAL CHANGE

It was said at the beginning of this chapter that once a hierarchical and controlling culture has developed, it is difficult to break the mould. There are, however, a number of factors that can change a culture. Some are opportunities or threats presented by an external factor, for example a change in the world market, or a loss of funding for a major project. Other changes in culture can come about by internal factors, for example a radical change in the senior management team, or the steady long-term effect of lack of recognition for best practice or creativity. In this part of the chapter we are considering some of the factors that act as change agents. Whether a particular factor has affected a

Table 8.1 *Missed opportunities for learning*

Missed opportunities for ...	Possible learning from this situation	Informal/formal learning
Open discussion amongst senior managers, and real consensus reached	• Transparent teamwork at SMT level	Informal
Open discussion between the senior manager and his section heads, so that they were fully informed about the overall company budget, the departmental budget, any contingencies, and their own budgets.	• Transparent teamwork in middle management	Informal
	• Being coached into a supportive model of leadership	Informal
	• Learning from the financial expertise of others	Informal and formal – training offered to the section head whose budget was always in deficit
Agreement that their budgets would be monitored monthly to avoid any crisis.	• Financial management	
An opportunity to discuss the needs of team leaders across the department.	• Team-building	Informal
The senior manager to explain to the team leader who approached him that all the budgets had been set by agreement with section heads, and that she would need to go back to her section head and discuss it with him	• The need to trust and confirm the role of your section heads	Informal
	• The management issue behind the challenge from the team leader	Informal
	• Dealing with conflict/negative responses	Formal – an opportunity to support section heads by offering training on dealing with conflict

company culture negatively or positively will depend on how aware people are of their existing way of working, and whether they are able and willing to transform themselves as individuals, teams or as a whole company.

Achievement of company kitemarks as an agent of change

Company quality marks, such as ISO 9001, IiP, Total Quality Management, Business Excellence, and the European Foundation for Quality Management, can radically affect company culture. IiP is the most obvious, in that its very title sums up a culture. In order to gain and keep this quality mark, companies have to demonstrate their commitment to the development of their staff, and build lines of communication and support. ISO 9001 is an audit of the process and procedures designed to improve the quality of the output of an organisation. The framework is concerned with involving a wider group of people in the responsibility of meeting customer requirements, and measuring customer reaction. It is true that this can be operated within a hierarchical framework, as well as within a culture that seeks to value and empower its workforce. However, many organisations operating ISO 9001 find that the spin-off from looking at systems and procedures leads people into a more transparent way of working, and encourages the development of individuals and teams. Similarly, most quality marks involve a process of reflection and review that can lead to changes of practice, relationship and systems.

Crisis

A crisis or the restructuring of a company can be a formidable change agent. British Aerospace (as it was called at the time) experienced such a change agent. The company had been formed in 1977 by bringing together a number of aerospace companies and was privatised two years later. It was a company built upon a history of incredible expertise and innovation, bringing together a number of: 'forerunners of modern aeronautics ... and becoming the country's biggest exporter of manufactured goods and largest employer' (Evans and Price, 1999: 5).

The crisis built up between 1990 and 1994. Evans and Price (1999: 2) describe it in this way:

> *Trouble came from all sides: our property company was hit with a lousy market. Sales of the Rover Group sank by about a fifth, and losses mounted ... Losses in our commercial aerospace division increased dramatically with the recession in the airline industry.*

The situation had deteriorated further by the middle of 1992, when British Aerospace recorded the then biggest single asset write-off in UK corporate history. With the share price at an all-time low, and the shareholders disillusioned, the company was close to crashing. There needed to be a radical rethink in the way they operated. Amongst the many complicated reasons for the crisis, Evans and Price identified the fact that, in spite of the resources of incredible expertise, a weakness in the formation of the company was their 'viability as a competitive organism' (Evans and Price, 1999). Strategies were devised to reduce costs but they also needed to move from being a group of companies working together and become an organism. Price Waterhouse were employed to work with the company and to support the process of what was being recognised as an urgent need for change of culture. Price Waterhouse identified the following barriers to cultural change, expressed in descending order of significance (Evans and Price, 1999: 65):

- competing resource priorities
- need for change poorly explained
- employee opposition
- lack of middle management support
- insufficient change management skills
- initiative fatigue
- inadequate communications
- unrealistic timetables for the change project
- inappropriate leadership at the top
- insufficient training and coaching
- lack of clarity of vision and objectives
- bottom-line benefits not understood.

These barriers had to be overcome and the change that ensued was radical. It is interesting to note that four of the bullet points above relate directly to communication. It is not surprising, therefore, that breaking the status quo meant new ways of communicating, often between one team and another. Sir Richard Evans, as the then Chief Executive of the company, sought, in the early days of the process of change to, in his words, 'improve the chemistry', and invited people to write to him personally. These 'letters to Dick' allowed open and direct criticism of the culture of the company at the time, and this was acknowledged by Evans and Price as 'one of the trickiest issues in a change programme'. This open channel of communication was influential in a process in which the status quo really changed. Of course, the open and honest communication presented taxing problems for Evans and required considerable personal skills on his part, and on the part of all those involved in following up the issues raised by the feedback in 'letters to Dick'. The cultural mould was broken, however, and there was a sharp learning curve for all those involved. Aptly, the Evans and Price book has, as part of its subtitle, 'British Aerospace's Comeback from Crisis to World Class'.

Support for personal development

Apart from being in a learning environment, there is another issue that can motivate learning and self-development, and that is to do with gaining personal credit. Many companies and organisations have excellent training schemes, open learning centres, Intranet facilities, virtual universities and good communication systems, but all these facilities and support systems are targeted at company values and aims. The company ultimately gets the credit. Of course this is to be expected – organisations naturally want a well-qualified workforce committed to the company's mission and values. In addition, companies often want company accreditation in terms of a quality kitemark, and whilst the process of gaining that involves them in a great deal of learning and change, there is no personal credit for an individual employee. Some companies recognise merit with individual prizes offered for innovation or outstanding performance. Whilst not wishing to criticise this, it doesn't carry the same weight as a national or international award, especially for future job-seeking.

Some companies feel that they could not afford to give everyone the opportunity to gain national or international awards. There are, however, many opportunities available for the individual to gain credit towards national/international awards by using work that has been carried out through company training or through processes leading up to and maintaining a company kitemark – for example, as evidence against the standards of NVQs, or undergraduate and postgraduate degrees in work-based learning. Positive support (study leave, mentoring, advising) can also be given to people in achieving chartered status with the various professional bodies, or in gaining traditionally delivered awards by part-time study. Case Studies 7.1 and 8.1 outline a situation where the CSB recognised that national accreditation was a motivating force for some of their staff. In a two-stage plan, they built a programme to facilitate this through their work practices and the employment of assessors and advisers. There was a cost, but much of the evidence for the appropriate award came through the workplace.

Case Study 8.1: *Building a culture of personal development*

The regional Citizens Support Bureau (CSB), in realising the lack of recognition of the skills of their volunteer staff, set up a system of support to help their staff develop CPD portfolios. Throughout the last year, a rota of senior staff and two facilitators from the local further education college have held monthly 'surgeries' for groups of staff wanting feedback or help with their portfolio building. The next stage is to encourage people in 'routes through' to further awards. Accordingly, the CSB management has set up a training information day. Three groups of people have been invited to set up stalls, and time can be booked for advice sessions during the day. The three stalls are NVQs (manned by staff from the local college of further education), work-based learning programmes in higher education (staff from the two universities in the region) and Diploma in Advisory Services (People Development Manager from CSB central staff). The CSB has also invited successful CSB students from this and other regions. Each of the students will make a short presentation on the particular award they have achieved, as well as being available for informal discussion during the day.

Other internal and external factors

Each one of the internal and external factors in Figure 8.1 could affect companies in different ways, depending on their culture and the current situation in their development. It is also true that a company could experience the whole range!

There is often a correlation between external and internal factors. An obvious example might be the external factor of takeover, leading to the internal factor of restructuring, and the dynamic effect that could have upon company culture. Because of the number of factors that could affect company culture, bodies such as IiP reassess organisations who have already been awarded the company kitemark on a regular basis (for IiP this is every three years). Sometimes positive factors can disappear completely over a three-year period. Staying with the example above, a takeover from a company operating in Europe could bring in new managers who recognise existing good practice, are delighted that the organisation has recently been given the IiP award, but are not familiar with it. In the two years following the takeover it becomes very obvious that some of the new managers were not aware of the need to sustain processes that were in place to meet the requirements of IiP. At the same time, the change of personnel has brought about a lack of motivation in some areas of the organisation.

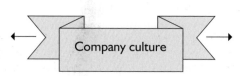

External		Internal
Political decisions		Restructuring
Mergers/takeovers		Redundancies
National/international crises	Company culture	Change of personnel
Financial constraints		Financial constraints
Tax and interest rates		Mergers/takeovers

Figure 8.1 *Some internal and external factors affecting company cultures*

THE MAINTENANCE OF A LEARNING CULTURE

As with British Aerospace, changes of culture nearly always involve the need to improve communication, and learning a new way of relating and operating. However, company cultures that are conducive to learning do not just remain so, once set up. They need to be maintained, and practices that support learning need to be embedded in the day-to-day operation of the company. If an organisation establishes and maintains this, they are in a stronger position to tackle new crises or other pressures. Some of these pressures are external and others come from within the company, as illustrated in Figure 8.1. For every organisation, strategies have to be in place to maintain and nurture the framework of development and communication, in order for CPD, in its widest sense, to take place. An important part of communication is listening. Listening in itself is a skill, which sometimes needs to be developed by formal training, but always needs to be practised! It is a crucial issue in maintaining and sustaining a learning culture, and so needs to be built into communication systems.

Physically listening is important, but messages can get lost or misinterpreted depending on circumstances and the personalities involved. What has been heard needs to be confirmed, and feedback mechanisms provide a natural and easy way of doing this. Strategies for feedback need to be employed in as many ways as possible, in order to build up a picture of the issues being discussed or evaluated. Surrey Satellite Technology Ltd (SSTL) (Box 8.2) has a whole variety of ways of listening and receiving feedback from its workforce. Many people work in an environment where the opportunity to speak and be listened to is minimal, but an organisation can build feedback into existing contacts with staff – not just the sheet of paper at the end of a training session, but as part of the preparation and execution of appraisal, in team meetings and in larger groups (team section, whole company) on specific issues. Feedback is unnecessary in certain circumstances, as it is built into the work activity, e.g. in technology and knowledge transfer. It is also an integral part of working towards a quality mark. On the other hand, very many aspects of work require personal skills, for example being able to deal with conflict. Giving feedback in this case requires expertise and sensitivity. Belbin (1993: 7), in discussing a strategy for 'finding the real self', states that: 'strategy rests on reconciling two strands of information, one derives from self assessment, and the other from the assessment of others'.

These two strands are brought together clearly in 360° feedback, and performance planning and review (see Chapter 7, Activity 7.7). Who is 'listening' to feedback is sometimes also an issue. Personality, status and skills all play a part in feedback. In some organisations the listening stops short of management. This is obviously counter-productive as people who are faced with no action on their feedback give up! A version of 360° feedback is useful in this context, as the basis of the system is to invite feedback from a range of people (managers, peers, direct reports, self and a choice of others). Their feedback builds up a picture of the individual's competencies and skills. Pedler *et al.* (1991) define a learning organisation in this way:

> *[it] has the capacity to transform itself .... It can be argued that all organisations learn, or they would not survive, but learning organisations demand proactive interventions to generate, capture, store, share and use learning at the systems level in order to create innovative products and services.*

> Pedler *et al.* (1991: 206)

SSTL is an example of a company that seeks to maintain a learning culture, or in Pedler's terms (above) has the capacity to transform itself. This capacity to transform arises directly out of being proactive about learning. Note the contrast between the company described in Box 8.1 and the company described in Box 8.2. Both are real companies, the first operating with some success, and the second named by *The Times* newspaper (28 September 2003) as one of the top 100 of Britain's fastest-growing technology companies. The culture of SSTL reflects what Pedler describes (above) as a learning organisation. It is also clear that if they stopped being proactive about learning, their Technology Transfer Programme would be seriously affected. In spite of this open and transparent culture, embedded in its regular practice, SSTL still sees a need to regularly review its way of operating. One example of its review of practice has been through a system called 'RapidScore', which is a means of self-assessment against the Business Excellence Model. A selection of staff from all levels in the company (including all senior managers) complete the standardised RapidScore questionnaire, which evaluates their perception of the company's performance in nine critical business criteria. The results can then be aggregated to come up with a single overall score, analysed at the criteria level, or even analysed on a question-by-question basis. Typically, the overall result is used to determine whether the company is advancing on its way towards excellence, and the criteria scores are used to find specific areas for improvement during the next year. The company's overall scores have improved year upon year, but more importantly, the RapidScore has provided an annual reminder that *all* aspects of the business need attention and improvement. This audit or review of practice is time-consuming, but maintenance of a learning culture is not an easy path. In addition the company is operating a programme of technology transfer, which promotes a multicultural environment that is not limited by an Anglocentric or even Eurocentric view, valuing a wider, richer spectrum of cultures. Its relationship with partners, therefore, is based on mutual respect and collaboration. Through this collaboration, teams from other countries develop the technology to build their own satellites. These academic/commercial collaborations provide opportunities for creative ideas to be developed. Combined, the technology transfer and academic activities that take place at the company engender an environment where learning and teaching are common and are valued – in fact, 50% of the company's contracts include a paid-for element of technology transfer and training. This approach is rare, as many organisations would be reluctant to 'give away' (or even sell) their expertise. SSTL seeks to maintain a learning culture by ongoing review of all aspects of the business, through more than one system (ISO 9001, Business Excellence Model/RapidScore), through an openness to collaboration and new ideas generated by technology transfer, and through open communication networks.

There are other aspects of technology or knowledge transfer that operate within one company. For example, BAESYSTEMS has had teams who have developed an aspect of the work to a high standard, and are then invited to visit another site in order to pass on their expertise. There are also instances where, as the business has restructured, strategies for transferring knowledge from one site to another have been developed. This has involved careful planning, thought about ways of transferring knowledge and considerable emphasis on personal skills (see Activity 8.3). The company is also engaged in offers of 'packages of its products and services' to other countries. This technology transfer not only relates to the design and in-country build of the product, but includes a support package for the life of the product.

Box 8.2: Surrey Satelite Technology Limited

SSTL is a company of approximately 150 people. Its day-to-day operations are characterised by regular open communication. For example they have:

- A weekly company newsletter with corporate, business, personnel, sporting and personal updates.
- A 'family' meeting each week that provides the whole company with an opportunity to exchange information in an informal and community setting (these are highlighted as being very effective).
- People can communicate with senior managers individually or in a group setting, formally or informally.
- Monthly meetings for leaders.
- Quarterly 'Corporate Update' meetings for all staff, including a presentation of financial results to date, the workload going forward, marketing prospects, and an open question/answer session with the MD.
- Annual appraisals and PDPs.
- Mystery outings, and efforts to engender team spirit.
- Technology transfer – customers (often overseas) send their engineers to work alongside the company's engineers to learn satellite engineering, engendering a multi-cultural learning and teaching environment.
- Academic/commercial collaborations – PhD students working alongside company engineers aiding communication and proliferation of ideas.

ACTIVITY 8.2

In the light of the examples of company practice in Boxes 8.1 and 8.2, review the way your organisation works, and see how strong the communication systems are. Sum up your company culture. What are the internal and external factors that impact upon it?

ACTIVITY 8.3

Go to the web site http://www.som.surrey.ac.uk/learnatwork and click on Portfolios Matched Against Standards 3 to review this evidence of knowledge transfer. This includes a summary of the planning and operation of the transfer (which took place over a period of 10 months) and observation of part of the face-to-face transfer.

The effect of knowledge and technology transfer shows itself in two ways. The first is that it builds an ethos within the company of openness, readiness to communicate, and readiness to learn from one another. This practice also sends the message that it is good to share knowledge and expertise, and that there is real benefit in exchanging ideas with others – very simple statements, but rarely embedded in practice. The second influence is upon learning per se. Technical expertise and knowledge are transferred to others, not by classroom teaching but in the workplace, and without 'taking time out'.

The contribution of 'non-work activities' to company culture

It is clear that companies who organise sporting activities, or have parties and away-days, build relationships across the company that add value to their workplace relationships. There are all kinds of side-effects of this, but an important one is that in stronger relationships there is less need to feel threatened by, and defensive towards, other people, which is often a 'full stop' in developing a learning environment in the workplace. Some working relationships are simply about meeting in meetings! On the other hand, effective company relationships:

- value people and teams
- recognise innovation and outstanding performance and facilitate their achievement of credit from formal qualifications
- are transparent in their management and leadership
- have ongoing plans for training and development
- have excellent communication systems that they work to maintain
- build a company ethos where knowledge, expertise and innovation are shared
- listen to feedback and take action upon it.

HOW CAN WE LEARN FROM THE WORKPLACE?

In addition to the creation of a supportive, learning environment, we need to identify what is being learned at work, and who is there to support the learning, and begin to track what is being learned from and through the workplace. This section of the chapter reflects and develops issues that have been discussed in previous chapters (specifically Chapters 2, 3 and 6) and will, through the activities, suggest ways in which individuals and teams can be proactive in the process of learning through the workplace. There is a variety of people who can support us, and a wealth of learning at work that we often do not recognise or value. Activity 8.4 is a starting point for this process.

ACTIVITY 8.4

Keep a record of new learning in the workplace, making a note *of when* and *how* you learned it. Leave two columns free so that you can review your entries and mark connections between them. It could be a personal skill (for example, dealing with conflict) or a technical one (for example, designing a database for failure mode analysis).

When you review this log (e.g. monthly), it might be helpful to mark what you see as strengths or learning points in the final column.

The effect of keeping a log in this way is that you begin to recognise your learning, and the development of skills from sources other than organised training. Over a period of time you can make connections between different ways of learning the same skill or competence – for example, to see the link between the various ways of developing communication skills through team meetings, in project work, in inducting staff into a new project, in presentations to line managers, and in effective use of email. Similarly, organised training may introduce you to a new system of financial accounting, but working with the expert may consolidate the knowledge that you have already gained, or may clarify issues not previously understood. Some would call the organised training 'formal learning' and working alongside the expert 'informal learning'.

The research of Eraut *et al.* (1998: 22) took account of both formal and informal learning, and they summarised organised, planned (formal) learning as: 'apprenticeships, induction, mentoring, coaching rotations, visits, work shadowing and reference to experts'.

The criteria for formal learning are seen here as the organisation and planning of learning. It is not easy to categorise in this way. It could be argued that the degree of planning by an organisation in reference to experts could simply be making appointments, or organising working arrangements, whereas the planning of an apprenticeship would be much more detailed. Eraut *et al.* (1998) also discuss self-directed learning, which relies on the employee being proactive in their own development – establishing what they see as their own needs and asking for support from the employer, or gaining support from outside of the company. This could amount to a combination of formal and informal learning. In fact, keeping a learning and skills log is itself an initiative in self-directed learning.

FORMAL LEARNING

This section covers a range of ways of learning formally at work. It includes Eraut's categories, but deals with other categories that we would also regard as formal learning (appraisal, performance development review, workplace observations, courses and training programmes).

It is perhaps helpful to first consider the term performance management, because it is used frequently and is sometimes confused with appraisal. Performance management is often used as an umbrella term for organised learning support, which is linked into work objectives and performance development planning and review. Appraisal is also sometimes used as a generic term covering the management of performance, but this is misleading, as appraisal (evaluating performance) is only part of performance management. Performance management is a system whereby a manager and employee/team member work together to improve or sustain performance. Bacal (1999: 3) describes it in this way:

> *This is an ongoing communication process, undertaken in partnership, between an employee and his or her immediate supervisor that involves establishing clear expectations and understanding about the jobs to be done. It is a system. That is, it has a number of parts, all of which need to be included if the performance management system is going to add value to the organisation, managers, and staff.*

Performance management therefore is seen to have two aspects. Firstly, it has the ongoing communication between manager and employee, a relationship that gives the framework to advising, coaching, mentoring, feedback, performance planning and review and informal ways of learning. Secondly, it has the clear aim of meeting work objectives to as high a standard as possible, and to deal with poor performance. It is not always easy to reconcile these two aims. A role that is concerned with developing the person, and at the same time managing their performance in meeting targets, requires skilled and sensitive managers and leaders!

Appraisal (Performance Development Review, 360° feedback)

Possible support for this process could be that, in general practice, appraisal is often carried out by line managers or more senior people in the workforce. Some companies give the individual a choice of appraiser, and 360° appraisal gives the appraisee the opportunity to draw upon a wide range of people (in addition to line managers and self-evaluation).

As it is best practised, appraisal can be a creative approach for facilitating learning at work. It involves individuals in their own development, with feedback and support from mentors and advisers, and gives a framework for review of performance and development, and action planning between reviews. As with performance management, there is sometimes a tension between the role of encouraging development and of meeting targets. This is particularly so when there is one appraiser, and they are also the line manager of the person being appraised.

The value of the 360° appraisal approach is that the focus is on a number of people who relate to the appraisee in different ways. This is an excellent tool. The system is structured to target certain roles, attributes and skills. Feedback is invited against those criteria from colleagues, managers and team members. The person appraised also carries out a self-evaluation against the same criteria. In addition to the written feedback, a mentor or adviser will go through the overall picture produced, to draw out the strengths and weaknesses and also to compare the self-evaluation with the evaluation of the other people feeding back. In the case of BAESYSTEMS, the feedback sheets are collected and represented as bar charts for ease of analysis and the results also analysed against company values. Bacal (1999: 151) sums up 360° appraisal as follows:

> *360° evaluation or appraisal. A method of collecting information, providing feedback and evaluating performance that relies on multiple resources of information, usually the manager, customers, co-workers and, if appropriate, suppliers.*

As already stated, the greatest amount of learning from this form of appraisal comes from the discussion that follows collation of the results. Again the quality of this feedback depends on the relationship between the individual and the adviser or mentor who is responsible for discussing the overall picture. Handling issues, for example, like why a manager perceives you as customer-focused, but the customer does not, requires not only openness and trust, but also honesty.

ACTIVITY 8.5

Go to the web site http://www.som.surrey.ac.uk/learnatwork and click on Personal Development 1 and 2 for examples of 360° appraisal.

As with many other systems, appraisal can be just a time-consuming exercise, and used by people not committed to continuous development of those in the workplace. There needs to be consensus amongst those 'cascading' the appraisal system throughout an organisation. Lecky-Thompson (1999: 9) asks some very pertinent questions, targeted at management:

- Why do I want to appraise staff in the first place?
- What are my business priorities and plan for the next year, and how will appraisal help?

- What are my management colleagues saying about the subject of appraisal?
- What do staff say and feel?
- How do my management and I regard the people practices in the organisation?
- Have my management and I been trained in non-technical skills, such as basic supervision?
- What kind of day-to-day feedback and guidance do I, and other managers, give to their staff?
- Do we use the word 'support' in our conversations about staff?
- How much time and resources will my organisation put into setting up or amending the appraisal process?
- How will I know that it is working properly?

There seem to be four important issues that arise from the questions above. The first is to do with the training and commitment of management. Groundwork needs to be conducted in communicating the reasons for, and benefits of, appraisal. Managers also need to know the extent and limits of what they can offer staff in terms of development. If they are asking about using the word 'support' in their feedback and guidance, the issue is obviously not clear! The second issue is whether there is already a system of self-development that appraisal can add to. If this is not in place, or is being put in place at the same time as the appraisal system, then it is hard to see how staff can be motivated to participate. The first two issues can be summed up in a third, which is how the staff regard appraisal. Fourthly, we can return to an issue raised above under the heading 'Performance Management', that is, the balance between development and meeting targets. In other words, will appraisal help the business?

ACTIVITY 8.6

Consider the following four questions in relationship to your organisation.

- Are management committed to appraisal, and are they trained to do it?
- Does appraisal relate to the day-to-day development of staff?
- How do employees regard appraisal?
- Will appraisal help the business?

Perhaps it would be helpful to compose a questionnaire based on these questions and send it to members of your team. In the light of the answers to these questions would you want to add to or change your description of company culture? (See Activity 8.2.)

How much learning goes on within an appraisal process will depend on how and why it is conducted, how much those involved are committed to the process, and the quality of the feedback given. Many organisations have launched appraisal schemes that have involved a great deal of time and money and they have become self-defeating. What was designed to be supportive has eventually become a source of disillusionment. Very often the four questions in Activity 8.6 have not been raised, and the purpose of the appraisal system is not clear to appraiser and appraisee alike. The 'day-to-day' development of staff only takes place in a learning organisation. Consider the example in Box 8.3. This appraisal process was introduced into an actual company, and the details given are, in principle, correct. The name of the company has been changed for the purposes of this

deal with the two issues of performance and personal development (an issue that was discussed earlier in this chapter), whereas other forms of appraisal focus on general issues of performance and, more specifically, needs for development or training.

ACTIVITY 8.8

Go to the web site http://www.som.surrey.ac.uk/learnatwork and click on Personal Development 2, for an example of a PDP and a PDR.

Workplace observations

Possible support for this process could be from peers, newly appointed staff in work shadowing, line managers, external verifiers, examiners or inspectors. As with other forms of appraisal, workplace observations need preparation and follow-up. The observer might be a manager or colleague (as part of ongoing staff development), or they may be an assessor for a certificated award. Many educational institutions have a rolling programme of observations as part of their quality systems, and to support staff development. Workplace observations are an integral part of NVQs and these are often face-to-face, but the use of web cams or videoed observations is increasing. In terms of the learning process, as with 360° review, feedback can tackle some tough issues, and the relationship between observer and observed is key. Observation can also be an opportunity for new staff to 'work shadow', which can be a form of training or coaching. Observations are also the bedrock of inspections and quality assurance visits.

ACTIVITY 8.9

Go to the web site http://www.som.surrey.ac.uk/learnatwork and click on Portfolios Matched against Standards 3 for an example of a workplace observation.

Mentor, coach or 'buddy'?

Possible support for this process could be from work colleagues or people from outside of the organisation completely. Buddies and coaches are people who know the job or system and can apprentice you into it. These three terms are often used synonymously, because the same person may offer all three roles. However, in order to clarify the differences between them this section gives a brief outline of each of the three roles.

Mentors

What is a mentor? (Cook, 1999: 106) gives us this definition:

> *Mentor – a wise loyal adviser. The word comes from Greek mythology; Mentor was friend and adviser to Odysseus and the teacher of his son Telemachus.*

Apart from skilled feedback in a good learning environment, there is certainly a need for wise loyal advisers to support learning in the workplace. Mentors have already been mentioned in terms of appraisal, but there are many mentors who are not involved in any kind of formal appraisal. For example, in the 1990s in one UK further education college, mentors were allocated to black students undergoing Business Management courses. These mentors, black business people themselves, were appointed as role models to the students. Their mentoring role involved spending time with the students in and out of college. For management NVQs the adviser role is sometimes taken up by mentors who have themselves gained an NVQ in Management. Other organisations have mentoring systems that are informal, and are simply there as wise loyal advisers.

Cook (1999) discusses the benefits of mentoring. He states that employees will be more motivated and productive as they begin to sense and exploit the possibilities in their job. He also argues that they will be loyal, and will still appreciate their friendship with a mentor, even after they have left the organisation. Self-development and motivation creates a vibrant ethos and, as people progress, new opportunities are opened up for others to move into the organisation, or for the current workforce to move into higher positions in the workplace. The mentor role, therefore, is key to developing a lively, motivated workforce.

ACTIVITY 8.10

How would you rate as a mentor? Could you, for example, mentor people in building CPD portfolios?

Draw up an annual mentoring plan either for a candidate developing a CPD portfolio, or for a new team leader.

Coaching

Possible support for this process could be from experts, colleagues and leaders. Many of the characteristics of coaching overlap with those of a mentor, but the difference is that the focus is on encouraging the person to achieve in their key work roles. Sports coaches are a good example. They have practical knowledge of the game, give advice, and demonstrate various aspects of performance. The training from the coach is focused on success for the individual and team, and the personal relationship between player and coach is one of trust and respect. Mentoring can sometimes be 'as and when' needed, but coaching is planned towards goals. Coaches need to 'know the business' and be able to pass on skills and knowledge to the people they are coaching. Coaching has one element in it that needs to be carefully considered. By their very nature coaches are expert in an area of work, and they pass on some of that expertise to the person they are coaching. The danger could be that the knowledge or skill might be very specifically the approach of that coach. In order to cope with this, care needs to be taken to monitor coaching and perhaps to change coaches if necessary. How do you rate as a coach? See Activity 8.11.

'Buddying'

Possible support for this process could come from team leaders, colleagues, experts and coaches. This is a fairly new term, and seems to bridge both coaching and mentoring. In one company it is used as part of the induction for new members of the IT team. After initial induction, new employees are allocated a 'buddy' to mentor the person into the organisation and the job role. Like the operation of mentors, buddy schemes are a way of welcoming in 'new blood' and supporting initiatives. They are also mentors in terms of friendship and advice. They do, however, have elements of coaching in that they are often involved in teaching someone the basic principles of their new job, and working with them to plan training relevant to their job role. Sometimes this also involves work

ACTIVITY 8.11

Identify someone in your workplace whom you could, or do, coach. Tick the chart below in terms of your role with this person. What are your strengths as a coach? How can you improve your coaching?

Characteristic	Never	Rarely	50/50	Frequently	Always
Positive					
Enthusiastic					
Supportive					
Trusting					
Focused					
Goal-orientated					
Knowledgeable					
Respectful					
Assertive					
Clear					
Patient					

(Adapted from Cook, 1999: 24)

shadowing. Work shadowing is also used in formal training, for example in induction, or in training people in external verification or inspection.

Courses and programmes

Possible support for this process could come from administrators, subject tutors, personal tutors and technicians. Of course any discussion of formal learning must include programmes drawn up by the company. Some are matched to company values, some encourage generic transferable skills. These programmes sometimes involve e-learning through virtual universities, or may involve self-study through open learning centres. These are normally recorded through training records or within personal profiles. In the most motivating circumstances the training arises from PDPs and PDRs, or when an employee is moving into a new role. Case Study 8.2 illustrates a two-stage plan by Transglobal. The company has worked through a first stage of staff development where the workforce has been encouraged to build CPD portfolios. It then moves on with a plan to encourage people to undertake national or international training. This second stage of the development plan is facilitated by the provision of advice and guidance from the HR department in selecting appropriate training.

Case Study 8.2: *A two-stage plan for self-development*

Transglobal has developed as a learning organisation, looking for ways to sustain support for the development of its workforce. The first stage in its action plan was the facilitation of online

CPD portfolios. This involved the development of software to integrate three previous systems (which recorded the achievement of core skills and competencies, performance development planning and review, and individual training records). The system has now been operating for 18 months and the company is ready to move into the second stage of its action plan. Transglobal has employed a consultant to work with the HR department in offering advice and guidance to anybody wishing to work towards a national/international award, or to apply to a professional body for membership or chartered status. Because it is a global company, the consultant has already produced his report on the scope of distance learning, and options for formal learning in the locality are also being investigated. The first cohort of people to be supported will be drawn from those who have produced CPD portfolios and who have been involved in company training when appropriate. The initial plan is for a three-year pilot.

INFORMAL LEARNING

Eraut *et al.* (1998) also considered less well-known sources of learning at work, for example 'exposure and osmosis' and 'consultation and observation'. The former is to do with knowledge about the company, its procedures and practices, which is built up simply by being alert to what is going on around people in the workplace, and absorbing the culture. It involves observing and learning from both day-to-day and specific work practices. The latter is to do with working with a colleague, in teams and in groups. Learning occurs in all kinds of ways in these circumstances – brainstorming ideas, asking questions to gain an overall view of a project, or to focus on a specific issue. Learning from one another is often an unrecognised form of learning at work.

Learning through teams

Possible support for this process could come from colleagues, experts, team leaders and facilitators. Teams can be formed for short- or long-term tasks or projects. There are teams who work together for a small part of the week, or who are together on a daily basis. Some teams are virtual teams, some face-to-face, and others are international. There are also teams of employees plus clients working together to improve company–client relationships. Teams need to be balanced in their composition. Experts or specialists are needed, but there also needs to be people who have the ability to elicit information from others to facilitate the teamwork itself, to be able to 'pace' work and to bring projects to closure. Once again, teams reflect the company culture. Belbin (1993) draws the distinction between the 'shaper culture' and the teamworker culture, but he recognises both as potential barriers to teamwork:

> *People at work meet in a particular context, being selected not because of who they are, but because of what they are. At a senior level most collective decisions involve heads of departments. Their positions entitle them to attend and so to express their views. The fact that they are all Shapers with the drive and determination to get their own decisions accepted may be seen as an impediment to good teamwork.*

He also argues that a teamworker culture may suffer from the same problems as a shaper culture if both resist input from things that are seen to be 'counter culture':

> *both models suffer from the genetic faults associated with in-breeding and cloning ...*
> *Only hybrids can withstand the disease and remain fruitful*
>
> Belbin (1993: 88)

This argument highlights the problem of 'set' practices and points to the need for openness, flexibility, a willingness to listen and the ability to select teams to fit tasks. However the team is operating, it needs to have concrete aims that are fed back or written up. There is often a wealth of undocumented learning being gained by each team member that is very frequently unrecognised. This undocumented learning can be a valuable source for reflecting upon learning and planning future development, both for the individual and the team. Debriefing sessions on what was learnt individually and as a team can be the stepping-stone to the next stage of learning.

A group of undergraduates completing a part-time degree (BSc Hons Professional Development through Work-Based Learning), when asked how they learnt from others in the workplace, offered the following:

- example/copying others
- presentation
- interact – discuss – listen
- appraisal
- communication/discussion
- factual procedures
- brainstorming
- in-service training/specific-subject training
- informal conversations
- feedback
- networking
- peer support
- interest
- team-building
- induction in different areas of your business (i.e. spending time in other departments)
- 1:1 training
- mentoring/buddy/becoming a student
- research into job role/seek relevant information.

ACTIVITY 8.12

Which of the above have been a source of learning for you in the last year? Add in your own 'sources of learning'. Revisit Activity 8.4 and add to your learning log.

Informal learning is usually underestimated and undervalued, but one result of the above activity is that we begin to see a wealth of knowledge and skills emerging from our daily contact with colleagues and from our workplace activities. It is worth taking time to assess these. In identifying these areas of knowledge and skills, an individual builds confidence and is empowered to build on strengths and plan self-development to tackle weaknesses. Learning, therefore, is seen not simply as occurring through organised programmes, but through participating in, reflecting upon and internalising knowledge in the workplace, and is 'at the heart of productive activity'.

Zuboff (1988, cited in Boud and Garrick, 1999) states:

> *Learning is no longer a separate activity that occurs either before one enters the workplace or in remote classroom settings. Nor is it actively preserved for a managerial group. The behaviours that define learning and the behaviours that define being productive are one and the same – learning is not something that requires time out from being employed in productive activity; learning is at the heart of productive activity.*

Feedback – a learning process for both parties

As can be seen from the various sections of this chapter, feedback is key in the learning process, both for the appraiser and the appraisee. This applies even if the results of appraisal seem self-evident. In the case of 360° appraisal, where most of the documents are written feedback, talking it through with a mentor or adviser can support honest reflection on practice and facilitate the planning of future development. There needs to be someone who can provide a sounding board to what the appraisee has seen, and who will also be a trusted adviser in drawing out the issues that were not initially recognised. Day (2002) places emphasis on the structuring of a feedback interview. Amongst the issues he raises are eye contact, open and honest feedback, giving praise and giving time for the learner to put across their view. These are all practical issues that demonstrate that feedback needs to be thought through and, if necessary, training in giving feedback offered to managers and supervisors.

If it is to be a learning process, then the feedback needs to be constructive and clear. In an informal situation, people can be tempted to give informal feedback. It is worth bearing in mind that a casual word can easily be misinterpreted and for that reason casual words need to be monitored. Written feedback in general has the advantage of being able to be given in advance, so that the individual has time to think it through before discussing it. However, it requires the appraiser to have very clear written expression. It needs to be remembered, as has already been stated, that learning may occur for anyone involved in the process. For example, the appraiser may need to improve their skills in giving feedback, and in the process of feeding back to their team members, they may become aware of the need for their own development in related skills (for example, listening skills, dealing with conflict, empowerment of others). Company culture needs to be such that appraisers are also expecting to learn from their workplace activities, and records of appraisal might well document that.

At the end of one phase of appraisal, the learning may still be at the stage of reflection upon actions, or it might have been internalised, conceptualised and able to be drawn upon for a wider number of issues, or in a range of circumstances.

Conclusions

Chapter 7 demonstrated how the move towards developing portfolios 'owned' by the individual increased motivation, and the engagement of the person in the process of their own learning. Reflection upon learning and review of practice are keys to self-development, and enable the concepts developed through previous learning to be drawn upon in a wider context. Although motivation for learning comes from the individual,

INDEX